ETHICS AND THEOLOGY FROM THE OTHER SIDE:

SOUNDS OF MORAL STRUGGLE

Enoch H. Oglesby

University Press
of America™

Copyright © 1979 by

University Press of America, Inc.™

4710 Auth Place, S.E., Washington D.C. 20023

Printed in the United States of America

ISBN: 0-8191-0706-9

Library of Congress Catalog Card Number: 78-62897

Dedicated to

Gloria, Josten, and Derek

with love

PREFACE

The aim of this work is not to critically develop a Black
Ethical Theology, but to grapple with understanding the importance of a viable perspective on the relation between ethical
discourse and the religion of the oppressed, in the long struggle
by Blacks to achieve full freedom and self-respect in America.
While the clamor for liberation and humanization is heard in
many sectors of our global community, it appears that it is the
religious and moral value-orientation of black religion which has
made a significant difference in black people's search for a
responsible freedom and a better way of life under God. Theologically, it is my basic conviction that the black church, for better
or worse, as a social institution has been the *moral cement* which
gave Blacks a sense of identity, hope, and solidarity in the face
of oppression and white racism. Ironically, the moral tragedy of
the contemporary Black Church is the growing awareness that we
are losing the vision and revolutionary ethical potential of the
Black Spirituals as we gradually become more and more integrated
into bourgeois middle-class America. We are becoming more and
more like the things we fight against: demonic Western materialism
and the subsequent internalization of the values of the white
oppressor. If the whole story about the black condition in
America were ever told, perhaps we would discover something surprisingly new. The surprisingly *new* of which I refer, relative to
ethical analysis of the black religious experience, is precisely
this: that the real cement of black Christian consciousness is
not to be found necessarily in mutual suffering, but in a common
hope that a truly human future can become a reality for the children of dark skin. I affirm that such an awareness demands a basic
shift in the way we do things in the black community as well as in
the way we perceive our role in the wider society. It is an awareness that calls for the radicalization of ethical responsibility on
the part of the oppressed themselves, particularly as a precondition for the creation of a new social order where all people can
live with dignity and human rights.

The personal struggle to say something of worth about *ethics
and theology from the other side* has not been an easy task for me.
The assistance and encouragement of which I have received came from
many people and sources. First of all, I wish to express my sin-
cere gratitude to the Mellon Foundation for providing financial
assistance to do part of the research while serving as Assistant
Professor of Christian Social Ethics on the Andrew W. Mellon Fund,

at the Interdenominational Theological Center, Atlanta, Georgia.

I wish to further acknowledge and thank my colleagues, Douglas Meeks and Allen Miller, of Eden Theological Seminary who found the time in their busy schedules to critically read the manuscript and offer helpful suggestions. In addition, I gratefully acknowledge permission by the Board of Editors of the *Journal of the Interdenominational Theological Center* to reprint Chapter 6, which appears here in a revised form.

I am also indebted to my typist, Dorothy Schroeder, who rendered invaluable assistance in the final preparation of the manuscript.

A special word of appreciation and thanks must go to my wife, Gloria, who provided me with an immense source of moral strength, support, and practical insight near the final stages of this work. As we shuffled between the many duties of parenthood, she also provided me with an atmosphere for reflection and study.

CONTENTS

vii

CHAPTER:

CHAPTER:

INTRODUCTION

Today as never before black Christians the world over are facing a new future. This future is dynamically creative and strangely paradoxical because it is wrought with new ethical challenges, political dilemmas, and socio-economic problems that will test--undoubtedly, for sometime to come--the very heart and spirit of black people. W. E. B. DuBois once remarked that the essential socio-ethical problem of the twentieth century is the "color line" that's used, more often than not, by the wider society to subordinate and exclude blacks and other oppressed minorities. While the color-bar has not been overcome and is interlocked with an amazing array of complex issues, the most critical problem confronting the black American as we approach the twenty-first century is essentially moral, economic, and spiritual in character. Theologically, the radical imperative of the black man today *is* liberation and economic justice in all areas of community life in light of the ethical demands of Jesus Christ, who is Liberator and Humanizer!

The crucial variables that will, undoubtedly, shape the black man's future destiny are not always crystal clear or apparent in a scientifically and technologically complex world. But from the perspective of the black religious experience, I think that the ethical and theological themes of liberation, justice and love, human oppression and suffering, the problem of authority in Scripture, and the question of man's loyalty or obedience to God in community will be the kind of "boundary concerns" with which the morally honest person must wrestle. To this end, I believe that those who do theology and ethics still have something significant to say, especially within the context of the black religious experience in America, relative to these boundary concerns.

Every book purports to have some purpose. However, this volume is not a sort of critical-analytical commentary about the legitimacy of Black Theology as a proper discipline of study and reflection for scholars, teachers, religious educators or theological students, primarily. It is not a book on the nature of Black Theology *per se* as much as how one believing Christian attempts to understand and grapple with the relation between ethics and black ethnicity, between ethical discourse and the religion of the oppressed in the long historical struggle on the part of the black man to achieve authentic freedom and self-respect in America. In yet another sense, this volume is about how the faith and ethical

1

spirit of the black church has been that moral cement which held together black people in times of trial and struggle; the very foundation of the black man's sense of social solidarity, of value and morality, of hope and moral promise--is essentially an expression of the religion of the black church. For the wider black community, one can safely say that the black church has been, and continues to be, not only a leaven which keeps alive the dream of a better life in *this* world, but also a "moral enabler" for the children of dark skin.

Perhaps of crucial importance for all right-thinking people today, this book raises a group of related questions which may be most simply put as follows:

- Is there an identifiable black religious ethic supportive of the liberation of blacks from white oppression? If so, what are its elemental characteristics relative to the nature of moral experience in black struggle?

- What is the ethics of the black church and black religion in light of the historical struggle of blacks to find self-fulfillment and human dignity on the American soil?

- Can ethical reflection make a positive difference in one's attempt to understand and critically interpret the meaning of black religious experience in a white-dominated society?

- How can Black Theology and Christian ethics be dynamically brought together as morally sensitive persons grapple with the meaning of the gospel of Jesus Christ and the plight of the oppressed today?

- What are the dimensions of moral responsibility in black life?

These are some of the questions, in varying degrees, which will press our conscience in the course of this ethical inquiry; they are amenable for analysis both by the social ethicist and theologian as well as the lay person who takes seriously the radical imperatives of the Christian faith in human community.

From a theoretical perspective, it may well be that the organizing-integrative radical imperative of the oppressed black in American society today is the development of, and coming to grips with, a black religious ethic viable enough to sustain the integrity and survival of black people. In a broad theological sense, the radical imperative is not purely *contextual*, but *universal*; for the most persistent cry heard the world over is for human liberation. Enrique Dussel points to this strange ferment of hope and despair relative to what God is doing in history to

2

root out oppression, while concomitantly establishing the moral preconditions for the oppressor in human society: "The process of liberation itself is," writes Dussel, "the only thing which will make it possible for the oppressor to undergo a real conversion. Hence only the underdeveloped nations of the world can enable the affluent nations to discover a new, more human model of human life...."[1] In a similar manner, the search for liberation--in all of its complex dimensions and processes--is one of the organizing-integrative *sounds* of ethics (in a black context) and Black Theology in modern society.

The use of the phrase "sounds" in the title can perhaps be best understood by referring to the significant role--sometimes engendering an unconscious manifestation of desire, will, and passion on the part of its participants--music plays in dealing with the ups and downs, the trials and tribulations, the joys and tragedies of black life in white America. Indeed, for oppressed blacks, sounds are indicators of the nature and character of moral existence. Nearly every place the individual person may go in the black community, for instance, one is greeted with diversified sounds: the sounds of men and women making love and funky boogie, of laughter and folly, of friendly debate and political fermentation; the sounds of struggle and suffering, of hunger and pain, of crying and weeping. Thus *sounds* are, in a more profound ethical sense, symbolic of the stubborn ingredients of black reality itself.

In the first part of this book the quest for black religious ethics, as I see it, is one of the vibrating and reverberating *sounds* of the black community. Theoretically, the quest itself is neither an exercise in acoustic redundancy and diffuseness, that is to say, a mere repetition of the popular theologies of Black Awareness and Black Radicalism warmed over again from the sixties. Nor is it a simple cryptonym for Black Theology which has had, especially in recent years, an indelible impact on the way in which black and white theologians perceive their work and reflect upon the meaning of human moral existence. Rather the quest for black religious ethics, at its most rudimentary level, is a search in part for a new style of moral being, a new consciousness about black folk that can reshape the old values and stereotypes of the past in light of current ethical reality. It is a mode of ethical sensitivity that must emerge in the community of the oppressed, if we are to fully understand the revolutionary potential inherent in the black religious experience.

In the midst of the challenge to make Christian theology and ethics more meaningful and relevant to the black condition, there has been an attempt by some black scholars to develop what may be called a "Black Christian social ethic." Whether or not one believes in the legitimacy of such a point of departure is not the issue. To be sure, the moral claim by black scholars and educators, *ipso facto,* implies the right to theologize and ethicize about certain dimensions of religious experience in black life; and to establish some basic ethical premises and methodological directions which may well be determinative in steps toward the creation of a more humane value system in the wider society.

In chapter one, therefore, this writer seeks to delineate the case for black religious ethics, the meaning and problematics implicit in defining the ethical task from a black frame of reference, and an explanation of how oppressed blacks in this society come to place certain positive and negative valuations on their own "blackness" and religious experience as a people of God, particularly in the midst of a world that's hostile to anything black.

In chapter two, the writer discusses the role of the Black Church as a key integrative institution in shaping the religious, moral, and social values of black folk. In a descriptive and appreciative manner, I specifically attempt to review the role of the Black Church, the Black Preacher, and the Black Spirituals as foundational sources in our understanding of the texture of the moral life of the black religious experience. For example, the black church may very well constitute, as aforementioned, the primary source of black religious ethics. Though unsystematized in terms of concrete ethical methodology and not always conforming to the alleged rational criteria of its white counterpart, the black church, without doubt, contains, I believe, some significant ethical canons which gave hope, historically speaking, to a destitute people, and moral courage to press against the dehumanizing system of chattel slavery.

Now chapter three seeks to understand the structure of Black Religion--not primarily from the vantage point of its emotive, social, and cultural importance--but rather a perspective which tries to take seriously the idea of black religion as a value-theory, as a rational and cognate discipline that has the cutting edge in illuminating the human condition, and thereby providing a different kind of insight into the broader social and theological problems confronting the church in the American cultural system.

In chapter four I have limited the discussion to a focus on Black Power that takes into account the social, historical, and moral struggles of blacks in America. Here I find it both interesting and instructive to uncover what may be called the "patterns of historical continuity" relative to the evolutionary development of the roots of Black Power, especially as reflected in the ethical and philosophical thought of Martin R. Delany, Frederick Douglass, W. E. B. DuBois, and Marcus Garvey. Given the similarity and dissimilarity of their moral views about the plight of the children of dark skin, these men gave coherent shape, character, and authentic expression to what some social critics regard as a confusing-misguiding-inflamatory concept: Black Power! Thus it is my fundamental ethical assertion and conviction that the real theoretical roots of Black Power--more than some dare to acknowledge or contemplate--is enshrined essentially in nineteenth century black thought and social struggle.

In addition, we may note that the contemporary cross-currents of Black Power are analyzed and interpreted, primarily as a basis for the emergence of Black Theology and black radicalism in chapter five. At this juncture in our ethical inquiry, I argue in part that Black Theology is problematic essentially because it tends to "hang loose" or fails to sufficiently take into account the ethical requirements of the Hebraic-Christian faith, in its delineation of the black religious experience in American society. I also see the failure of a number of black theologians to achieve some reasonable balance between ethical universal principles explicitly manifested *in* the Christian faith, on the one hand; and theological propositions *about* the Christian faith in terms of their application to human conduct in the community of the oppressed, on the other.

This observation does not suggest that various modes of theologizing about the black experience in recent years by such perceptive theologians as James H. Cone, J. Deotis Roberts, Gayraud Wilmore, William Jones, and others is without merit or methodological validation--quite to the contrary. But rather I am suggesting that the black religionist, who honestly grapples with the whole content of the Christian faith, is also obligated or compelled to bring ethics to bear upon the dynamically complex and creative life of the black community--socially, culturally, and religiously.

The last two chapters of this book are oriented, to a greater or lesser degree, around both the thought of Martin Luther King, Jr., and the residual task to achieve more methodological clarity between those who do Black Theology and Christian ethics. These latter chapters, six and seven, therefore, attempt to point toward new directions and a process of constructive dialogue between ethically sensitive persons in both the black and white communities. To be sure, it is my hope that the moral and ethical mandates of the whole Christian faith can be discerned anew and reappropriated in such a way as to speak to the deeper yearnings of the human spirit: liberation, coherence, divine purpose, human solidarity, and self-fulfillment.

CHAPTER I
THE QUEST FOR BLACK RELIGIOUS ETHICS

THE PROBLEM OF ETHICS AND THE
BLACK RELIGIOUS EXPERIENCE

The problem of ethics in the collective life of the black community is the problem of values. The paramount importance of values is evident in, for instance, the methodological unclarity surrounding the popular contemporary discipline of Black Theology. Indeed, the significance of values and the need, apparently, for value clarification on life-and-death issues is in part a major task of ethics. To the extent that ethics is concerned with evaluative reflection upon the moral foundations of human behavior, the black religious experience *per se*, as a viable point of departure, can no longer be ignored. The problem of ethics, then, is one of values and the systematic attempt to delineate and understand the values of the human agent since man himself is a valuing creature.

However, the problem itself, from a black frame of reference, is a complicated and deep one; it requires coming to grips with some type of radical imperative which has the impetus to compel black folk to develop new ideals, principles, and strategies in preparation for the next harvest. For example, genuinely concerned Christians of the black community are challenged by the magnetic pull-of-the-future to commence a new harvest, to be literal "seed sowers" for a new culture that has the moral tenacity and cohesiveness to set all oppressed people free. Perhaps the real mission and task before the black community, is, I believe, illustrated best in the New Testament parable of the Seed Sower. Jesus of Nazareth once said, "Behold, a sower went forth to sow; and when he sowed, some seeds fell by the wayside, and the fowls came and devoured them up: some fell upon stony places, where they had not much earth...and some fell among thorns; and the thorns sprung up, and choked them: but others fell in good ground, and brought forth fruit, some an hundredfold, some sixtyfold, some thirtyfold." (Matt. 13: 3-8). Theologically speaking, if we take seriously the parable of the "seed sower," as recorded by the writer Matthew, the implication is crystal clear: it is time for black people--especially young black youth, radicals, intellectuals and scholars,

7

as well as lay folk alike--to begin to sow seeds for the next harvest in the American culture. In a real sense, one of the problems that demands ethical reflection in the black community, particularly at the practical level, is the problem of "operational unity" or coming together in order to work for the next season.

In large measure, the vast majority of blacks in America have already perhaps reaped, to recapitulate for a moment the painful historical struggle of black leaders who sowed seeds of discontent during the forties and fifties, the bulk of the harvest of the Civil Rights Movement in the sixties. To be sure, it is no time for euphoric sentimentalism and blissful celebration; it is time for tilling the soil for the next harvest. Etymologically considered, we may observe that to "sow" simply means to scatter in, on, or to plant beneath the soil. Here the burden of the ethical is the force with which it niddles black folk to sow their seeds not upon "stony places" or "among thorns" where the fowls of our society--both in and outside the contours of the black experience--can readily devour that which is sown.

Further, the problem of ethics in the black religious experience is also one of loyalty to God, on the one hand; and the inherent conflict arising out of loyalty to some lesser man-made value depicting the black condition, on the other. To assert, as many black theologians do, that black people themselves must value their own humanity as an object of moral worth, does not mean that blackness *per se* is antithetical to God's humanizing activity in the world. Nor does it mean that black people, by their very nature, are necessarily more righteous and morally virtuous than others. To the contrary, it may very well mean ethically that the notion of loyalty itself has a bifocal character: namely, the full actualization of one's identity as a person-in-community requires trust in God and obedience to his moral command.

Perhaps the complicated texture of the problem, implicit in one's quest for a viable black religious ethic, is expressed in this perceptive comment by Professor Preston N. Williams:

> Either one is loyal to the God who works on behalf of the oppressed, most of whom happen to be black, or one is loyal to the Blacks, most of whom may be oppressed and some of whom may have a peculiar place in the plan of God for this day. My alternative is loyalty to God or whatever symbol may stand for the ultimate and eternal source of meaning and value.[1]

In any case, the morally earnest person, either in the black community or the white community for that matter, cannot afford to ignore the fact that the magnetic pull of contemporary events requires a fundamental reassessment of our values and loyalties in America. In one's quest for basic human rights and a sense of self-fulfillment, there seems to be no easy way to avoid reflection upon such critical questions as::

- Can there be a viable ethic, emanating from the black religious experience, which has the capacity to give vitality and hope to oppressed blacks in America?

- What kind of values and directional principles ought we to pursue, particularly at a time when the Civil Rights impetus or Black Power rhetoric has been taken off the front burner and put on the back burner?

- How can blacks and whites, as moral agents, come to terms with the ethical meaning of the religious experience in black, essentially in a society that equates blackness with evil?

- What is the nature of the ethical task in relation to Black Theology and third-world theologies?

These are crucial questions which demand honest attention, moral perceptivity, and practical response in our churches today. In this particular chapter, however, we shall attempt to engage the reader in a fruitful discussion, largely in a descriptive and appreciative manner, on the following issues:

1. the nature and style of the ethical task in the black experience;

2. some preliminary reflections on the meaning of Blackness as a moral force; and

3. a seminal proposal in regard to elemental characteristics for the construction of a viable black religious ethic.

DEFINING THE ETHICAL TASK IN BLACK EXPERIENCE

Any legitimate quest, in one's attempt to understand the nature and style of Black religious ethics, would seem to involve some procedural statement on the ethical task in black experience. Many contemporary Christian social ethicists would, undoubtedly, agree that arriving at, or seeking to delineate a common definition of what the ethical task is, viz., what one who calls himself an ethicist ought to be about, is problematic in itself.[2] The ambiguity is even more evident in those who seek to take seriously the ethical task from a non-white perspective. This is so

9

particularly because of the difficulty involved if one advocates the stance of rational objectivity and value-neutrality as cardinal rules of scholarship; or if one seeks to isolate racial sentiment *ipso facto* from the larger socio-cultural system. One cannot be sure that it is either possible or always desirable to claim standards of objectivity and moral neutrality in defining the ethical task with regard to the black religious experience. Ethics, at its best, is more a pattern of normative and critical reflection--in which man confronts and responds to the living word of God out of his fragmented condition of despair and hope--than it is a purely analytic science of human conduct.

All ethically sensitive persons, I believe, recognize the importance of being historically situated. Obviously, the Black Christian social ethicist, largely conditioned by his social environment and his peculiar religious and cultural context, is no exception. Nathan Hare, a noted black social scientist, illuminates our consciousness regarding the task of the black scholar in a white dominated society. Professor Hare emphatically declares:

> The black scholar must look beneath the surface of things and, wherever necessary and appropriate, take a stand against the bias of white scholarship. He must be biased against white bias, must be an iconoclast, rallying to the call to arms of all the black intelligentsia, to destroy obsolete norms and values and create new ones to take their place.[3]

It seems logical, I think, that the first place to begin in defining the ethical task is with the black experience itself. One of the obligations of the Black Christian social ethicist, or the social scientist for that matter, is to "look beneath the surface of things." In a crisis-oriented society where the racial factor still tends to be more determinative in evaluating one's basic humanity and worth, the legitimate task itself becomes a rather dangerous and intriguing one; it involves the radical affirmation of the need to "destroy obsolete norms and values and create new ones to take their place." Thus the first and clearest duty is one of digging into the "stuff" of the black religious experience, to literally probe into, and to disclose its basic pattern and moral character. The task of ethics therefore--whether Christian, social, philosophical, humanistic or otherwise--is the task of "digging."[4]

Secondly, critical reflection upon the ethical task involves what may be called a descriptive analysis of the *cultural ethos*. The quest for a black religious ethic, methodologically and theoretically speaking, is to be engaged in a conscious self-critical struggle to understand the moral role and purpose of black existence as a value in and of itself; moreover, critical reflection upon black existence in the modern world also presupposes in part an ethical perspective informed by, and sensitive to, a whole network of mutually interdependent relationships within the black community and the larger social system. This means that the ethical task in the black experience is *relational* in character, that is to say, it must be understood in light of the search of black people for a more palatable value system in the wider community of faith.

At the bare existential level of black life in contemporary society, the key question here can be posed very simply, yet critically: What does it really mean to do ethics? Or, to put the matter in political perspective, how can ethical valuation engage our consciousness, especially in light of the struggle of oppressed blacks to be free and self-determining? This, I believe, may very well be the real normative question with which we must grapple in order to understand the ethical task as it relates to the whole social system. To do ethics, therefore, in a black context means existentially to commit oneself to a serious analysis of the *cultural ethos* in which black folk live, move, and work-- the very essence of black life. To be sure, the task of ethics is in part the task of probing, of self-critical reflection--not for the purpose of intellectual ego-tripping, but for the purpose of illuminating and reconstructing black reality itself. That is to say, we must struggle to understand the "isness" of black life, so much of which is saturated by human misery, suffering, and oppression, in the light of what "ought to be." Therefore, the prevailing cultural ethos of today and new emergent lifestyles of blacks demand ethical inquiry and reflection, particularly from the perspective of the Christian faith.

Lerone Bennett, in *The Challenge of Blackness*, sets the stage for the development of new moral and theoretical frontiers in black thought. He challenges his social critics and contemporaries to put the ethical task in sober perspective, precisely when he says to us that

> It is necessary for us to develop a new frame of reference which transcends the limits of white concepts. It is necessary for us to develop and maintain a total intellectual offensive against the false universality of white concepts....By and large, reality has been conceptualized in terms of the narrow point of view of the minority of white men who live in Europe and North America. We must abandon the partial frame of reference o of our oppressors and create new concepts which will release our reality....[5]

Thirdly, the ethical task in the context of the black experience involves the motif of *discernment*. The concept of discernment is a key integrative principle as well as a necessary

11

methodological tool for any scholar seriously engaged in doing Christian social ethics or theology in modern society. Thus the burden of ethical inquiry into the "funky facts" of black life is the burden of *radical moral discernment*.

The capacity to discern engenders a certain kind of moral perspective. For the oppressed black community, it incorporates the power to see between things, to catch sight of, sometimes with a piercing and penetrating eye, the deeply spiritual and moral dimensions of existence, conditioned by always having to view life from the bottom upward. Moral discernment encompasses a mode of "seeableness" which is not, at first glance, visible by those who seized the chance of formulating the social system to their own advantage--deliberately fostering a view of ethnic relations from the "top" downward. The capacity to discern thereofore as a moral agent of the black religious experience, is a significant part of ethical inquiry and reflection.

James Gustafson, in his article entitled, "Moral Discernment in the Christian Life," speaks of discernment as an important principle in the life of the Christian believer.[6] It is both theological and contextual; it is both sociologically ameliorative and historically relevant for the oppressed black community. While the principle of discernment, obviously, has much to do with an adequate understanding of the state of black reality in America, individual persons themselves are very much a part of the discerning process--regardless of whether they appeal to formal religious belief systems or to merely subjective criteria in making moral judgments. In any event, the role of the individual person, as a moral agent, is important in discerning the ethical task. Moral perceptivity seems to come through persons who are themselves discerning. James Gustafson articulates the matter in a rather succinct way by arguing that

> It is persons who discern; and persons have histories that affect their discernment. Some have never been seriously challenged to examine the bases of their judgments; others are highly self-critical and introspective. Some have developed characters on the basis of critical evaluations of past experiences and of the exercise of their initiative in becoming what they are throughout their personal moral histories....Some have acute senses of justice and injustice by virtue of having been the victims of oppression, or by virtue of being members of groups that have histories of being oppressed.[7]

Thus the moral logic of discernment, as reflective of the ethical task in black experience, deeply implicates the black man as an individual person in the total process. To be sure, moral discernment means to ability to see how things come together, or do

12

not fit together in the black man's struggle for his own manhood, autonomy, and the development of a critical self-
consciousness. For example, the ethically sensitive person of
the white community must consciously and persistently seek to
discern in order to affirm what some perceptive individuals of
the black community have known all along: namely, that the
oppressed black man, in spite of his perennial victimization by
white racist theories of innate inferiority, is not without
rational concepts, morality, culture, religious philosophy.

In short, the notion of discernment as a reflective part of
the ethical task gives us, more acutely, a sense of identity,
purpose, and direction as a people of God. All in all, the idea
of discernment means that black folk must develop and be about
the business of formulating their own ethical concepts consistent
with their own history, culture, religious values, eschatological hopes and dreams.

Preliminary Reflections on the Meaning of
Blackness as a Moral Imperative

In the whole of Western society, Christian religion has
helped to perpetrate a negative perspective on the word "black."
In the view of many Christian thinkers, the term "black" con-
jures up the negative: it connotes "evil," "sin," "misfortune,"
"rejection," and "alienation." Conversely, the term "white" in
Western society, according to conventional ethics, connotes positive virtues, i.e., "purity," "innocence," "goodness,"
"majesty."[8] I believe that the thrust of our ethical reflection,
then, in terms of its viability and promise is the force with
which it attempts to redeem the term "black" from the traditional
Western stereotype.

Concretely speaking, there appear to be three basic attitudes
implicit in the concept of "blackness" which require illumi-
nation in the context of the black experience in America. These
may characteristically include:

(a) blackness as a *designative* category;

(b) the idea of blackness as an *appreciative* category;[9] and

(c) the notion of blackness as a *moral imperative* or moral
force in the American cultural system.

We may note that the first type is simply a way by which to identify the subject, i.e., a mere sociological recognition of Black Americans as distinguished from other social groups. Put another way, it refers to an awareness on the part of the wider society that black people as a social entity do, *ipso facto*, exist. Further, that their presence can no longer be ignored either by the nation or the world.

The second type for consideration, which is what I refer to as an appreciative category of thought, tends to be more ideological and culturalistic; it reflects to a greater or lesser degree the entire history, culture, social philosophy, thought-form, and personality of an oppressed black people and their struggle to make sense out of human existence. As an *appreciative* category, the ideal of blackness, first and foremost, tells the story of what it means to be "black" in a predominantly white racist society. Moreover, it tells the story about what may well be called the existential-otherness of the American experience, about the world within the veil, a world silent and asleep; indeed, a world that is so far removed from the heartbeat of white America's conscience. The real anguish and wretchedness of black life, though often hidden beneath the surface of things, is partially disclosed in these powerful poetic lines by Paul Lawrence Dunbar:

> We wear the mask that grins and lies,
> It hides our cheeks and shades our eyes--
> This debt we pay to human guile;
> With torn and bleeding hearts we smile,
> And mouth with myriad subtleties.
>
> Why should the world be overwise,
> In counting all our tears and sighs?
> Nay, let them only see us, while
> We wear the mask.
>
> We smile, but, O great Christ, our cries
> To Thee from tortured souls arise.
> We sing, but oh, the clay is vile
> Beneath our feet, and long the mile;
> But let the world dream otherwise,
> We wear the mask.[10]

Paradoxically, the idea of blackness as an *appreciative* frame of reference is a kind of spiritual leaven. It gives black men and women, seemingly, unrelenting courage to "wear the mask." Though burdened with the pains of everyday existence, there is nevertheless a quiet dignity in being black which echoes from the soul of black folk; and moves them to ethically internalize the rhythm of their own psychosocial condition, the result of which is the power to believe in themselves. For the dispossessed, there is a point at which self-assertion replaces self-doubt, and a place at which one's soul reaches out for a greater sense of identity and self-esteem. So then, the irony of "wearing the mask" is the stern courage which it musters for those with "torn and bleeding hearts."

We now come to a consideration of blackness as a moral imperative. This third consideration of blackness, largely viewed on the part of this writer as a *moral force*, has as its primary task the articulation and interpretation of the desires, needs, and yearnings of the oppressed black man in America. In one sense, we may observe that blackness is morally neutral; it is merely the expression of human vitality, activity, and service in the drama of life itself. Depending on the particular context, the idea of blackness is neither overwhelmingly positive, nor decisively negative. It is morally neutral.

However, the ethically sensitive person may very well recognize that the notion of blackness as a *moral force* has deeper ontological significance, in a world where the exploitation of the poor is real. For many contemporary thinkers like Albert Cleage, James Cone, and others, the idea of blackness is related to the being of God and his majestic creation. Ethically and theologically considered, blackness is the affirmation of the humanity of black people. It means that "God came into the world," writes James Cone, "in order that black people need not be ashamed of who they are."[11] I think that the positive religio-moral connotation of blackness is also captured in this comment by Professor Cone:

> Being black in America has very little to do with skin color. To be black means that your heart, your soul, your mind, and your body are where the dispossessed are.[12]

Now for some social critics of the theology and ethics of James Cone, I must hasten to add that this statement appears to be problematic and ambiguous; especially in regard to the obvious disvaluation and depreciation of "black skin color" in the larger cultural system.

Nevertheless, one must be cognizant of the fact that the notion of blackness as a *moral imperative* forthrightly presupposes the need on the part of black people to create their own value system in order to repudiate theoretically and pragmatically, the widely held claim in racist America that "blackness" is a symbol of depravity, of sinfulness, of evil in our social system. To argue, as I do, that many white theologians and Christian ethicists in particular, of European religio-cultural origins, have problems with the idea of "blackness" as a moral consideration is to put the case rather mildly. To be sure, this

15

need not be the case. But it is. For reasons complex and perhaps deeper than any of us can fully understand or comprehend, white theologians and ethicists cannot apparently incorporate a notion of "blackness" into their ethical scheme of reflection. Therefore, the black man as moral agent is compelled to commence the difficult task of laying bare the misery and grandeur, the frustrated hopes and noble strivings of people of African descent in America. Herbert O. Edwards seems to come close to the truth concerning the implications of blackness as a moral force in his observation that "to be black...is to be engaged in a conscious, deliberate struggle against suffering, misery and oppression which this community of color has experienced, mainly at the hands of white people."[13]

In a communitarian sense, blackness is not only a significant part of our humanity; it is our humanity! Ethically discerned, it challenges us to raise our goals and moral perspectives. Blackness challenges us to create new tools of insight not only for the expressed purpose of clarifying the black condition in the modern world; but in a very profound sense, to *change* the condition that frustrates our hope, our determination, our vision.

Furthermore, it is my conviction that the idea of blackness as a moral force seeks the release of the total humanity within us. This does not mean the often conceptual contours of the black community only; but it refers to a sort of qualitative moral force to be released within a nation, indeed, a post-bicentennial nation desperately grasping for new breath, for a new value-orientation. Thus the ultimate task and challenge of blackness, I believe, is the creation of a humane value system in a society that disvalues anything resembling "black." Moreover, the notion of blackness as a moral imperative seems to be implied in this cogently relevant observation by Lerone Bennett. He writes:

> Blackness is a challenge because it raises the whole question of values and because it tells us that we must rise now to the level of teaching this profoundly ignorant and profoundly sick society. And in order to do that, we must create a new rationale. We must create a new rationality, a new way of seeing, a new way of reasoning, a new way of thinking. Our thinking... is Europe-centered, white centered, property and place-centered. We see now through a glass whitely, and there can be no more desperate and dangerous task than the task which faces us now of trying to see with our own eyes.[14]

In addition to our perspective of blackness as a moral force, there are other scholars of the black religious community such as Bishop Joseph A. Johnson, Jr., who attempt to set forth a theological rationale from the standpoint of the Christian faith. His theoretical aim, for instance, is to provide theological content and vitality to the concept of "blackness" by casting it within the framework of the Christian faith; and thus to establish credence for the use of the term "black" with the term "theology." Therefore Bishop Joseph A. Johnson argues the case that

> Blackness is an ontological-philosophical-theological concept. It is ontological in the sense that it affirms the existence of the black man as a legitimate and significant part of a God-given humanity to which all other races belong. Blackness is a philosophical concept in the sense that it requires a critical examination of fundamental ideas about God, world, man, good, and evil which have arisen out of the black Christian experience. Blackness is a theological concept in that it affirms with the Hebraic Christian tradition that all of God's creation is good....Blackness represents a man's commitments, his beliefs, his ideologies.[15]

Here it is important for us to note that any theological, philosophical, or ontological affirmation of blackness as a concept does not negate its ethical dimension; rather it points--in a more profound way--to a dynamic convergence, seeking always to illuminate the whole of the black religious experience. In the past, blacks have had to subscribe both to an "ethics of deception" and an "ethics of freedom" in order to survive in a society that socially and spiritually discriminated against the children of dark skin. The scheme for addressing this pattern of value-orientation in black life may be depicted as follows:

VALUE-ORIENTATION IN BLACK LIFE

THE ETHICS OF SURVIVAL	THE ETHICS OF FREEDOM
Blackness as Deception	Blackness as Moral-Force
"Me-ness"	"We-ness"
Social-Acceptance (victimization)	Moral-Resistance (progress)
Moral-Tolerance	Social-Conflict

17

The conceptual scheme describes some of the dynamics and interrelational elements that help to make up the value-orientation in black community. Ethical consideration of the harsh realities of being black in a white-dominated society tends to develop within the souls of black folk a diversified pattern of responses for coping. Now in the American society, the two main patterns or poles around which black life seems to revolve are reflective of the "ethics of survival" and the "ethics of freedom." Depending on the crucibles of the existential situation, black response to white oppression may be mixed, and at times, ranging from mere "moral tolerance" to radical violent conflict; from "social-acceptance" (i.e., a process of victimization where whites define the black man's "place" and self-identity in society) to "moral-resistance" (the process of struggle wherein the person determines his or her own identity, religio-cultural values, and ethical disposition toward society--hence "progress").

In terms of relational character, the elements of "blackness as deception" and "blackness as moral-force" in our scheme point to a difference more in degree than in kind. Notwithstanding, the crucibles of black wisdom indicate that oppressed blacks, historically, have overwhelmingly lifted their voices to sound the trumpet of the "ethics of freedom." In the black religious experience, the main ethical attention is on the "we-ness" instead of the "me-ness." While the reality of the "me-ness" is important, it can only be fully authenticated *in* and *through* community. Man is both a spiritual and social human being; and as such, it is only within the community of faith theologically where persons find their ultimate fulfillment under God (koinonia). Ethically and theologically considered, the black religio-cultural heritage, then, holds more central to the concept of the "we-consciousness" than to the "me-consciousness." In short, blackness as a moral imperative--and in the light of our conceptual scheme--gives positive ethical content to human existence, not simply because it is supportive of the "ethics of freedom" in particular, but also because of its crucial relevance to black religious ethics in general. In any event, the concept of blackness enables the oppressed black man not to be ashamed of who *he is*, of his life-style and cultural heritage. In a word, blackness means the struggle on the part of the black man to stand tall and firm against anything that negates his humanity, his basic sense of integrity, and his dogged determination to be free! Let us turn now, however, to some of the elemental characteristics implicit in the construction of a Black Religious Ethic.

FIVE CHARACTERISTICS OF BLACK RELIGIOUS ETHICS

Black religious ethics expresses in part the "soul" of the black experience. For purposes of explication, we may functionally define black religious ethics as *a socio-political ethic of liberation, which aims, objectively, at changing the conditions of oppression and sees God's will as congruent with the solidarity of the dispossessed.* For Blacks, this means in part that we must begin to understand and interpret the norms and radical imperatives implicit in the Christian faith from a different theological posture. Thus far we have already ventured to indicate something about the nature of the ethical task and the meaning of blackness as a moral imperative. Our remaining task in this chapter, however, is to identify, in a brief descriptive manner, some of the characteristic elements of Black religious ethics.

The first major characteristic of Black religious ethics is the *moral conviction*, particularly in one's examination of folk-wisdom of the black tradition, that *God cares about the poor and the oppressed.* The moral conviction that God cares about what happens to the poor, needy, and dispossessed--in this world--is an integral part of black ethical thought. It seems to me that any viable Christian understanding of God, as reflected in the ethical teachings of Jesus Christ, must take into account that God Himself is deeply involved in the human condition; that he knows and understands the sufferings and afflictions of his people; and that the Almighty God will deliver the poor and the oppressed of the land.

Ethically and theologically speaking, the sensitive black Christian is acutely aware that the Bible teaches: "Rob not the poor, because he is poor: neither oppress the afflicted in the gate: for the Lord will plead their cause and spoil the soul of those that spoiled them." (Proverbs 22: 22-23) Thus, Black religious ethics is an ethic of radical concern for the poor. Because God in the person of Jesus Christ identified with the poor and outcast, the Black Christian, then, believes God to be the highest source of moral good, the supreme pattern of moral conduct in human community. Howard Thurman, in his volume *Jesus and the Disinherited,* identifies the central thrust of the ministry of Jesus as one that was oriented around the poor and the oppressed. He argues:

> ...The basic fact is that Christianity as it was born in the mind of this Jewish teacher and thinker appears as a technique of survival for the oppressed. That it became, through the intervening years, a religion of the powerful and dominant, used sometimes as an instrument of oppression, must not tempt us into believing that it was thus in the mind and life of Jesus....

19

Whenever his spirit appears, the oppressed gather fresh
courage; for he announced the good news that fear,
hypocrisy, and hatred, the three hounds of hell that
track the trail of the disinherited, need have no
dominion over them.[16]

A second major characteristic of Black religious ethics is
the fact that it is *biblical* in character. As one old black
preacher once remarked: "Sisters and Brothers, 'dis O Bible is
a road map and guide; it's a plan of salvation for de sinner man,
for a rejected and demoralized people!" It is quite evident to
those who are acquainted with the crucibles of black history that
"slave morality" and the slave's particular mode of social conduct were very much influenced by what we now call biblical
ethics. The concern on the part of slaves to understand the moral
laws, the ten commandments, and ethical mandates as disclosed in
the Word of God constitutes an important ingredient in Black
religious ethics. Here we may observe that Black religious
ethics, in the life of the community of faith, is an ethic of
loyalty to God. This is, undoubtedly, the case because black folk
have always demonstrated a peculiar capacity to discern the meaning of existence and the moral truths of the universe primarily
in light of the Word of God as disclosed in the Bible.

Moreover, the morally sensitive person can perhaps see, far
from any accident of history, that the first book many slaves
learned to read was the Holy Bible. Indeed, Black religious
ethics, in a very real sense, is not only biblical--boradly con-
sidered--but also *theocentric* in character. Here it would appear
that the genesis and *telos* of Black religious ethics is God; a
God who was apparently viewed by slaves to be the source and norm
of human existence. To be sure, black slaves certainly perceived
the God of the Bible as one who gives supreme importance to the
norm of justice as a requisite for all people in human society.
This particular theme relating to God's justice was vividly
stressed by nineteenth century black leaders such as David Walker
and Henry Highland Garnet.[17]

As an articulate and prophetic spokesman of the black community, David Walker, for instance, believed that the wretchedness of slavery in America was an obvious abomination to the
righteousness and justice of God. And that white Americans in
particular are accountable to the Almighty for their deeds of
hatred perpetrated against blacks. Walker proclaimed:

Can the Americans escape God Almighty? If they do, can
he be to us a God of Justice? God is just, and I
know it--for he has convinced me of my justification--
I cannot doubt him.[18]

Again, in a similar fashion, Walker speaks of God's retribu-
tive judgment upon the Americans in their perennial oppression of
the black slave:

> For God Almighty will tear up the very face of the
> earth!!! Will not that very remarkable passage of
> Scripture be fulfilled on Christian Americans? Hear
> it Americans!! "he that is unjust, let him be unjust
> still:--and he which is filthy, let him be filthy still:
> and he that is righteous, let him be righteous still:
> and he that is holy, let him be holy still." I hope
> that the Americans may hear, but I am afraid that they
> have done us so much injury, and are so firm in the
> belief that our Creator made us to be an inheritance to
> them forever, that their hearts will be hardened, so
> that their destruction may be sure....[19]

A third characteristic element of Black religious ethics, as
I see it, is its emphasis upon a *sense of community*. From a
theological perspective, the concept of community is both descriptive and normative. It is more than a place or common terri-
tory where people meet based on formal contractual arrangements
that are regulated to a greater or lesser degree by vested
interests. The idea of community is far more than social organization, or a collection of individuals living in proximity to one
another. I agree with Professor Walter G. Muelder's comment that
"it takes a whole range of values mutually interpenetrating to
constitute a community, or even a culture."[20] So then, our reflection upon community in a normative sense, as an important ingredient of Black religious ethics, means to place emphasis on the
"we" relationship. It is in the black community where individuals
black Christians find a strong sense of "belonging," group
identification, and social solidarity as a pilgrim people of God.
Here it is also important to point out, at least in a brief
descriptive way, that Black religious ethics affirms the black
family as a value-shaping center. At the practical level, Black
religious ethics suggests that we must have a strong emphasis upon
black family life as an instrument for providing ethical guidance
for our youth.

We may note, with approval, the comment made by Andrew
Billingsley, in his book *Black Families in White America*, concerning the normative instrumental value of the black family in
developing the personality of the young. Billingsley rightly contends that "it is within the intimate circle of the family that
the child develops his personality, intelligence, aspirations, and
indeed, his moral character."[21] He further argues that "...the
Negro family...must teach its young members not only how to be
human, but also how to be black in a white society."[22]

A fourth outstanding feature of Black religious ethics is its concern for *moral achievement* in the collective life of the black community. From a historical perspective, any morally earnest person would be impressed with the fundamental concern among blacks for social advancement, growth, and the general amelioration of the black condition in America. It was this same America, by the way, that systematically raped their daughters, lynched their men, and forced their women and children to become literally a "suffering servant class." But in spite of this horrible American reality, the creative and expressive genius of black people, perhaps largely due to their religious persuasion and ethical orientation, was not to be denied. Only in recent years has there been considerable recognition of the contributions of black people to the building of America and Western civilization as a whole. For example, Alain Locke, in his article, "The Negro's Contribution," documents the black man's ethical spirit of achievement in terms of his contribution and the meaning of his presence in America in particular. He writes:

> The Negro's contributions have been made as reactions to white civilization; its elements have been the basis of these reactions and its attitudes often the stimulus thereto. Christianity, the plantation, freedom, democracy, justice were all imposed ideas, ideals, and social facts. But to each of these the Negro has given a peculiar and definite contribution from a double point of view: first, as a passive presence influencing the institutional development of each...in the second place, actually making...a constructive contribution to these same ideas.[23]

Again, Alain Locke alludes to the qualitative moral achievement as well as to the eschatological promise of black presence by contending further that

> It is obvious, in spite of the great necessity for practical and economic contributions in the future on the part of the Negro, that the main line of Negro development must necessarily be artistic, cultural, moral, and spiritual. Because of the complementary character of such contributions in contrast with the predominantly practical, economic, and scientific trend of the nation, the part which the Negro will play is all the more desirable and promising.[24]

From a comparative point of view, the noted historian Benjamin Brawley, in his classic work A *Social History of the American Negro*, also makes a rather perceptive comment concerning the black man's moral achievement. He declares that the real quality and value of the black man can be readily observed especially in the areas

of the arts, aesthetics, and religion. In terms of the motif
of achievement as an elemental expression of Black religious
ethics, Brawley argues that the black man "brings nothing less
than a great spiritual contribution to civilization in America.[25]
"His is a race of enthusiasm, imagination, and spiritual fervor,"
writes Brawley, "and after all the doubt and fear through which
it has passed there still rests with it an abiding faith in
God."[26]

What many social critics and theologians fail to recognize,
however, is the fact that the black man's religion often functioned
as perhaps the only real "cohesive center of values" in a con-
fusing and mixed-up world where white folk called the shots and
set the ground rules of the "American-Culture-Game" of which black
folk were forced to play and adapt to. In any event, it seems to
me that one cannot deny that an integral part of Black religious
ethics is its concern for *moral achievement* in all areas of black
life. The principle of achievement has always been a significant
cornerstone in the ethical spirit of the oppressed black community.
Indeed, the dynamic chronicles of American history would testify
that the black community has not been without discipline, fortitude,
and a persevering ethical spirit in matters pertaining to the
advancement of the black struggle.

From a methodological perspective, a fifth characteristic
mood of Black religious ethics is its radical concern for the
"right" course of conduct in matters of decision-making and moral
action in human community. Some Christian social ethicists on
the contemporary American scene recognize that there are at least
two procedures, broadly considered, of human moral reflection.
Either the moral agent begins by seeking to define the end of human
action and thereby relate one's conduct to an ultimate good or
end; or the agent can choose, as his ethical point of departure, to
identify the primary duties, laws or requirements which must be
obeyed.[27] These two distinctive modes of moral discourse are often
referred to by some theologians and scholars as the "ethic of the
Good" and the "ethic of the Right," especially in one's theoretical attempt to interpret the meaning of reality. Methodologically,
Black religious ethics tends to belong to the latter category of
moral thought.

Here ethical reflection upon the black condition is concerned,
moreover, with the question, "What is the right?" or to put the
matter another way, "What is the best thing for the Christian
believer or black moral agent to do?" The ethical wisdom of the
black religious tradition responds to this question by suggesting
normatively that mankind, black or white, etc., ought to live
according to the moral requirements implicit in the Word of God.
That we ought to live, all things being considered, rightly. It

is in this context, I believe, that Black religious ethics may be viewed as primarily an "ethic of the right." Indeed, the value-orientation of black Christians postulates the "right" as a normative pattern for social conduct. For example, an interesting piece of ethical wisdom of the black religious tradition is set forth in this old moral dictum: *"It is always best to do right, because it is right to do right!"* I must hasten to add, however, that while the precise nature of the right is, in and of itself, problematic, the implication to be discerned in the case of the black Christian points toward a sort of inner "feeling" that each person knows the right as a child of God. For instance, black brothers and sisters of the community of faith are often quick to point out that the "right way," as they say, "is the way of the Lord!" In short, it is the "way of the Lord (the politics of God) and the ethical reality of his presence in the world (the Christian community of faith) that constitute, I believe, the vital nexus in our understanding of Black religious ethics; and subsequently, the emergent role of the Black church as a pattern of moral guidance.

Questions for Additional Study

1. In what ways can Black religious ethics be regarded as a
   seminal quest on the part of the black man to recover "bits
   and pieces" of the normative African culture?

2. Is the central problem of ethics in the black Christian
   community essentially one of identifying the moral foundations of our actions and conduct in a given social situation in American society, or is it primarily a matter of
   the agent's loyalty to God who promises to set the oppressed
   free?

3. What is the relation between the biblical materials and Black
   religious ethics in the light of the ethical imperative for
   social justice, brotherhood, and equality among the people
   of God?

4. Is Black religious ethics necessarily Christian?

5. Because of the black man's unique experience in North
   America, does Black religious ethics foster a radically different response to the traditional ethical question, "What
   ought I to do?"

6. Why is a positive concept of blackness important for young
   black people in church and society today?

7. Ethically and theologically considered, should young blacks
   be taught to magnify or glorify everything that's black in the
   light of the ever-present reality of white power?

8. How does the Bible contribute to our understanding and interpretation of a constructive perspective on blackness and
   ethnicity?

RELATED READINGS

Allen, Richard, *The Life Experience and Gospel Labors of the Rt. Rev. Richard Allen.* Nashville: Abingdon Press, 1960.

Baldwin, James, *Go Tell It on the Mountain.* New York: Dell Publishing Co., Inc., 1953.

Carpenter, Edward, *Common Sense About Christian Ethics.* New York: The Macmillan Co., 1962.

Franklin, John H., *Reconstruction After the Civil War.* Chicago: The University of Chicago Press, 1961.

Foner, Philip S., ed., *The Black Panthers Speak.* New York: J. B. Lippincott Co., 1970.

Herskovits, Melville J., *The Myth of the Negro Past.* Boston: Beacon Press, 1941.

Hughes, Lanston, *The Panther and the Lash.* New York: Alfred A. Knopf, Inc., 1967.

Lyman, Stanford M., *The Black American in Sociological Thought: A Failure of Perspective.* New York: Capricorn Books, 1972.

Means, Richard L., *The Ethical Imperative.* New York: Doubleday/ Anchor Books, 1970.

Murray, John, *Principles of Conduct.* Grand Rapids: Wm. B. Eerdmans Publishing Co., 1957.

Paschal, Andrew G., ed., *A W.E.B. DuBois Reader.* New York: The Macmillan Co., 1971.

Schulman, L. M., ed., *Come Out the Wilderness.* New York: Popular Library, Inc. 1965.

CHAPTER II

THE BLACK CHURCH AND MORAL DISCOURSE

THE TRADITIONALIST'S FAILURE OF PERSPECTIVE

One fact seems undisputed by theologians and scholars who have studied black religious institutions: namely, that the Black Church is an amazing and complex phenomenon of modern day society. Certainly, many scholars would not disagree that the Black Church as a social institution of formidable status does not lend itself to easy definition or simplistic ethico-theological interpretation. I wish to elaborate the ethical view that to do otherwise, would in fact, lend itself to what I call the "traditionalist's failure of perspective."

A number of volumes in recent decades have been written on the nature, character, and role of the Black Church in the Black community. Any cursory glance of the literature in this area would, undoubtedly, point toward the vital role that the Black Church has played in shaping the lives of black people in American society. For example, some writers and scholars have emphasized in varying degrees, the social and cultural role of the Black Church as a primary center in the Black community for the socialization of the young, and a place of cultural adaptation and assimilation into the larger society (Frazier's The Negro Church in America). On the other hand, some scholars and religionists have stressed the role of the Black Church along lines of the prophetic-charismatic tradition of the Hebraic-Christian faith (e.g., H. H. Mitchell's Black Preaching, and M. J. Jones' Black Awareness: A Theology of Hope, especially chapter 3, in what he calls the "Pre-Civil War Black Church"). Then, too, there are still other black religionists who have placed much emphasis upon the politico-revolutionary role of the Black Church as a potential power-base for black solidarity and unity--surreptitiously in search of the elusive "American Dream" to be included within the mainstream (e.g., J. R. Washington's The Politics of God). On whose terms, I might add, one cannot always be sure.

In each of the above cases there is an apparent neglect or failure of perspective to seriously examine the Black Church as a source of ethical guidance, to organically relate its theology

27

and ethics in a dynamic process of interaction. The failure of
perspective, however, is also evident in the traditionalist's posture of the black religious community. Here we may observe that
the term "traditionalist" is used to refer to any person or
Christian believer whose theological, social or philosophical persuasion prevents him from seeing the Black Church as a relevant
source of moral decision making and power. The current "crisis
of perspective" in the Black Church is perhaps illustrated by a
recent comment made by a visiting black lecturer at a major
theological seminary of the East: "The Black Church is a
'sleeping-giant,' drifting farther and farther away into slumber-
land, and away from the cries of our youth in particular, and the
oppressed in general!"

Some contemporary critics have gone so far as to outrightly
call the Black man's church little more than an "Uncle Tom Institution," a place for broken-hearted old ladies, and irrelevant for
the young, gifted, and black! Albert Cleage, for instance, comes
close to this view when he argues: "Look around in the black community now. What does a black child have to attach himself to?
He can go to some Uncle Tom Church, but he will find only the
image and power of the enemy."[1] Cleage further asserts that:

> ...there is nothing in an Uncle Tom black Church for an
> alienated black child....He is not going to come to Church
> and make any exceptions for a little white Jesus. He
> can only say, "If that's what they are putting down in
> there, forget it." So he doesn't go to Church. And
> Uncle Tom Churches are crowded--with old folk.[2]

Whether or not the harshness of this particular indictment
against the Black Church is totally justifiable is really not the
point here. The point is not whether Uncle-Tomism is relevant.
The point is whether or not the church in the black community is
true to the radical imperative of Jesus Christ. The point is not
church growth but moral responsiveness. The point is not church
doctrine but the call to revolutionary discipleship in behalf of
the poor and disadvantaged. Further, it seems to me that the real
point of contention centers in the traditionalist's failure of
perspective to adequately view the church as a significant source
of ethical guidance for all oppressed people--the old and young,
the skilled and unskilled, the learned and unlearned. What the
traditionalist fails, apparently, to understand is that the primary mission of the Black Church is to learn how to "take care of
business," relative to the areas of crucial concern in black life.
To be sure, the connections between the Black Church and ethics
or moral discourse in the social life of black people have not
been crystal clear. But the black Christian's moral struggle to
understand the church's witness to the meaning of its own faith is

28

deeply joined to its "boundary concerns" for liberation from oppression, justice and love, humanization and reconciliation under God in human society.

In varying degrees, the scheme that seeks to address these boundary concerns in the life of the Black Church can be depicted visually, relative to normative sources/resources, as follows:

Orientational Typology
The Black Church and Moral Discourse

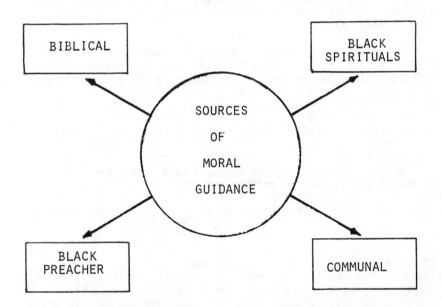

In the black Christian community, the scheme or orientational typology attempts to partially describe the dynamic patterns of interaction between the "biblical" and "communal," the "black spirituals" and the "black preacher" as sources and resources of ethical and moral guidance in black community life. At the practical level, the Bible for blacks has always served as a central source, as well as normative resource for the Christian moral life. In the life of the black Christian community, the Bible is perceived not simply as *a* book, but *the* book, wherein the oppressed

meet God in their suffering and toil; and this Almighty God is
perceived to give not only freedom but residual moral guidance to
the children of dark skin. So then, the "biblical" is a central
moral paradigm for right living. For black Christians, it is
both a *normative* source and *practical* resource.

For the morally sensitive person therefore, the wider meaning
of ethical reflection in a black context is the awareness that
the Black Church's ethics is not simply *black*, but *biblical*.
Attention is also given in this scheme to the "communal" category
as source for moral guidance. For example, the black man as
agent is always compelled to assess the judgments of moral
value brought to bear upon his existential situation of oppression in white America. Here the actual doing of ethics may
emmanate both from the "black spirituals" as well as from the
"black preacher" as resource and interpreter of God's Word to the
oppressed. A more careful discussion of these elements will come
later in this chapter.

With respect to the Black Church, I believe that serious
ethical inquiry or ethics itself, then, becomes a manner of
thinking that encourages one not to accept things at face-value,
not to accept life in our culture as it is or appears to be--
but rather to attempt to understand *what is* (reality) in light of
a moral concern for what *ought to be* (potentiality), particularly
for the common good of all human beings in the wider society.
In any event, the Black Church's ethics may very well have its
true birth in the ashes of discontent with the way things are
(status quo oriented), with an eye upon moral transformation
and humanization; the recognition and awareness that what is,
need not be, and cannot remain if we are true to the rudimentary
principles of God's liberating word as revealed in Jesus Christ.
From the ethical stance of Black Church this means, in some
sense, that black Christians must do battle with the sins of
social injustice, oppression, greed, racial bigotry and idolatry,
and white cultural arrogance manifested in so-called "high
places" in the American society! Concretely speaking, I wish
to elaborate further in this chapter the need to take a closer
look at three primary media that may illuminate the pattern of
moral discourse in Black religious experience: (a) the Black
Church, (b) the Black Preacher, and (c) the Black Spirituals.

THE BLACK CHURCH AS A SOURCE OF ETHICAL GUIDANCE

Historically, the Black Church has been one of the vital media
through which Christian communicants, devoted believers and non-
believers, as well as ordinary black folk have received ethical

guidance. For black folk, moral logic would suggest that the most permanent institution responsible for a reasonable amount of moral direction, from the cradle to the grave, is the Black Church. This reality was evident in the pre-Civil War black community; and it continues even today. Though often clouded by the peculiar drame of historical events, the most coherent norm of the Black Church, particularly in the social arena of life, is the norm of freedom. It is for this reason, but not for this one only, that the Black Church has been in the forefront of the black revolutionary struggle; and that its claim to freedom is a practical moral claim. So then, the norm of freedom is evident in both black religious activism and social agitation. We may observe this perceptive remark by C. Eric Lincoln concerning the Black Church's moral claim:

> The Black Church has always stood as a symbol of free-
> dom, even when the exigencies of the times made it a
> "Negro" Church. But it was never completely unanimous
> on the issue of whether it must not also be the
> *instrument* of freedom--a dilemma which shadows it to
> this day. Perhaps it is enough that it has produced some
> of freedom's most celebrated leadership--Nat Turner,
> Henry McNeil Turner, Adam Clayton Powell, Jr., Martin
> Luther King, Jr., and Malcolm X, to name a handful--but
> the Negro Church qua Church traditionally courted such a
> conservative image as to have seldom been considered a
> threat to prevailing social values.[3]

The Black Church is deeply rooted in the history of black folk in America; and in order to adequately understand its role as a source of moral guidance, a brief descriptive analysis is, I believe, appropriate. We have seen that in the literature of some scholars the ethic of freedom, with reference to the Black Church, is accented. In the course of our reflection, however, evidence would suggest that the Black Church has made an ethically relevant contribution to the black man's sense of personhood, and moral character. For example, one would be hard pressed to believe that the black slave in the pre-Civil War black community could have actually survived the brutalizing forces of chattel slavery were it not for the existence of the Black Church. Historically, the social and moral value of the black man's most prestigious institution is perhaps captured in part in W. E. B. DuBois' volume, *The Negro Church*. In a report of the Third Atlanta Conference of 1898, he clearly links its rudimentary religious and moral character with the African heritage by contending that

> The Negro Church is the only social institution of
> the Negroes which started in the African forest and
> survived slavery; under the leadership of priest or

31

medicine man, afterward of the Christian pastor, the
Church preserved in itself the remnants of African tribal
life and became after emancipation the center of Negro
social life. So that today the Negro population of
the United States is virtually divided into church
congregations which are the real units of race life.[4]

Here it is important for us to recognize that by any reasonable
standard or criterion of judgment, the Black Church has been the
key institutional center of black community life. Whatever
religio-moral and social values of African culture that remained
as a result of the enslavement of blacks by whites, was largely
preserved by the Black Church. Indeed, it is a peculiar chroni-
cle of modern history that this very institution--which receives
so much criticism on both sides of the color line, within and
outside the black community--shows, even today, a remarkable moral
and theological resilience. Theologically considered, the Black
Church is still a place wherein oppressed blacks can find
strength, hope, and encouragement that "things are going to get
better after while," even in a society largely dominated by white
immoral power. This type of moral strength on the part of the
oppressed is shown, literally deep down within black folks' souls
because they believe that God Almighty is on the side of the
oppressed; that he controls everything.

Now ethically considered, the Black Church is not only a
place where people of color go to find strength and social
acceptance; but in a rather profound sense, it is a *prima facie*
center of ethical guidance as well. After critically analyzing
the status of the Black Church, assessing its structural and
theological weaknesses, Mays and Nicholson emphatically proclaim,
in their volume *The Negro's Church*, that the Black Church itself
possesses a peculiar moral and spiritual "genius" of its own.[5]
They hold the view that

> ...there is in the genius or "soul" of the Negro Church
> something that gives it life and vitality, that makes
> it stand out significantly above its buildings, creeds,
> rituals and doctrines, something that makes it a
> unique institution.[6]

From a historical perspective, we may observe that part of the
ethical "soul" of the Black Church may well have been captured by
W. E. B. DuBois--in what I think to be a reflection of the
religio-moral African character of the Black Church, even to
this day--when he argued that after two centuries of white
missionary effort and association the religious rituals and rites
of the Black Church had only what he called a "veneer of
Christianity" and that much of the "old customs" lingered on
in their services.[7]

In any event, there is the recognition of the fact that many writers and social historians clearly document the important role of the Black Church as a source of ethical guidance relative to oppressed blacks who sought the opportunity for a better life in American society. Concretely speaking, part of the Black Church's genius is precisely this: that it functions as a practical pattern for moral guidance, a foundational source for the ethical development of the self. In our reflection upon the moral role of the Black Church in the development of individual character, Mays and Nicholson appear to be right on target by reminding us that

> With races and individuals, there must be an opportunity for the development of initiative and self-direction if real character is to be developed, and if hidden potentialities are to be brought to the fore. Certainly the Negro Church has been the training school that has given the masses of the race opportunity to develop.[8]

Or again, in a similar fashion, these authors emphatically assert:

> The opportunity found in the Negro church to be recognized, and to be "somebody," has stimulated the pride and preserved the self-respect of many Negroes who would have been entirely beaten by life, and possibly completely submerged. Everyone wants to receive recognition and feel that he is appreciated. The Negro church has supplied this need.[9]

To be sure, the Black Church has been a self-conscious, self-assertive and self-directed training ground for the shaping of character, a place where real character is literally "brought to the fore." But it is precisely here, I think, that we must raise some critical questions: What is the meaning of, indeed the ethical implications of, the notion of "character" in the black religious experience? Does it mean the same thing for black and white Christians in our culturally pluralistic society? How does "character" normatively described become an important ingredient in illuminating the structure of the moral life in Black experience? For example, the *Webster's New International Dictionary* speaks of several key words to define the notion of character such as "sign" or "token," a distinguishing attribute or personal quality. Ethically, some social thinkers refer to the concept of "character" as a kind of moral virtue, a sort of relatively permanent structure which underlies the moral conduct of a person as a whole. As a unique positive mark implicit in moral conduct, character may be said to denote those qualities or traits that distinguish one human being from another. In the psychological sense, however, the term character is almost synony-

33

mous with "personality," and tends to connote an *evaluative* judgment relative to individuals and social groups. For some psychologists, notably Gordon Allport, the evaluative connotation, for instance, persists in referring to certain "character traits" or particular stages in the psychobiological and social development of the individual person. Thus character refers, generally speaking, to typical or characteristic aspects of an individual's personality; it indicates some basic qualities unique to individual persons. All of this sounds well and good.

However, it is my contention that critical ethical reflection must go a bit further, especially when mirrored against the corpus of black life in America. In the context of moral experience in black life, there are many popular words and "catchy phrases" used by some blacks to disclose the ethical meaning of the phenomenon of character. To illustrate this point, let's take the following two popular phrases: (a) "being for real," and (b) "up-tight" or "together." The concept of "being for real," when used by the brothers and sisters, often means a kind of natural self confidence which one displays to the external world; it connotes personal integrity in moral behavior. For many blacks, the concept of "being for real" means the rejection and negation of all negative external images placed upon black people by the wider society. For still others, theoretically speaking, it means the repudiation and disvaluation of Anglo-Saxon norms, principles, and moral rules which are antithetical to the development of personhood and a full sense of wholeness in human relations. At the gut level of black community life, the notion of "being for real" connotes the negation of all acts of "phoniness" in the individual and collective life of the black community. In short, the idea of "being for real" expresses part of the essence of character because it points toward self-authentication.

Secondly, the use of the term "up-tight" by many black brothers and sisters is another way of discerning the ethical meaning of the phenomenon of character.[10] Perhaps the principal use of the term "up-tight," in ordinary social usage by blacks, particularly the youth, usually refers to a sort of positive self-acceptance and self-respect. As a feeling of positive self-awareness, it fosters a profound sense of personal pride in the agent's capacity to be himself and to become the kind of person he ought to be. So then, there is deeply interwoven into the moral fabric of the oppressed black man, a strong existential ethic of "pressing on"--a gnawing feeling in his gut that he can *be* and *become* something more than what white society says that he is. In any case, serious reflection upon these two popular phrases-- "being for real" and "up-tight"--reveals, I believe, part of the ethical significance of the phenomenon of character in black life.

34

In summarizing our reflections on the Black Church as a
source of ethical guidance, three observations at this time seem
appropriate. First, the Black Church, the only social institution which black folk fully own and control, serves as a vital
center of socialization and religious inspiration for a poor
and oppressed people. Religiously speaking, it still inspires
a destitute people to look ahead for a "brighter day" as children
of God. Secondly, the Black Church as a source of moral guidance
provides an opportunity for self-expression and leadership on
the part of the ex-slaved, dehumanized black man; an opportunity
which was usually denied in the larger American system, especially
in the white Church. Further, we have noted that historical
studies on the Black Church--particularly by such scholars as
W. E. B. DuBois, Carter G. Woodson, Mays and Nicholson, to name
a few--unequivocally repudiate the popular racist assumption that
the black man is without ethics, morals, rational principles,
and culture.

Thirdly, the Black Church was and still is a place where the
lowly and the outcast can come and receive recognition and
become "somebody." This is precisely what the noted historian
Carter G. Woodson meant when he once remarked that the Black
Church was "the school of experience for the Negro community."[11]
"The church furnished the opportunity for this experience and the
people learned their lesson well," writes Woodson. "They learned
how to discriminate, how to think for themselves, how to take care
of themselves in a critical situation, in short, how to be self-
sufficient."[12] Finally, we may note that the social value of the
black man's church stems also from the fact that it literally
stands as a "bridge over troubled waters," a refuge in a
hostile white-dominated society. Indeed, the Black Church as
moral teacher is the place where so many sons and daughters of
the race get their first lessons in the art of living. Thus it
is one of the principal shapers of the moral life in the black
experience.

THE BLACK PREACHER AS A SOURCE OF ETHICAL GUIDANCE

If the Black Church, as we have argued consistently, is one
of the chief sources through which the masses of the black race
receive ethical guidance, the black preacher, then, is its principal
actor in the drama of religious life. Just as the Black Church as
a whole became the center of social, moral, and spiritual growth
among black people, on the one hand; the black preacher eventually
became the chief moral teacher and theological interpreter of the
black religious experience, on the other. The black preacher, in
no small way, exerts a dominant influence in the lives of the masses
of black folk.

In Carter G. Woodson's study of black religious life in America, particularly in his work *The History of the Negro Church*, the observation is made that the black preacher was not only the key actor who occupied the prestigious position of community leader and orator but moral spokesman as well.[13] As moral spokesman, the black preacher was that individual, perhaps more than any other, who inspired a persecuted people to "think and to think on their feet," to express themselves in such a manner that enhanced dignity and self-respect among all persons in human community. E. Franklin Frazier reminds us that it was the black preacher, during the pre-Civil War period of American history, who gave moral and religious instruction to his enslaved brothers and sisters; and he accomplished this important task in spite of the perennial external threats to his own life, primarily through the medium of sermons, and the force of his own personal life as an example.

Theoretically speaking, it is important to note that Mays and Nicholson, in *The Negro's Church*, make a cogently relevant distinction between different types of sermons by dividing them into three classes: "those that touch life situations, sermons that are doctrinal or theological, and those that are predominantly other-worldly."[14] Although each of these sermon types is considered important for analysis, it would appear, I believe, that the first class of sermons is particularly relevant for ethical discussion. Obviously, the black sermon type that touches upon "concrete life situations" is crucial for ethical reflection, primarily because it deals with the "nitty-gritty" aspects of black life in white America.

In discussing the thought content of black sermons, Mays and Nicholson cite several important examples that reflect the ethical dimension of the minister as moral teacher. These include sermons with special emphasis upon race pride and group awareness such as "Teaching Negroes to be satisfied with their race and stop imitating others," "Teaching Negroes to be mentally and morally free," "Teaching Negroes to be thrifty and courageous," and "Teaching Negroes group self-respect."[15] We may observe here, generally speaking, that many of the sermons by the black preacher reflected to a greater or lesser degree four dominant ethical themes, in my own view, as a source of guidance for the black religious community:

1. sermons that stressed a strong reliance upon God, as the One who is just, all-powerful, loving and merciful;

2. ethical themes expressing a sense of faith that things that be and persist will not always be and persist;

36

3. the envoking of the love principle as a guide in
   how blacks, slave or free, should treat one
   another and others; and

4. a positive emphasis upon self-reliance and group
   solidarity.

Here it is important to point out that this writer is by no
means suggesting that other religious, social, and cultural
factors are less important in our description of the ethical
content of the black sermon. Rather, that the ethically sensitive person cannot afford, I believe, to neglect these vital
moral indicators in one's treatment of the black preacher's
sermon. That they represent a clue in our understanding of the
black preacher as a source of ethical guidance in the light of
the plight of the poor and dispossessed in America. Bishop
Joseph A. Johnson seems to capture part of the significant moral
role which the black preacher has played in the historical
struggle of black people in American society. He declares:

> The early black preacher was primarily the preacher
> of the word. His messages were determined by the
> reality of death, the difficulties of life, and the
> saving word which he discovered in the Bible. His
> ultimate purpose was one of bringing healing and
> liberation to a despised and depressed people who
> were exposed to the vast ambiguities of life. He
> sought by the word of God to bring healing and
> liberation to the broken personhood of black men
> and women whose lives had been disrupted and degraded
> by slavery.[16]

Indeed, the author goes a step further to indicate something about
the black preacher as "moral interpreter" but peculiarly
associated, perhaps always, with the medium of sermon and the
preaching of God's word. He argues that

> The black preacher was an interpreter of the black
> experience. He interpreted it in the light of God's
> revelation in Jesus Christ and thereby provided the
> moral dynamics for living. He believed that even
> though the black people had suffered, there was the
> conviction that God had brought them to this
> country for a divine mission to become...the medium
> of God's new revelation, the proclaimers of his
> loving mercy to a decadent and morally corrupted
> society.[17]

I must point out here that the ethically sensitive preacher of the
black community realizes well the need to keep alive a dynamic

interplay between the preaching of the word of God and the teaching of the word of God. Through the crucible of experience, the black preacher soon learns that effective ministry in the world involves both preaching and teaching; they are different parts of the same coin. To be sure, the black preacher must ever keep before his own consciousness the reality that God established a function of teaching in his Church as well as a function of preaching. In terms of our understanding of the moral life, neither is overwhelmingly effective without the other. After all preaching is, generally speaking, the proclamation of the living word of God (*kerygma*), the proclamation of the good news, i.e., the proclamation of the gospel of Jesus Christ--a gospel of liberation and redemption to a sin-sick world. It seems to me that for the black religious community this means that preaching--through the instrumentality of the black preacher--addresses itself always to the high and low, the poor and oppressed as well as the whole of humanity. In short, preaching addresses itself to the pitiful state of the human condition: a condition of estrangement from one's neighbor, one's sense of internal moral coherence, and one's sense of the "Holy Other." Thus it is for this reason, but not this one only, that the black preacher realized the prophetic importance and ethico-theological indispensability of the *kerygma* in the collective life of the black religious community.

Moreover, the black preacher is also cognizant of the fact that teaching is an essential concern of the Church. Concretely speaking, teaching is ethical instruction. The preacher as moral teacher guides his own congregation, for instance, in a quest for understanding of the moral life through a study of scriptures, and through serious reflection upon the ethical teachings of Jesus Christ as a standard for social conduct in the world. Normatively discerned, this reality of Jesus Christ is the reality of his moral presence in the world as the ethical guide for all people. Further, it is my conviction that the same Jesus who saves and liberates is the same Christ proclaimed by the black preacher to be the ideal model for the moral life, the One in whom oppressed blacks find comfort and unspeakable joy! The Reverend James Cleveland, a popular black gospel preacher, goes a step further by describing Jesus as "the joy of my salvation, yes He is!" In any event, Jesus Christ stands as the concrete socio-revolutionary paradigm for ethical guidance in the religious life of the black community; and the black preacher is normatively perceived as his *ethical instrument* and prophet who must "feed the sheep" and lead the oppressed into the pastures where the grass is greenest and most abundant, where the most refreshing waters of strength, courage, and freedom can flow.

In a profound existential sense, the black preacher is a man for others. By this I mean that he is one who feels the pain and experiences the sufferings of his own people in their struggles, trials, and tribulations. He is deeply implicated in their pathos; yet he speaks a word of comfort and guidance in order to give character to the poor, and to restore a sense of "soul" to the fainting heart. As moral leader, moreover, the black preacher attempts to acquaint the people with the essential truths of the Biblical message by stressing the centrality of moral duty in public life, of the necessity of love and forgiveness in neighbor relations, of justice and righteousness in ethnic relations, and of good deeds as a manifestation of discipleship in the world. In short, the black preacher as moral leader reminds the people that "everybody is somebody, and God is all." Thus the black preacher used religious insight--sometimes ascertained through revelation and personal experience, sometimes derived from scriptures--primarily as a source that enabled oppressed blacks to make ethical decisions relative to the everyday struggles of human existence. In no small way, therefore, the black preacher is an indispensable part in our understanding of religious and moral values in the collective life of the oppressed.

THE BLACK SPIRITUALS AS A SOURCE OF ETHICAL GUIDANCE

In centering our attention on the Spirituals as a point of departure for ethical guidance, we will, undoubtedly, be drawing upon one of the rich wellsprings of the black religious experience. As with the Black Church and the black preacher in America, voluminous literature on the Spirituals has been produced by writers and scholars of many disciplines. The primary thrust of much of this literature, however, focuses on the historical origins, development, and structural composition of each Spiritual as a valid expression of the image and culture of oppressed blacks. For example, we may observe this perspective in volumes of black religious music such as *Religious Folk-Songs of the Negro* by R. Nathaniel Dell, *The Negro and His Songs* by H. W. Odum and G. B. Johnson, and *Blues People* by LeRoi Jones, just to name a few. These volumes, as I see it, tend to share one basic thing in common, in spite of methodological and theoretical variables, namely: they all seek an appreciative understanding of the black experience essentially through the use of the historical-analytical and structural-comparative approaches to black religious music.

To be sure, there are a number of legitimate methods of treating the Spirituals. Here this writer's present purpose, however, is to argue the thesis that the Black Spirituals also contain ethical content and valuable insight into the wellspring

39

of human existence. Thus I wish to pose the basic question in a rather simple manner: Normatively described what is the subject matter, ethical significance and meaning of the Spirituals in terms of the moral life in black religious experience? From a historical point of view, some social thinkers have suggested that--as a result of the rape of Africa of millions of men, women, and children--the Black Spirituals were purely noble creations of a slave culture and a certain mode of adaptation on the part of blacks to a strange new world.[18]

Geoegraphically cut off from their native African culture, black slaves had to adapt themselves to a strange and hostile land, under one of the most harsh systems of oppression ever devised by man for man: the American system of chattel slavery. Thus it was from the crucibles of slavery, seemingly, that the noble Spirituals sprung.[19] Ethically speaking, the Black Spirituals express, I believe, a common moral identity, even to this day, of an oppressed people. Under the harsh system of slavery, the Spirituals perhaps constituted a unique moral language, a peculiar pattern of communication, a secret mode--in some instances--only obscurely visible to the outside world. But nonetheless a mode of moral language that was acutely relevant to the children of oppression and sorrow. The words of each Spiritual, whether we take, for example, "Deep River," "Steal Away to Jesus," "Go Down, Moses," or "Don't Leave Me, Lord," tend to possess dignity and reveal a kind of moral philosophy of the heart's cravings.[20] In spite of the opinions of some critics who suggest that the Spirituals are not really the black man's own original creation, there can be little doubt, however, that the Spirituals themselves are not void of ethical content. Indeed, the Bible is a paramount source of material for the Black Spirituals, particularly Old Testament characters and the ethical teachings of Jesus.

Further, there are certain guiding principles and ethical themes implicit in the corpus of the Black Spirituals. Chief among these we may observe, at least ethically viewed, are the following motifs which are readily discernable:

1. a concern for freedom in earthly life;

2. songs of concerns expressing moral admonition and guidance for human conduct; and

3. songs of aspiration expressing essentially an ethic of hope.

While many of the Spirituals do, indeed, emphasize sorrow, pain, death, and other-worldliness--we believe, overwhelmingly, that there is a sort of life-affirming character, encouragement, and

moral quality about them. The ethically sensitive person can
perceive in such soul-energizing songs, e.g., "We Are Walking in
de Light," "We Are Climbing Jacob's Ladder," an eloquently moral
pattern taking form and shape:

> We are walking in de Light,
> We are walking in de Light,
> We are walking in de Light,
> We are walking in de Light of God.
>
> Children, we are walking in de Light,
> Hallalujah to de Lamb,
> We are walking in de Light.

Or, we may be invited to experience, at first hand, the joy,
encouragement and enthusiasm for life itself evident in such a
song as:

> We are climbing Jacob's Ladder,
> We are climbing Jacob's Ladder,
> We are climbing Jacob's Ladder,
> Soldiers of the Cross.
>
> Every round goes higher, higher,
> Soldiers of the Cross.
>
> Sinner, do you love my Jesus?
> Soldiers of the Cross.
>
> If you love Him, why not serve Him?
> Soldiers of the Cross.

Practical experience shows the necessity, in most cases, of having
norms and values to live by. For example, the possibility for
failure or stumbling is far greater for the aimless wanderer
than for the person who has some moral directives and ethical
principles by which to live and to govern the affairs of human
existence. Perhaps nothing can be worse for a given individual,
a social group or nation than a loss of a sense of direction and
purpose. For the alienated black slave the Spirituals pointed
toward the moral life. The Spirituals gave moral direction in
seemingly what may be described as a "directionless world" where
the white man called all the shots. They breathe a childlike
faith in the "moral promise" of human existence, precisely at
a time when most other social groups would have perhaps undoubtedly
given up the struggle.

For the alienated slave it is important then to see that
the Spirituals constitute in part what may be called a *normative
light* which enabled the oppressed and alienated black man to

literally walk through the wilderness of slavery and not get irrationally disturbed. Because as the brothers and sisters would often say, "there is going to be a reckoning day, down here, after while!" So then, the morally earnest person can, perhaps, discern that when the slave talked about "walking in de light" or "climbing Jacob's ladder," he was referring in part to a God considered to be the ultimate judge and ethical guide for a pilgrim people. But even more, there is implicit in these slave songs something fundamentally human: a norm by which to live, a moral philosophy by which to unravel and disentangle a complicated universe where men, women, and children were dehumanized and systematically oppressed for no other apparent reason--after having isolated the socio-economic material motive in white America--than the color of their skin. To be sure, the Spiritual "walking in de light" is suggestive of the slave's intent to follow the Lord Jesus Christ and to resist the forces of evil and strife in the world.[21]

From the standpoint of form, emotional expressiveness, and ethical meaning, the Spirituals reveal the slave's faith in the possibilities of life. For example, the hymn "Walk Togedder, Childron" speaks of this life-affirming element implicit, apparently, in the slave's ethical view not only of the things that be, but things not yet.

> Oh, Walk Togedder Childron,
> Don't yer get weary.
>
> Oh, Walk Togedder Childron,
> Don't yer get weary.
>
> Dere's a Great Camp-meetin'
> In de Promised Land!

This particular humn was made and sung by slaves who were forbidden by their master to sing or openly pray, but when the old master died the mistress looked upon them with pity, and subsequently granted the opportunity to come together and sing at night.[22] It seems to me that the hymn itself, analytically speaking, expresses in its rudimentary nature an ethic of social solidarity and unity. Here we can discern a morally relevant insight into all human existence: that there is a kind of power and vitality in social solidarity as reflected in "Walk Togedder, Childron"; that the lone individual or solitary wanderer could not sustain his existence for long. For the oppressed slave community, it is important for us to recognize that real solidarity could only possibly come through their common striving, their common pressing, and their common religious communion with one another as children of God. To be sure, the moral admonition, "not to get weary," constantly rekindled their faith in the possibilities of tomorrow.

42

The second ethical theme and attitude implicit in the
Spirituals, besides those reflecting moral admonition and
encouragement, is the theme of freedom. To examine the Black
Spirituals as a source of ethical guidance, we find a perennial
concern for freedom in human existence. Perhaps the real
ethical significance of the Spirituals is partly disclosed,
though often hidden and covertly enshrined beneath the melodic
surface of each song, in the human drama for moral freedom
itself. The exact measure of freedom anticipated by the oppressed
black man under the yoke of slavery was often contemplated in
proportion to, or in relationship to the probability of death
in one's attempt to struggle for freedom. The life of freedom
for the slave, and the imminent possibility of death in his
quest for it, has always been an intriguing theme of the Black
Spirituals. For example, Howard Thurman's important work,
The Negro Spiritual Speaks of Life and Death, is a classic
illustration of this interwoven drama.[23] The concern for freedom on the part of the alienated slave is reflected in this
familiar song:

> Oh Freedom! Oh Freedom!
> Oh Freedom, I love thee!
> And before I'll be a slave,
> I'll be buried in my grave,
> And go home to my Lord and be free.

Ethically discerned, we may note that the temper of this
song infers that in every situation, even in the most gruesome
circumstance, the slave himself has some choice as to what to
do with his own life--whether to acquiesce and accept bondage
as his lot or to "strike a blow" for freedom. Moreover, it is
also reasonable to assume that even an alienated slave had a
kind of *moral choice* in a life-death situation, though in human
bondage. But the odds against his survival, in the latter case
as a rebel, would be dangerously great. Yet it is also apparent
that the greater danger or tragedy, I believe, to the human
spirit, with reference to the slave's situation, would not be
the perennial threat of death by a demonic master but the loss
of one's sense of human dignity, of self-respect, of the loss
of moral tenacity and character.

To be sure, there are some things in human existence worse
than death: the loss of selfhood, the slave's sense of personal
worth, the loss of a feeling of being "somebody." So then, the
morally earnest person is compelled to recognize the fact that
the Spirituals accent freedom as a pivotal norm of ethical
guidance. Again, the theme of freedom is beautifully disclosed
in such songs as "Slav'ry Chain," "Go Down, Moses," and "Children,
We All Shall Be Free." The characteristic norm of freedom is
intensely expressed as a mode of religious and moral experience,

43

especially in the latter song:

> Children, we all shall be free,
> Children, we all shall be free.
>
> Children, we all shall be free,
> When the Lord shall appear.
>
> We want no cowards in our band,
> That from their colors fly,
> We call for valiant hearted men,
> That are not afraid to die.

    The third ethical theme or tenet which can be found in the Spirituals, as we reflect upon their implications for the moral life in black religious experience, is the theme of aspiration. It is apparent from existing evidence and historical events that black slaves knew, existentially speaking, that this old world of "sin and suffering" was not their home. They had their hearts and minds set on "lofty heights," on "higher goals," and on a "heavenly place" beyond the temporal wilderness of physical slavery. Perhaps the important point to be discerned here is the fact that in the Spirituals we observe a peculiar theological phenomenon: the convergence of ethics and eschatology in one literary frame or musical composition. For instance, we may observe how the following slave songs express both a transcendent point of reference as well as a passionate concern for moral freedom and the good life through persistent struggle in this world.

> Don't you let nobody turn you roun',
> Turn you roun', turn you roun'
> Don't you let nobody turn you roun',
> Keep the straight an' narrow way.

Again, in a similar manner, the black slave bleeds together an ethic of aspiration with eschatological hope.

> Lord, I'm bearin' heavy burdens,
> Trying to get home;
> Lord, I'm climbin' high mountains,
> Trying to get home;
> Lord, I'm standin' hard trials,
> Trying to get home.

Or still again, the aspirational ethical posture of the black slave as reflected in his songs was directed also toward the actualization of God's eschatological promise. Thus the alienated slave could sing, though despised and socially rejected, with joy and praise to Almighty God:

I am seekin' for a city, Hallelujah,
Seekin' for a city, Hallelujah,
For a city in de heaven, Hallelujah;
City in de heaven, Hallelujah.

Dere is a better day a-comin', Hallelujah,
When I leave dis world O' sorrer, Hallelujah.
For to jine de holy number, Hallelujah,
Den we'll talk de trouble ober, Hallelujah.
Lord, I don't feel no-ways tired, Hallelujah!

These slave songs reveal a powerful ethic of aspiration and
a profound eschatological vision of the future community.
Ethically speaking, they describe the black slave as a climber,
as an aspirer. Moreover, they depict the oppressed black man
as a "mountaineer" in a wilderness of slavery and socio-economic
exploitation. Yet behind the web of oppression one could find
moral guidance and eschatological hope in God's future; black
slaves fervently believed that the God of history holds the
future in his hand. By using this type of moral logic as an
operational assumption, they could sing, "Don't you let nobody
turn you roun'"! "They looked beyond the condition of their
servitude," writes Professor James Cone, "and perceived that the
real meaning of their existence was still to come. The absurd
present was not eternal, and they were free to change it according to their vision of the future."[24]

In any event, the norm of aspiration proves to be a significant dimension of the Black Spirituals. In a very real sense
the norm of aspiration is the *intentional character* of black
religious experience; it is one of the foundational cornerstones
of black religious values. Descriptively considered, the very
heart of the norm of aspiration implicit in the Spirituals can
be simply expressed this way: it is an ethical disposition that
repudiates all static and fixed boundaries--superficially imposed
by the white establishment for the purpose of keeping the black
man in his "place" or in his current social position in the
American social system.

Perhaps it is the *intentional character* of the Spirituals
that rekindles the fire in the black man's soul to dream the
"impossible dream," to strive unrelentlessly for a "Promised
Land" beyond the day-to-day vissitudes, anguish, and despair of
his lowly existence. Further, the intentional character of the
Spirituals means that the black man must literally "keep his eyes
on the star" of freedom. Theologically speaking, the intentional
character of the Spirituals express, as I see it, the conviction
and foundational belief that the "Promised Land" will be
ascertained because God is on the side of the oppressed. That
God Almighty has his finger in the plan of liberation. As one

45

old Southern Baptist preacher once remarked concerning the historical struggle of black slaves: "Sisters and Brothers, we took a big lickin' (the horrors of slavery); but we kept right on tickin'" (undoubtedly referring to the "promise" of freedom). In short, it is this "tickin'" dimension of the Spirituals that reveals, at rock bottom, an ethic of aspiration.

In summarizing our reflection upon the Black Spirituals as a source of ethical guidance, the following two points seem significant. First, the moral logic or strength of the Spirituals stems largely from the fact that they provided the alienated slave with a means of coping in a society that exploited and subordinated him; one that literally attempted to destroy all vestiges of his common humanity. Secondly, a major implication of the Spirituals is the recognition that they enabled the oppressed black man to have an ethico-theological point of reference beyond the boundaries of the white race and the social caste in America. The peculiar irony of all of this, however, is the precise awareness that the ethical burden of white racism and its subsequent patterns of domination and control over slave life was in part a principal *raison d'etre* for the existence of the Spirituals in the first place, which expressed so much sorrow and pain, yet joy and hope in the possibility of overcoming, if not in this life, certainly in the next.

As a cultural and moral idiom of the black religious experience, the Spirituals were what white America was not: a majestic source of religious inspiration, a moral pattern of guidance, an extremely important reference point for a better life through self-acceptance. LeRoi Jones speaks of the strength, which the black man receives from his music, in this manner:

> The Negro could not ever become white and that was his strength; at the same point, always, he could not participate in the dominant tenor of the white man's culture. It was at this juncture that he had to make use of other resources, whether African, subcultural or hermetic. And it was this boundary, this no-man's land, that provided the logic and beauty of his music.[25]

In short, the black man's music, especially the Spirituals, represents part of the historical genius of the black experience. The Black Spirituals, to be sure, still remain a perennial source of ethical guidance for black people in America and elsewhere in the world community. We may now turn our attention to a consideration and ethical analysis of the contemporary phenomenon of Black Religion as a value in understanding a neglected dimension of the American experience.

QUESTIONS FOR ADDITIONAL STUDY

1. Can the contemporary Black Church, in a manner of speaking, afford the luxury of paying only "lip service" to constructive programs of economic self-development and self-help, particularly since it has a clear biblical mandate to ameliorate the social condition of the weak and disadvantaged?

2. How can the Black Church in the community make real the radical imperative of liberation?

3. Can the church universal accomplish the tasks of liberation as well as other ethical and theological requirements of the Christian faith without, at some points, engaging in politics?

4. Since theological reflection often arises from the believer's struggle with pressing issues in the work-a-day world, to what extent can the Black Spirituals contribute to the development of a moral climate where persons may better understand the *spiritual character* of moral struggle?

5. What role does the Black preacher play in relating Biblical faith and ethics to the concrete realities that confront blacks in white America today?

6. At what points can ethics and theology be dynamically brought together as the black Christian community seeks a more relevant articulation of its mission in the world?

7. Ethically speaking, why is it that some critics still feel that the black man in American society is victimized by a so-called "slave mentality"?

Related Readings

Berton, Pierre, *The Comfortable Pew*. New York: J. B. Lippincott Co., 1965.

Browning, Don S., *The Moral Context of Pastoral Care*. Philadelphia: The Westminster Press, 1976.

Carter, Harold A., et al., *The Black Church Looks at the Bicentennial*. Elgin, Ill.: The Progressive National Baptist Publishing House, 1976.

Drake, St. Clair, *The Redemption of Africa and Black Religion*. Chicago: Third World Press, 1970.

Frazier, E. Franklin, *The Negro Church in America*. New York: Schocken Books, 1963.

Hicks, H. Beecher, Jr., *Images of the Black Preacher: The Man Nobody Knows*. Valley Forge: Judson Press, 1977.

Niebuhr, H. Richard, *The Purpose of the Church and Its Ministry*. New York: Harper and Row Publishers, 1956.

Puckett, Newbell N., *Folk Beliefs of the Southern Negro*. Chapel Hill: University of North Carolina Press, 1942.

Smith, J. Alfred, ed., *The Church in Bold Mission*. Atlanta: National Baptist Home Mission Board, 1977.

Careers in the Christian Ministry. Wilmington, N.C.: Consortium Books, 1976.

48

CHAPTER III

CAN BLACK RELIGION BE ETHICAL?

For the contemporary Black Christian ethicist a fundamental point of departure of ethical reflection--both in terms
of our understanding and interpretation of black presence in
America--is black religion. Quite apart from its emotive and
experiential dimensions, black religion has value and credence
as a rational and cognate discipline in the theological community. Perhaps for the ethicist and theologian alike, whose
consciousness has been informed by a black perspective, the
ethical issues raised by black religion have implications far
beyond the pale of the black community.

In the black community's continuous quest for truth, identity and self-definition, it is reasonable to assume that we
must take more than a cursory glance at the ethics of black
religion. At this state in the development of black consciousness, it appears ironic that more systematic reflection in this
regard has not been so widespread.

The purpose of this chapter is to explore and identify in
a precise manner, some of the pertinent ethical questions raised
by black religion in context of the American cultural system.
Accordingly, I wish to investigate three important centers of
attention in black ethical thought, namely, (1) the consideration of black religion as a value theory; (2) the ethical relevance of black religion as a crucible of white Protestant
Christianity; and (3) the contemplation of three basic-ethico-
theological motifs in the structure of black religion.

While we are often appreciative of, and responsible to, the
various ways in which contemporary black religionists perceive
their work, there is always room for procedural diversity in
ethical and theological deliberation upon the black condition.
Thus what may follow will not be an attempt to force a consensus
relative to a common definition/explanation of what black
religion *is*, but rather to delineate how one black ethicist perceives the ethical task and its subsequent implications for the
amelioration of black life in white America. In any event, the
reflective mood of this chapter shall be descriptive, comparative, and interpretive. It is not the purpose of this writer to
deal with the relational character of black religion and the black
church or its assumed historical continuity with African culture--

49

although such a venture obviously has merit. Rather, our reflection shall be limited to some of the ethical questions posed by black religion in the light of value-formation of black folk in America.

Theoretically discerned and quite apart from the term "black," religion itself may be functionally defined as a symbolic system of meaning and value; it is the condition of being ultimately concerned about matters of life and death, and about the profound questions raised by human existence. Etymologically, the term religion is derivative from the Latin words *religere* and/or "*religio*," which means that which binds; *religio* refers to a constraint that no one can evade; and *religere* describes that which repeats itself, in the sense of a verdict of which we return again and again. The cumulative ingredients of these Latin terms, then, are the notion of binding constraint from which we cannot escape and to which we feel deeply committed.[1]

In the volume *Exploring Religious Meaning*, the authors argue religion implies, at least operationally, loyalty to and reliance upon a "pivotal value" as the center of meaning for individual persons in human community.[2] Now once the term black—a very powerful adjectival modification, indeed--is linked with the notion of religion, there is an interesting interplay and dynamic operative. Thus we are compelled to explore in part the essence of this dynamic, i.e., black religion as a value theory.

BLACK RELIGION AS A VALUE THEORY

Ethical reflection on black religion as a value theory begins with the affirmation of the being of black existence. It begins with an attempt to understand and to clarify the "isness" of existence, i.e., black people's primary images or theories of reality in the light of a sense of "oughtness." Theoretical reflection upon black religion is important, to say the least, because "theory is not just the end point of research," writes Richard L. Means; "it is also its beginning, the alpha as well as the omega of systematic thought."[3] What is being suggested here, I believe, is the recognition that black religion has merit as an independent religious force. It is not simply another cryptonym for white religion in America.

Although the ethics of black religion may embrace some of the historical normative values of both the Euro-American and the Afro-American traditions, its orientation is not essentially cryptonymatic. Descriptively, black religion is neither primarily cognitive nor emotive in its attempt to make sense out of the historical particularities of the black condition. Rather, I wish to argue the case here that the primary concern of black religion

50

is the question of values in the life of the oppressed in their search for wholeness and a new moral nexus under God.

I believe that the ethical question undergirding the structure of black religion is, therefore, the issue of values; the heart of black religion centers in value-affirmation of the worth of black people. These values are, in varying degrees, both theological and cultural in the black religious experience. Even from a comparative framework, a number of social scientists of Western society--e.g., such men as Durkheim, Weber, Parsons, Simpson and Yinger, to name a few--have argued the position that our values determine what we select as the cause of a cultural reality or event as well as a catalyst for the unfolding of moral action itself. While there is no absolutely "objective" and scientific analysis of human values, the focus on black religion as a value theory does, in the main, say something about the ethical significance and the nature of black reality.

Even the notion of black culture is essentially a value concept. Values are existential expressions of preference, with distinct moral overtones. From the perspective of black religion, they are implicit and explicit manifestations of the actual behavior of the oppressed in light of their struggle for liberation. Norms, on the other hand, differ from values in that norms are specific prescriptions of behavior relative to a particular situation of oppression.[4]

For example, James Cone, in his work *Black Theology and Black Power*, makes an assessment of the oppressive black situation in America and concludes blacks must struggle for liberation "by any means necessary."[5] Regardless of the merits and demerits of such a methodological posture, the norm for behavioral response is identifiable relative to the situation of black oppression.

In any event, the dispositional character of black religion stems in part from its value assumptions. What, then, is the nature of values in terms of a viable theoretical construction? The new *Roget's International Thesaurus* (3rd edition) speaks of three key words, primarily, to convey the essence of the term "value," namely, usefulness, meaning and worth.[6] The notion of *usefulness* pertains to the locality and efficacy of an object or act; *meaning* refers to the substance, impact, and intent of an idea or concept. *Worth* has to do with the moral content of an agent's behavior in a concrete cultural situation. So then, the cumulative significance of the idea of "value" implies an object of worth and a qualitative experience relative to the intentional character of practice.

Values determine the choices we make in the light of what is existentially occurring. Thus values are contextually

validated; they emmanate from the wellspring of lived experience.
For black people in America that experience is largely one of
oppression. It is only in this sense, therefore, that we may
speak of black religion as a value theory because it sensitizes
our conscience to the absurdity and immorality of oppression.
Theologically, black religion is not simply a matter of logic
and theory but of life and struggle, because it is the condition
of being ultimately and morally concerned about what happens to
black people in the lived world of experience.

Thus the use of value terminology, from a black frame of
reference, means that the oppressed black man has always had
some perception of the "good," the "right," and the "virtuous"
in human society. Further, it is reasonable to assume that the
basic source of his experiential encounter with the "holy other"
and the "ethical" is in all probability something different from
his white middle class counterpart, whose existence is not
pejoratively limited by the barrier of skin color. It is precisely at this point that the ethical question raised by black
religion, especially in the context of the historical black community, is survival.

Black religion is pragmatic, it is about the business of
improving the quality of life and the social status of the
oppressed black man in this land. The politics of "survival"
has been, and continues to be, a perennial strand in the black
man's history and culture. Joseph R. Washington, in his
articles "How Black is Black Religion?" points to this moral insight in black experience. From a historical perspective,
Washington reminds us of the dynamic interplay between black culture and black religion. He contends:

> Black culture has its special domain in black folk
> religion, the locus where black people have proved
> and preserved their identity. Black folk religion is
> experiential first and foremost. It begins and ends
> in the experience of the people through uninhibited
> feeling expressed in the powerful tones.

Whatever else we may say about the ethics of black religion,
its value orientation arises in part out of the corporate life
of black people in their search for identity, meaning, and purpose as children of God. The plight of the black in a white-
dominated society has been a stormy one; however, the ethical
values implicit in Black religion, particularly the prevailing
survival motif, have enabled black people to weather the stormy
seas of racial injustice and institutional subordination.
Professor Wilmore, in *Black Religion and Black Radicalism*,
describes a historical dimension of this value orientation by
pointing to a fusion between the African religious past, on the

52

one hand, and the radical-pragmatic demands of modern secularism on the other. He argues that

> this search for meaning and direction by an analysis of the development of Black religion in America from the period of slavery to the emergence of the new theological currents which have impelled Black churchmen into the center of the civil rights movement of the last decade....Its basic theoretical postulation is that there was, from the beginning, a fusion between a highly developed and pervasive felling about the hierophantic nature of historical experience, flowing from the African religious past, and a radical and programatic secularity, related to the experience of slavery and oppression, which constituted the essential and most significant characteristic of Black religion.[8]

BLACK RELIGION: THE CRUCIBLE OF
WHITE PROTESTANT CHRISTIANITY

From the outset, we have argued that one of the basic ethical assumptions undergirding the phenomenon of black religion is its emphasis upon values. In addition to the motif of "survival" as a pivotal value of black religion, the principles of freedom and equality are also integral parts of its value orientation. From the vantage point of teleological ethics, the idea of freedom and equality appears to be the end goal or telos of black struggle.[9] Indeed, the dynamic character of black religion demands freedom and equality as minimum moral requirements in black-white relations in order to balance the scale of social justice.

In 20th century white America, however, the scale of social justice has been largely set against the amelioration of the black condition. The alienative values of contemporary American society have been, in the main, reinforced by what may be called "white Protestant Christianity" or "organized white Christian religion" rather than challenged by the cries of the oppressed. For black folk, white racism is still the chief barrier to racial progress. Ethically discerned, racism is, for many minorities in this country, synonymous with the dominant white culture; it is the primary expression of alienative values in our national life.

It is a bit ironic and strange, to say the least, that black religion embraces a set of values--in varying degrees indigenous

to our democratic character--to which America pays only lip-
service. In this sense, black religion may be viewed as a viable
ethical paradigm to critically evaluate white Protestant
Christianity. Black religion, I believe, affirms the assumption
that all values--theological moral, social, cultural, artistic
or otherwise--must be tested by their capacity to contribute to
the freedom, health and integrity of persons living together in
community. As moral beings, values are determinative for
decision-making and action. If those values be clouded by what
Reinhold Niebuhr calls "social pride" or man's "inordinate desire
for power," then white Protestant Christianity is, indeed,
ethically problematic and theologically corrupted.

Basically, it is my thesis here that black religion is not
only important for the survival and integrity of the black man--
especially in terms of our understanding of the evolution of
values in the black community--but also because it has played a
peculiar spiritual role in the testing of white Protestant
Christianity and the American democratic ideals in Western
society. W. E. B. DuBois, in his volume, *Gift of Black Folk*,
describes this reality from a historical-comparative perspective
of the convergence of American religions:

> ...the American Church, both Catholic and Protestant
> has been kept from any temptation to over-righteousness
> and empty formalism by the fact that just as Democracy
> in America was tested by the Negro, so American religion
> has always been tested by slavery and color prejudice...
> It has compelled American religion again and again to
> search its heart and cry "I have sinned," and until the
> day comes when color caste falls before reason...the
> black American will stand as the last and terrible test
> of the ethics of Jesus Christ.[10]

Historically, the traditional interpreters of American
Christianity and culture have largely depicted the black to be
without a legitimate religion, law, and/or artistic-cultural
symbolisms. Evidence suggests nothing seems further from the
truth; the black man did not come to America empty-handed and
empty-headed. For the Black American, it is reasonable to assume
that his philosophy and world view are reflective of an integrative whole, which have their source in the traditional religions
of Africa.[11] So then, our understanding of the ethical and
spiritual character of black folk did not start with the intro-
duction of Christianity to the black slave community. There was
something before. DuBois writes:

> ...Religion in the U.S. was not simply brought to the
> Negro by missionaries. To treat it in that way is
> to miss the essence of the Negro action and reaction

upon American religion. We must think of the transplanting of the Negro as transplanting to the U.S. a
certain spiritual entity, and an unbreakable set of
world-old beliefs, manners, morals, superstitions and
religious observances...[12]

Here the fundamental issue is the meaning of black religion as
the crucible of white Protestant Christianity. Paradoxically,
the very reality of black religion in the U.S.--with its own
cultural idioms and moral beliefs--reveals, at even a deeper
level, the inherent contradictions of American democratic values.
Black religion, I believe, is a viable alternative socio-
cultural value system, because it affirms the beauty and
strength of black life rather than social victimization.

The ethics of black religion reveal how the black man--
in his quest for meaning and truth beyond the narrow structural
limitations of white society--has persevered as a pilgrim in a
strange land. DuBois writes:

From the first his (i.e., the black man's religion)
was the concrete test of that search for truth, of the
strife toward a God, of that body of belief which is
the essence of true religion. His presence rent and
tore, and tried the souls of men.[13]

Metaphorically, DuBois seems to be suggesting that the black man's
religion not only provided him with an integrative principle
for interpreting the pain and suffering of black reality, but
there is also a self-critical moral dimension of black religious
experience which lays bare the absurdities and ethical contradictions inherent in white Protestant Christianity.

The absurdity is precisely this: the prevailing gap between
what white Christians profess as Christians, on the one hand, and
how they actually live and treat their black brothers and sisters
as Americans, on the other. Indeed, this is the moral cutting
edge of black religion. And its presence in America tries the
"souls of men," i.e., the souls of white men who turn a deaf
ear to the cries of the poor and the oppressed.

To be sure, institutionalized white religion on the contemporary scene appears to be more in tune with the maintenance
of the status quo than with serious deliberation upon the implications of the revolutionary ethics of Jesus--a normative ethic
of justice and love. Sociologically, the mainstream religious
belief systems of today tend to be assimilated to the ideas and
values of what Will Herberg calls the "American Way of Life."[14]
The conventional religions--Protestantism, Catholocism, and
Judaism--are typically understood as an expression of the "American

55

Way," or the "Common Faith," thoroughly secularized and
homogenized, and quite apart from the ethics of Jesus and its
concern for persons in human community. In this sense, white
Protestant Christianity aids one in conforming to the status
quo. It seems to me that the moral cutting edge of black
religion informs our conscience that the white church must move
beyond a kind of "mindless loyalty" to American culture to the
posture of "radical faith" under the righteousness and love of
an Almighty Sovereign God.

Seemingly contradictory at points, there is yet another
level of ethical interpretation of DuBois' perception of black
religion relative to American democratic values. For DuBois,
historical ethical discernment enables one to perceive--though
difficult at times to describe--a kind of positive resonant
quality of black religion with respect to the American religio-
culutral ethos. Reflecting on this moral and qualitative
dimension of the black religious experience, on its humanizing
effect on modern civilization, DuBois declares:

> Perhaps least tangible but just as true, is the
> peculiar spiritual quality which the Negro has in-
> jected into American life and civilization. It is
> hard to define or characterize it--a certain spiritual
> joyousness; a sensuous, tropical love in life, in
> vivid contrast to the cold and cautious New England
> reason; a slow and dreamful conception of the uni-
> verse...an intense sensitiveness of spiritual values...
> all these things and others like them--tell of the
> imprint of African on Europe in America..."[15]

At the current juncture in American history, this classic work
by W. E. B. DuBois, *Gift of Black Folk,* is just another reminder
of the religious, ethical, and cultural contributions of the
black man to modern thought. In short, religion and morals in the
black experience are not existentially or socially compartmenta-
lized; but rather they express the integrative character of the
being of black folk, an expression of their common life, thought,
and striving.[16] We now turn our attention to a descriptive
analysis of three basic ethical motifs implicit in black religion,
in terms of developing a more constructive, normative posture.

THREE CONSTRUCTIVE ETHICAL MOTIFS

In the discourse of moral reflection, I believe there are at
least three interrelated motifs of black religion which are
important to clarify for the health and integrity of the black

community. For reasons of identification, I shall speak of
these respectively as (1) the motif of purposive struggle;
(2) the socio-political motif; and (3) the theological-
eschatological motif relative to the development of a theonomous conscience. Such labels are a bit arbitrary; however,
I do believe that they will provide a sort of framework for
wrestling with the ethical content of black religion. First,
there is the motif of *purposive struggle* implicit in black
religion which has to do with certain identifiable goals,
values, and the moral aspirations of black people themselves.
While this particular motif is complex, we can, nevertheless,
grapple with its significance. Theoretically, the notion of
purposive struggle inherent in black religion comes under the
rubic of teleological ethics, which tends to identify the good in
terms of a moral aim or end of human action.[17] In this sense,
black religion is goal-directed; it is oriented toward the
achievement of true freedom on the part of the oppressed under
God, who is Liberator. To further illuminate this dimension,
we may observe the following diagram on the role of religion in
Black slave experience:

FREEDOM-HUMANIZATION MODEL

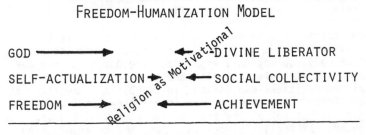

CONTEXT: BLACK SLAVE EXPERIENCE

The model or diagram seeks to address the reality of Black
slave experience in the context of white racist America. On each
side of the diagram the arrows indicate the flow and interaction
between the elemental components; it illustrates that *freedom,*
in ante bellum times, was morally and theologically perceived as
a goal to be *achieved* through struggle; and that *self-actualization*
cannot be adequately understood apart from the community (social
collectivity). At yet another level, the focus is on how God
participates, as *Divine Liberator,* in the concrete human affairs
of the oppressed--taking sides with them in the struggle for true
freedom and human dignity.

Ethically speaking, it is ironic that the "same religion"
the white master introduced to the slave--essentially as a means

57

of domination and social control--became the *elan vital* that
did most perhaps to inspire his fundamental yearning for
freedom; and to sharpen his religious perspective and moral
belief that God, the Divine Liberator, has no "step children"
but only "children" who are all created equal, free, and with
human worth. For the slave, freedom then was deeply connected
with a religious belief about God as Liberator and Judge.

Although the basic thesis set forth in Joseph Washington's
book, *Black Religion*, is problematic for some contemporary
theologians, I do think that he is correct in his assessment of
the "protest/freedom" character of normative black religion.
Professor Washington declares:

> Born in slavery, weaned in segregation and reared in
> discrimination, the religion of the Negro folk was
> chosen to bear roles of both protest and relief.
> Thus, the uniqueness of black religion is the racial
> bond which seeks to risk its life for the elusive but
> ultimate goal of freedom and equality by means of
> protest and action...from the earliest days, the
> Negro was much more concerned with the freedom of
> this world than with the religion of the next...[18]

Second, there is, I believe, in the structure of black religion
what may be called a *socio-political* motif. Here the ethics
of black religion not only emphasizes freedom as an end-goal
of purposive struggle, but also the need for recognizing its
social and political expressions in the black community. It is
reasonable to assume that the socio-political motif of black
religion arises out of the pragmatic concerns of the oppressed
for power. Ethically, blacks must have the power of being.
Indeed, the process of responsible decision-making in the black
community cannot be effectively executed without the "power of
being." By this I mean the power to grow and to participate in
shaping one's own history and moral destiny.

Politically considered, the power of being means freedom
from the restraints of a dominative white culture, from the
diabolical effects of racism and the institutional oppression of
black life in America. In essence, the "power of being" is the
power to become what God has created the black man to be: a
responsible and creative human being with moral choice.

Ultimately, it seems to me that the ethical questions
raised by black religion enables man as a moral being to see
beyond the contingent boundaries of cultural ethnocentrism,
religious history and social custom. Here one does not need to
appeal, necessarily, to some metaphysical system of universal
values in order to validate the claims of black religion.

Conversely, the moral claims of the religion of black folk
seem to have always reflected a kind of "universal element" in
the people's attempt to make sense out of existence and to
assume the awesome burden of freedom. One might hasten to add,
however, that the appropriation of the "universal" in black
religion, as I see it, must be understood primarily in
"emotive-pragmatic" rather than in "cognitive-metaphysical"
terms.

A third distinctive element, in our reflection upon the
structure of black religion, is the *theological-eschatological*
motif. I contend that ethics and theology in black religious
experience are inseparable. The confluence of the "ethical"
and the "theological"--in the black man's quest for identify
and liberation--is a neglected aspect of moral reflection in
contemporary black thought, especially for those theologians
whose primary frame of reference is the Christian faith.

Any serious reflection upon black religion, I believe, must
include the *theological-eschatological* element, i.e., a frame
of reference which seeks to deal with a realistic basis for
hope in terms of black people's own understanding and knowledge
of God--a God who is deeply concerned about the cries and sufferings of the oppressed. C. Eric Linclon, in the volume,
The Black Experience in Religion, makes a cogently relevant
observation in terms of the theological motif by arguing that:

> Black religion has had the anomalous distinction
> of depending upon a body of theology unsympathetic
> to its basic presuppositions for its interpretation
> of the faith. Black religion begins by affirming
> both the righteousness of God and the relevance of
> black people within the context of divine righteous-
> ness. White theology upon which black Christians
> depended has given little attention to the black
> individual or to the collective black experience in
> its concern with what it considered the significant
> aspects of the faith.[19]

In the perceptive work, *The Identity Crisis in Black Religion,*
Cecil W. Cone has made a valuable contribution to the
theological discussion. He emphasizes the theological motif
of black religion as a viable point of departure. For Cecil
Cone it is in the context of the black religious experience--
not black power or Euro-American theology as is the case with
some black theologians--where oppressed blacks in Pharoah's
White America encounter God in their human struggle for freedom
and personhood. From an ethico-theological perspective, the
primary focus of black religion is God. In *The Identity Crisis
in Black Religion,* Cecil W. Cone even goes a bit further in

stressing the theocentric character of black religion by
arguing that

> The divine and divine alone occupies the position
> of ultimacy in black religion. Indeed, an encounter
> with the divine is what constitutes the core or
> essence of that religion. Such an encounter is
> known as the black religious experience. This
> experience is continued in black churches today and
> is to be found whenever two or three are gathered in
> the name of God for prayer, song or sermon.[20]

In any event, it is this Almighty Sovereign God of black
religion who gives black people "strength for today and hope for
tomorrow." Perhaps the intrinsically binding meaning of the
"ethical" here is the degree to which it contributes in the
development of a theonomous conscience, i.e., the normative purpose undergirding black existence is understood in terms of our
appropriation of the humanity of God (theology) on our behalf,
and the humanity of man (anthropology). Put another way, the
meaning of the "ethical" in black religion is aimed at a type of
freedom rooted *not* in man-made morals, customs, and manners, but
rather in God's liberating activity in human history. In this
sense, the *theonomous* conscience implicit in black religion provides a deeper basis for ethical construction because its
existence emanates from the belief of black Christians in the
divine activity of God, manifesting itself on the behalf of the
oppressed, and all who affirm the inclusive principles of the
community of faith.

QUESTIONS FOR ADDITIONAL STUDY

1. On the practical level, to what extent can black religion function as a viable instrument in the struggle by the contemporary Black church to reclaim its prophetic tradition and revolutionary mission in the world?

2. Is black religion enough in a highly competitive and technologically complex culture?

3. Theologically, how can "black talk" about God and religion help in developing a broader perspective on the structure of American religious pluralism?

4. Can black religion transcend race or serve as an important corrective to the white cultural bias and ethical contradictions inherent in American civil religion?

5. Is the ethic of the Black church and black religion the same? If not, why not?

6. List at least three ways in which black religion may aid in reshaping our thinking about the value of community, of sharing and caring, and responding to the needs of other human beings in the context of society.

7. In a white-dominated society of moral indifference to the suffering of oppressed people, what constitutes a viable strategy on the part of the clergy for radical social change and value reconstruction?

Related Readings

Ahmann, Mathew, *Race: Challenge to Religion*. Chicago: Henry Regnery Co., 1963.

Bellah, Robert N., *The Broken Covenant: American Civil Religion in Time of Trial*. New York: The Seabury Press, Inc., 1975.

Birch, Bruce C. and Rasmussen, Larry L., *Bible and Ethics in the Christian Life*. Minneapolis, Minn: Augsburg Publishing House, 1976.

Drisko, Carol F. and Toppin, Edgar A., *The Unfinished March*. New York: Doubleday and Co., 1967.

DuBois, W. E. B., *The Negro*. London: Oxford University Press, 1970.

Gandy, Samuel L., ed., *Common Ground*. Washington, D.C.: Hoffman Press, 1976.

Hughes, Langston, *An African Treasury*. New York: Pyramid Publications, 1960.

Jones, William R., *Is God a White Racist?* New York: Anchor Press/Doubleday, 1973.

Lincoln, C. Eric, ed., *The Black Experience in Religion*. New York: Anchor Press/Doubleday, 1974.

Plumpp, Sterling D., *Black Rituals*. Chicago: The Third World Press, 1972.

Richey, Russell E. and Jones, Donald G., eds., *American Civil Religion*. New York: Harper and Row, Publishers, 1974.

Thurman, Howard, *The Centering Moment*. New York: Harper and Row, Publishers, 1969.

Washington, Joseph R., Jr., *Black Sects and Cults*. New York: Anchor Press/Doubleday, 1973.

CHAPTER IV

NEW NOTES ON BLACK POWER: HISTORICAL ROOTS

SOCIAL HISTORY AND BLACK STRUGGLE

In this chapter I wish to examine some of the major sources of information about the historical and intellectual roots out of which Black Power emerged, particularly as reflected implicitly or explicitly in the works of Martin R. Delany, Frederick Douglass, Marcus Garvey, and W.E.B. DuBois. In our analysis of their thought we will focus primarily on those themes which may shed light on the historical evolution of Black Power.

This analysis will not be a systematic survey of important dates and events in black history; rather it will attempt to present an understanding of the intellectual development of Black Power in order to explore the following ethical propositions. First, there are patterns of continuity between the historical and contemporary strands of Black Power. Secondly, the current Black liberation struggle--either in its secular or religious form--cannot be adequately understood in isolation from its historical context. Thirdly, the idea of Black Power, as it relates to the black man's collective struggle for freedom, justice, and social equality, is a dynamic and creative phenomenon in the wider society.

Fourthly, the dynamics of Black Power--largely viewed from a historical perspective--are reflected in the integrationist-separatist tendencies of certain black abolitionists prior to the Civil War, as the black community sought to define its future goals and objectives. Fifthly, the idea of Black Power was not only a negative reaction to the force of white racism and oppression, but also a positive affirmation of black pride and self-determination. The historical documents show that black social activists have been shouting Black Power--each in his own way, with different approaches--for a long time.

The emergence of the inflammatory phrase, Black Power, is not a recent phenomenon or purely a byproduct of the sixties. Evidence shows that Black Power has been a continuous refrain in the history of Black Americans. Nathan Wright argues the view that slave uprisings continually reiterated the Black Power

63

theme.[1] The cry for "black power" reverberated in the thoughts of many black abolitionists; two of whom were Martin R. Delany and Frederick Douglass. These black activists raised their militant voices in outrage and protest against the dehumanizing system of slavery.

At this point, it is important to differentiate between the contemporary slogan, "black power," and what we might call the historical expression of Black Power as self-determination. From a social and historical perspective, Black Power as self-determination means the yearning of blacks for real freedom and human dignity, i.e., freedom from the bondage of slavery, white oppression, and exploitation.

In the mid-nineteenth century, both Delany and Douglass were two of the most articulate black abolitionists in the black man's struggle for freedom and human dignity. Early Black Power took the form of protest against the black condition of enslavement. For the slave community, the right to rebel became a key form of Black Power. The slave's right to rebel for the purpose of gaining his freedom was a right generally acknowledged by many abolitionists. Morever, it was a right deeply rooted in the democratic American creed and based on the Declaration of Independence. Carleton Mabee, in his book *Black Freedom,* held that it was inevitable that the "Founding Fathers" of this nation would rebel against the British crown in order to win their freedom and independence.[2]

A more careful analysis of the critical question, "What is Black Power?" is needed in order to understand the complexity of the black struggle under the adverse circumstances of oppression and exploitation. Broadly speaking, the idea of Black Power is both dynamic and multi-dimensional; it means many things to many people. Historically, the dynamism and multi-dimensionality of Black Power may be expressed in certain dominant themes which tend to run through the thought of Martin Delany, Frederick Douglass, Marcus Garvey, and W. E. B. DuBois.

The themes of freedom and the black man's right to self-determination tend to be consistent strands in the thought of the writers under discussion. From a historical perspective, these dominant themes represent the two major aspects of Black Power. Freedom and self-determination are the two main dialectical poles of Black Power. They are not antithetical-- one moves naturally from the other in light of the historic evolution of Black Power. This means that freedom is a precondition to self-determination. Therefore, these dominant themes, in varying degree, embody the ultimate goal of black people in white America. Yet the residual problem centered not in the desirability of the ultimate goal *per se,* but in the question of how the ultimate goal should be approximated.

SEARCH FOR FREEDOM:
THE INTEGRATIONIST/SEPARATIST DILEMMA

Prior to the Civil War, there was a conflict emerging among prominent black leaders over the future of oppressed blacks in America. Harold Cruse, in *The Crisis of the Negro Intellectual,* identifies the emergent conflict by suggesting that some black abolitionists favored a return to Africa or emigration to Latin America, while others firmly believed that they should remain and struggle for freedom, justice and equality in America.[3] Quoting from George Shepperson's article, "Notes on Negro American Influences on the Emergence of African Nationalism," Cruse describes the nature of this conflict:

> Some Negroes in America showed an interest in Africa before the 1860's--usually in the face of the criticism of the black abolitionists such as Frederick Douglass who considered the African dream a dangerous diversification of energies which were needed in the fight for emancipation and civil rights at home.[4]

The quest for freedom by the oppressed is morally dramatized in the "integrationist/separatist" dilemma. On the one hand, the prototype leader of the integrationist strain is reflected in the thought of Frederick Douglass, the great black abolitionist of the mid-nineteenth century. On the other hand, Martin R. Delany, Harvard-trained physician and the acclaimed "Father of Black Nationalism," represents the separatist strand of thought. Thus the conflict within the Negro ethnic group between integrationism and separatism was vividly dramatized in the contrasting positions of Delany and Douglass. Martin Delany and Frederick Douglass were contemporaries in the struggle for freedom, justice and elevation of oppressed blacks who labored under the demonic system of slavery.

There are striking similarities in the thought of Martin Delany and Frederick Douglass. Both Delany and Douglass were champions in the cause of freedom for an enslaved and oppressed people. Both opposed the American Colonization Society in its philosophy that all Negroes, including those who had won their freedom, should be deported from America. Both established newspapers that strongly criticized the institution of slavery; and both fought for the elevation and self-determination of black people. In spite of these similarities, Delany and Douglass had

65

conflicting philosophical views over the future destiny of black people in America.

Dorothy Sterling describes the intellectual and social differences between Delany and Douglass in her book, *The Making of an Afro-American*. Sterling writes:

> Where Delany was likely to ask, "Is it good for our
> black brothers?" Douglass would say, with Garrison,
> "My country is the world; my countrymen are mankind."
> Yet their difference had a meeting point. Each, in
> his own way, believed that America in a white skin
> could never be truly free as long as it continued to
> oppress America in a black skin.[5]

In the mid-nineteenth century, Martin Delany wrote his most important and controversial work, *The Condition, Elevation, Emigration and Destiny of the Colored People of the United States*. In this volume, Delany sets forth his philosophy of political and ideological separatism. Themes of freedom, pride, and black self-determination penetrate the whole of his thought. In contrast to Douglass who emphasized the integrationist theme, Delany believed that oppressed blacks would never achieve justice and equality in America and that the black man's redemption and salvation would come only through separation. Delany wrote:

> Our race is to be redeemed; it is a great and
> glorious work, and we are the instruments by which
> it is to be done. But we must go from among our
> oppressors; it can never be done by staying among
> them. God has...designed this great portion of the
> New World, for us, the colored race; and as certain
> as we stubborn our hearts...his protecting arm and
> fostering care will be withdrawn from us.[6]

Delany advised his contemporaries that "a new country and new beginning, is the only true, rational, political remedy for our disadvantageous position." He felt that separatism or political independence was the sole means by which the black man could win his manhood and determine his own destiny. Constantly faced with the reality of prejudice and white racism, Delany would perhaps say to the oppressed, in the words of Bishop Turner: "White men are not to be trusted. They will betray you..... Don't fight for a country that refuses to recognize your rights.[7] On the other hand, Frederick Douglass, as an exponent of integrationism, believed in the American Dream of "freedom, justice, and equality" for all people.

Although racial bigotry, prejudice, and oppression were inescapable realities, Douglass felt that blacks must fight vigorously for their right to self-determination within America rather than separate. For Douglass, the American soil was conducive to the attainment of freedom and social reform. Douglass wrote:

> I know of no soil better adapted to the growth of reform than American soil. I know of no country where the conditions affecting great changes in the settled order of things, for the development of the right ideas of liberty and humanity, are more favorable than here in these United States.[8]

It is important to note that Douglass felt at home in America and regarded Delany's philosophy of separatism as "unwise" and "dangerous," a mere subterfuge for another type of slavery.[9] Benjamin Quarles, in his book *Frederick Douglass*, argues that Douglass "had completely assimilated the pattern of American culture. He had nothing in common with the native Africans except skin color." He further contends that Douglass disliked Africa because (in Douglass' words) "the human race becomes indolent in a warm climate."[10]

It seems that Douglass used this type of argument against Delany to reinforce his integrationist position which suggests that oppressed blacks must unite and struggle for freedom, justice and social equality here in America. For Douglass, this is the only plausible means by which the black man can win self-respect and human dignity. In the thought of Douglass, the struggle for freedom, justice, and social equality represents the essence of black self-determination. This struggle must be waged within the framework of the American society in order to transform rather than accommodate to its political, social, and economic structures. For the oppressed and disinherited, this struggle must be perpetual without which no progress or reform will be achieved. In an oratory fashion characteristic of many abolitionists, Douglass declared:

> If there is no struggle, there is no progress. Those who profess to favor freedom, and yet depreciate agitation, are men who want crops without plowing the ground. They want rain without thunder and ligtening. They want oceans without the awful roar of its many waters. This struggle may be a moral one; or it may be a physical one; or it may be both moral and physical; but it must be a struggle. Power concedes nothing without demand.[11]

Here the theme of black self-determination is made explicit as the oppressed struggle not only for freedom, which is a precondition to all reform, but also for power. Black self-determination means that black people must be free to determine their own destiny. "We ask nothing at the hands of the American people but simple justice," wrote Douglass, "and an equal chance to live."[12] Here it seems appropriate to raise two important questions: By what means will oppressed blacks achieve freedom and self-respect? Or, by what means will the dispossessed determine their own destiny?

From a socio-historical perspective, these are pertinent questions which must be faced realistically if we are to validate our case for Black Power. So far in this analysis we have suggested that Martin Delany and Frederick Douglass were articulate spokesmen in the cause for freedom--one of the dominant themes of Black Power. We have also suggested that Delany's philosophy of separation stood diametrically opposed to the type of integrationism advocated by Frederick Douglass, although both fought for the elevation and progress of black people. Philosophically, Delany and Douglass were of different moral and intellectual persuasions. Frederick Douglass, unlike Martin Delany, was influenced by the Garrisonian abolitionist school of thought, which emphasized the doctrine of non-violence and "moral suasion" as instruments of black liberation in the achievement of an integrated society.[13]

Frederick Douglass believed that violence was not a viable strategy or means by which freedom and self-respect could be achieved. The "only well-grounded hope of the slave for emancipation," he wrote in his *North Star*, is the operation of moral force."[14] Following in the footsteps of William Lloyd Garrison on the question of violence, Douglass felt that the use of "moral force" would inevitably end slavery. In contrast, Martin Delany believed that the use of "moral suasion" alone would not be sufficient to abolish the evil demoralizing system of slavery. Instead, he advocated the principle of self-defense and felt that the oppressed must resist all forms of oppression. As for the philosophy of non-violence, Delany insisted:

> Should we encounter any enemy with artillery, a
> prayer will not stay the cannon shot; neither will
> the kind words nor smiles of philanthrophy shield
> his spear from piercing us through the heart. We
> must meet mankind...prepared for the worse, though
> we may hope the best. Our submission does not gain
> for us an increase of friends or respectability--as
> the white race will only acknowledge as equal those
> who will not submit to their will.[15]

Martin Delany, unlike Frederick Douglass, de-emphasized the ethic of non-violence as a viable strategy and means in the achievement of freedom and self-respect on the part of the oppressed. In his judgment, the oppressed must meet "force with force" in order to attain the goal of freedom. In a letter to William Lloyd Garrison, Delany touched upon the theme of Black Power by emphasizing the black man's uncompromising determination to be free. He wrote: "Were I a slave, I would be free, I would not live to live a slave, but boldly *strike* for liberty--for freedom or a martyr's grave."[16] Here there are two observations that must be made.

First, critical reflection would suggest that the desire for freedom in the hearts of the oppressed tended to be stronger than the fear of death. This passionate desire to be free-- which is perhaps one of the deepest impulses of human nature-- is reflected in the militant-aggressive poetry of Claude McKay. Concerning the cost of freedom, he declared:

> If we must die, let it not be like hogs
> Hunted and penned in an inglorious spot,
> While round us bark the mad and hungry dogs,
> Making their mock at our accursed lot.
> If we must die, O let us nobly die,
> So that our precious blood may not be shed
> In vain; then even the monsters we defy
> Shall be constrained to honor us though dead!
> O kinsmen! We must meet the common foe!
> Though far outnumbered let us show us brace,
> And for their thousand blows deal one deathblow!
> What though before us lies the open grave.
> Like men we'll face the murderous, cowardly pack,
> Pressed to the wall, dying, but fight back![17]

The second observation concerns the question of "means" in the quest for freedom. Comparatively, Martin Delany sought to resolve the issue of means by advocating the right to self-defense and the possible use of violence in the attainment of the goal of freedom, while Frederick Douglass emphasized the use of "moral force" in the black man's struggle for freedom.

As we have already observed in the thought of Delany and Douglass, the question of "means" reflected a conflict in social philosophy. The question of "means" is important because of its moral implications in the black struggle; thus it is a residual problem in the intellectual and evolutionary development of Black Power. Inthe black man's continual struggle for freedom and self-determination, the twentieth century gave birth to a new crop of Black Power advocates, among whom were Marcus Garvey and W. E. B. DuBois. We will now turn to their thought in the revolutionary development of Black Power.

Black Self-determination:
W. E. B. DuBois and Marcus Garvey

Thus far one of the basic premises underlying this chapter has been that the contemporary call for Black Power cannot be adequately understood in insolation from his historical context. The present-day Black Power movement grew out of a long history of struggle and protest. As crusading abolitionists, Martin Delany and Frederick Douglass spoke for oppressed and disinherited blacks during the mid-nineteenth century. Although Delany followed the path of ideological and political separatism, the overarching goal of freedom was the central thread of his thought.

As the drama of black life unfolded on the American scene during the first three decades of the twentieth century, Marcus Garvey and W. E. B. DuBois emerged as the most prominent Black Power spokesmen in the cause of freedom and the elevation of oppressed blacks.[18] Concretely speaking, both Garvey and DuBois were products of the same social and historical period. The first three decades of the twentieth century churned up many ingredients from the depths of American society, giving rise to a number of ideologies ranging from nationalism and socialism to reformism and radicalism—all of which had implications for the black struggle. In his work *Dusk of Dawn*, DuBois described the social period in this way:

> My thoughts..and others (Garvey, Washington, etc.) were the expression of social forces more than our own. These forces or ideologies embraced more than our reasoned acts. They included physical, biological, and psychological forces.[19]

Both Garvey and DuBois were influenced by similar social forces emanating from the same period in American society.

Thus the historical "integrationist-separatist dilemma"—largely understood as conflicting valuations over the destiny of black people in white America—finds fertile soil in the thought of these two personalities. Theoretically and philosophically, Marcus Garvey followed in the footsteps of his intellectual predecessor, Martin R. Delany. W. E. B. DuBois, on the other hand, tended to emphasize integrationism; as such, his work bears a correlation with the intellectual orientation of Frederick Douglass. However, DuBois was not an integrationist in any rigid sense. During the whole of his life, "DuBois had periodically swung back and forth between the ideological poles of integration and nationalism," says Harold Cruse.[20]

As Black Power exponents, both emphasized the theme of freedom and the right of the black man to self-determination. However, each had a different approach, a different understanding of the black problem in white America. Edmund D. Cronon, in his book, *Black Moses*, argues the position that the social philosophy of Marcus Garvey revolves around the themes of race pride and African nationalism.[21] These themes tend to form the core of his social philosophy.

In his principal work, *Philosophy and Opinions of Marcus Garvey*, the author speaks of the necessity of race pride and self-esteem. "Be as proud of your race today as our fathers were in the days of yore. We have a beautiful history," wrote Garvey, "and we shall create another in the future that will astonish the world."[22] Garvey came to the United States from Jamaica in 1917. While in America he observed the dehumanization, powerlessness, and political disenfranchisement of black people. He concluded that America was a white man's country and that the black man's only hope for freedom and self-determination is separatism. As a Jamaican black separatist, he called upon oppressed blacks to return to Africa and redeem the land. Garvey declared:

> We are determined to solve our problem, by redeem-
> ing our motherland Africa from the hands of alien
> exploiters and found there a government, a nation
> of our own, strong enough to lend protection to the
> members of our race scattered all over the world,
> and to compel the respect of the nations and races
> of the earth.[23]

Garvey's social philosophy of race pride and African nationalism was optimistically received by many blacks who had been relegated to an inferior social status in the American society. Garvey's appeal to race pride gave to black people a new sense of dignity and self-respect. As E. Franklin Frazier has said, Garvey made black people "feel like somebody among white people who had said they were nobody."[24] In essence, the core of Garvey's social philosophy centered in the fact that he gave a despised and dispossessed people a sense of pride in being black. Thus the theme of "race pride" became a means by which he inspired black Americans to pursue African nationalism.

W. E. B. DuBois, on contrast to Marcus Garvey, did not advocate out-and-out separatism or nationalism as the only hope for oppressed black Americans. As a Black Power exponent, DuBois emphasized the themes of freedom, social equality, and the black man's right to self-determination in much the same way as his intellectual predecessor--Frederick Douglass. Like Douglass, DuBois encouraged the Negro to be morally vigilant and to fight for his political, civil, and social rights as a person within the American society as well as within the world community. Acquainted with the reality of prejudice and acutely aware of the subjugation of black people by white society, DuBois, in his book *The Souls of Black Folk,* contended that "the problem of the twentieth century is the problem of the color line--the relation of the darker to the lighter races of men in Asia and Africa, in America and islands of the sea."[25] Because of racism in American life, DuBois felt that any serious attempt by white society to discuss issues of interracial justice, equality and brotherhood must begin by recognizing the "problem of the color line." The problem of "race"--with all of its manifest and latent ramifications--constitutes the key problem for the modern world.

Existentially and morally speaking, the source of the black man's strength and weakness, joy and sorrow, triumph and tragedy springs from his unrelenting struggle to understand the meaning of his "blackness" in white America. To be "black" in white America means oppression; yet it also means pride in the reality of one's blackness. As a social philosopher, DuBois grasped the paradoxical nature of black life in white America in the following manner:

> The Negro is a sort of seventh son, born with a veil,
> and gifted with second-sight in this American world....
> It is a peculiar sensation, this double-consciousness,
> this sense of always looking at one's self through the
> eyes of others...One ever feels his twoness--an American,
> a Negro; two souls, two thoughts, two unreconciled
> strivings...in one dark body, whose dogged strength alone
> keeps it from being torn asunder.[26]

Here DuBois describes the paradoxical nature of the black experience, the never-ending struggle of the Negro to gain human selfhood and dignity in a society that degrades his cultural heritage and relegates him to an inferior status. In the larger arena of human life, this struggle is not only interracial, that is, between blacks and whites; it is one that goes on also *within* the group and *within* the black people themselves. At the personal and psychological levels, it is a struggle of conflicting valuations of the self--the perpetual struggle and longing of the Negro to "attain self-conscious manhood, to merge his double self into a better and truer self."[27]

In the thought of DuBois, Black Power raises the question--especially for the black male in America who has given so much in human toil and received so little in honest recognition--of manhood. What constitutes manhood in light of the paradoxical nature of the black experience? This question is crucial if we are to understand the deeper meaning of Black Power. For DuBois, the question of manhood--similar in many respects to Garvey's emphasis on race pride and independence--involves one's understanding of the nature of freedom. To be free means to be self-determining. Therefore, the black man cannot be his own man unless he is free. As black activists, both Garvey and DuBois understood freedom to be a pre-condition to self-conscious manhood. DuBois wrote:

> That freedom is the heritage of man and by freedom we do not mean freedom from the laws of nature, but freedom to think and believe, to express our thoughts and dream our dreams, and to maintain our rights...[28]

In the American society where blacks have been victimized by racial injustice, bigotry, and oppression, freedom means the right of self-determination. In this sense, freedom is the essence of manhood; it is the perennial struggle on the part of the black man to understand and cope with the "two souls, two thoughts, two unreconciled strivings" within himself. In our culturally pluralistic society, the black man "simply wishes to make it possible for a man to be both Negro and an American," wrote DuBois, "without being cursed and spit upon by his fellows, without having the doors of opportunity closed roughly in his face."[29] As a black activist, DuBois called upon the black man to affirm his manhood and demand white society to recognize it. In this sense, the social philosophy of DuBois is consistent with the emphasis Garvey placed on race pride and the necessity of self-respect.

Comparatively speaking, both Garvey and DuBois attempted to lead their people from a wilderness of degradation and despair into a promised land of freedom, self-autonomy, and human fulfillment. As black activists, both demanded justice and equal opportunity for disinherited blacks--despite their different ideological and philosophical orientations. In man's perennial quest for freedom, both envisaged a world where human beings would not be divided by the accidents of history. In short, they envisaged a world--in the words of DuBois--where "men will be judged by their souls and not by their skins."[30]

Thus far we have outlined some of the major strands of continuity in the evolutionary development of Black Power, as reflected in the thought of Martin R. Delany, Frederick Douglass, Marcus Garvey, and W. E. B. DuBois. Our purpose has not been to focus on their philosophy in any great detail--to do so would constitute a separate study. Our purpose, primarily, has been to demonstrate that the concept of Black Power is not a new phenomenon on the contemporary scene. It grew as a seminal idea out of the historical experience of black people in American society. With this view in mind, we will now turn our attention to a critical-comparative evaluation of the black activists under discussion.

A Positive Critical Assessment

The deeper meaning of Black Power for the oppressed creature is expressed in the passionate desire to be free from the bondage of slavery. Thus the theme of freedom was a basic similarity as well as the most consistent strand of continuity in the thought of the black activists presently under discussion--Martin R. Delany, Frederick Douglass, Marcus Garvey, and W. E. B. DuBois.

Critically speaking, however, these black activists had sharp differences not over the goal of freedom *per se*, but over what form freedom should take. For example, the feud between Delany and Douglass over whether blacks should "integrate or separate" was itself premature and immaterial. The "integrationist/separatist dilemma" was a premature argument because neither Delany nor Douglass had sufficient power to actualize their goals. As articulate spokesmen of the oppressed, both had the type of charismatic power to move the masses of blacks, but neither had the political or economic power to make effective their optimistic and often idealistic goals for an estranged people.

During this period of history, the conflict between Delany and Douglass over the destiny of black people was also premature and unfortunate because it proved to be inimical to the principle of unity--the fundamental ground of Black Power as understood in its political and economic dimensions. John H. Franklin, in his book *From Slavery to Freedom*, suggested that black abolitionists such as Delany and Douglass--who were themselves former slaves freed either by their masters or through deeds of manumission--were only quasi-free.[31]

Theoretically speaking, both Delany and Douglass had the same constitutional rights to freedom as any other American, but many states "carried on a campaign of vilification," writes Franklin, "against the free Negroes in order to keep them in their place."[32] The integrationist/separatist dilemma between Delany and Douglass was immaterial because it presupposes that each had a *real choice*. Neither of the black abolitionists had a real choice in determining his own destiny since both were only quasi-free, particularly in a society where predominant norm setters held the trump card.

74

Thus the conflicting philosophy of Delany and Douglass over the direction or form freedom should take was itself superficial. Furthermore, it is a matter of record that many quasi-free Negroes during this era of American history prided themselves in the lack of race consciousness and refused to identify themselves with any social cause--whether political separatism or radical integrationism. Benjamin Quarles, a noted historian, observed that the quasi-free Negroes--"having no culture peculiar to black skin"--had become a congeries of groups with diverse interests that reflected a typically American individualism.[33] The strange irony of Black Power, as reflected in the conflicting philosophy of Delany and Douglass, grew out of the inescapable fact that it was itself enslaved in the midst of freedom, waiting patiently yet impatiently to be released from the bosom of white racism, economic domination and political control.

The philosophy of integrationism, in contrast to ideological separatism, may have led Frederick Douglass to a type of uncritical acceptance of the great American ideal of freedom, justice, and equality for all people. There is, however, nothing inherently unethical or inconsistent about these ideal principles-- which undergird American democracy--within themselves, except for the fact that blacks have been excluded from participation in them.

From a comparative perspective, Frederick Douglass perhaps believed too strongly in the possibility of the realization of the principles of freedom, justice, and equality for black Americans, while Delany--acutely aware of the bitter fruits of prejudice and white racism--believed too little. Martin Delany, unlike Frederick Douglass, felt that because of the black man's legacy of slavery and oppression, he would never gain true freedom and the right of self-determination except through separation from the American society altogether. Thus the black struggle was torn between the cataclysmic forces of separatism and integrationism.

Another important observation in our evaluation of Delany and Douglass is the recognition that both seemed to have understood Black Power to be more reformist rather than revolutionary in character. But neither seemed to have made a formal distinction between the aims of Black Power as being essentially reformist or revolutionary. In the intellectual and evolutionary development of Black Power, the same critical observation may be made with respect to the social philosophy of Marcus Garvey and W. E. B. DuBois. However, our analysis for the moment concerns Martin Delany and Frederick Douglass.

Theoretically, it may be said that a "Black Power reformist" is one whose purpose is the alleviation of distress and

75

maladjustment *within* the social system without attempting to alter the basic structure of society itself. The "Black Power reformist" seeks to alleviate the cancerous distress of white racism and oppression which is inimical to authentic freedom and the progress of black people. On the other hand, the "Black Power revolutionary" aims at the radical transformation of the basic social structures of society, either through peaceful or violent means.

The "Black Power revolutionary" tends to advocate a form of radical social change which would rapidly procure the goal of freedom and self-determination. In light of these formal distinctions, we may conclude that the conflicting philosophy of Delany and Douglass tended to be more reformist than revolutionary in nature. However, their failure to make this formal distinction between the reformist and revolutionary character of Black Power may have contributed to the confusion over the goal and form freedom should take. Moreover, the perennial conflict between the integrationist and separatist forces in the intellectual and evolutionary development of Black Power is also reflected in the thought of Marcus Garvey and W. E. B. DuBois-- two militant voices of twentieth-century America.

Further, we may observe that there are at least three striking similarities in the thought of Marcus Garvey and W. E. B. DuBois in terms of their perspective on the black condition:

1. Being products of similar historical and social forces, each felt compelled to deal constructively with the reality of oppression, subjugation, and the general disenfranchisement of black people.

2. Each advocated a philosophy of struggle and militant resistance against the demoralizing forces of white racism and injustice.

3. The social philosophy of each--in spite of their ideological conflict over the ultimate destiny of disinherited blacks--inspired people of African descent in their quest for true freedom and the right of self-determination.

These main similarities were also reflected in the thought of Martin Delany and Frederick Douglass in varying degrees.

It is interesting to note, however, that when we compare further the Black Power stance of Garvey and DuBois, there is what we may call a lack of ideological consistency in the thought of the latter on the question of integration. Because of DuBois' lack of ideological consistency--which means that his thinking,

76

according to Harold Cruse, tended to oscillate between a philosophy of integrationism and black nationalism--the effectiveness of the black freedom struggle may have been weakened, at least politically.[34]

For example, in the twenties, DuBois advocated integrationsim as a viable goal for oppressed blacks in American society. By 1940, the integrationist posture had been abandoned in favor of the concept of economic, political, and cultural rehabilitation of the black community.[35] However, Harold Cruse observed that by 1953, DuBois had changed his mind again on the question of integration and the destiny of black people. At that time DuBois believed that oppressed blacks should continue their struggle for political integration, since they did not form a nation.[36] The result was that the black community was torn between the force of the integrationist argument on the one hand, and the force of the separatist argument--as vividly dramatized in the social philosophy of Marcus Garvey--on the other.

The ideological feud between Garvey and DuBois concerning the destiny of black people points to what may be called the tragedy and triumph of Black Power in twentieth-century white America. Ironically, Black Power is both tragic and triumphant. It is tragic in the sense that most of the "Back-Africa" movements of this century--though promising the hope of true freedom, human dignity, and political independence--must be regarded as deferred dreams nurtured in the fertile soil of optimistic idealism. Invariably, the "Back-to-Africa" impulse tended to provide no more than a convenient form of escapism for disadvantaged blacks hard-pressed by the brutal forces of white economic domination and social inequality.

In terms of the energetic leadership of Marcus Garvey and perhaps in spite of his influence and popular acclaim among the black masses, he still "remains a tragic, even pathetic figure, who is today remembered more for the size of his dreams," wrote Edmund D. Cronon, "than for the practical accomplishments of his once imposing race movement."[37] Black Power is tragic also in the sense that its adherents, particularly those of the separatist or black nationalist persuasion, have often misinterpreted the degree of attachment black people have to the American society. Ethically, this awareness is suggestive of the fact that the value system of black people tends to be more "Afro-American" than purely "African."

Moreover, Cronon further observed that many black Americans "scoffed at the Back to Africa talk and loudly proclaimed their desire...to remain in the United States."[38] This misinterpretation of the degree of attachment of black people to the American society by some spokesmen perhaps led inadvertently to a kind of "fragmentation" of Black Power as a viable force in the black community.

However, Black Power is not only tragic, it is also triumphant. At this stage, we may briefly summarize the legacy of Black Power. First, the legacy of Black Power must be understood in the light of its triumphant character. The triumphant character of Black Power, as expressed in the thought of Martin Delany, Frederick Douglass, Marcus Garvey, and W. E. B. DuBois, centered in its rational and moral capacity to inspire dispossessed blacks in American society in their struggle for freedom and human dignity.

Secondly, Black Power provided disinherited blacks with a sense of race pride and a new awareness of individual worth. It calls the attention of black people to the intrinsic value of Frederick Douglass' famous dictum: "No Progress Without Struggle." Thus Black Power contributes to one's capacity to struggle against white exploitation, domination and control. In the intellectual and evolutionary development of Black Power, this struggle tended to be both moral and physical. This struggle-- as reflected in the thought of Delany, Douglass, Garvey, and DuBois--was not only a negative reaction to white oppression, but also a positive affirmation of black pride and the determination of black people to be free.

Thirdly, one is compelled to recognize that Black Power is not *exclusively* a contemporary phenomenon; rather, it is an outgrowth of the persistent and stubborn effort on the part of the black man to define his place in a society not of his own making; nonetheless, a society in which he dare not fail to participate in shaping the future destiny and moral existence of humankind.

QUESTIONS FOR ADDITIONAL STUDY

1. Is there a new politics of Black Power developing in Southern Black churches in the light of the moral promises of the Carter Administration to do something about the plight of the poor and disadvantaged minorities in this country?

2. Identify some of the new directions in the Black community's continuous quest for freedom and a full measure of human rights.

3. What type of support systems must be specifically developed in Black community organizations and institutions in order to foster the importance of moral discipline and Black self-determination, particularly among young people?

4. List five constructive ways in which Frederick Douglass' famous dictum: "If there is no struggle, there is no progress" can be applied to the Black social condition today.

5. Some critics and students of history observe that the integrationist/separatist question is a false dychotomy. If this be the case, what constitutes a more accurate assessment of the Black American's ideological-moral dilemma?

6. What evidence exists to support the view that there is and always has been a sort of prototypal, though not clearly articulated, "Protestant work ethic" which undergirded the Black man's ethical spirit to make his own way in America?

7. Ethically and politically speaking, could there have been a contemporary Black Power movement without the historical context of chattel slavery in America?

RELATED READINGS

Brawley, Benjamin, A *Social History of the American Negro*.
    New York: Collier Books, 1970.

Cruse, Harold, *Rebellion or Revolution*. New York: William Morrow
    and Co., Inc., 1968.

Ehrlich, Paul R. and Feldman, S. S., *The Race Bomb: Skin Color,
    Prejudice, and Intelligence*. New York: The New York Times
    Book Co., 1977.

Frazier, E. Franklin, *Race and Culture Contacts in the Modern
    World*. Boston: Beacon Press, 1957.

Pettigrew, Thomas F., *Racially Separate or Together?* New York:
    McGraw-Hill Book Co., 1971.

Quarles, Benjamin, *The Negro in the Making of America*. New York:
    The MacMillan Co., 1969.

Schuchter, Arnold, *White Power/Black Freedom*. Boston: Beacon
    Press, 1968.

Washington, B. T., and DuBois, W. E. B., *The Negro in the South*.
    New York: The Citadel Press, 1970.

Washington, Joseph, Jr., *Black Sects and Cults*. New York:
    Anchor Press/Doubleday, Inc., 1972.

Wynn, Daniel W., *The Black Protest Movement*. New York:
    Philosophical Library, 1974.

CHAPTER V
CURRENT SECULAR AND THEOLOGICAL
DEVELOPMENTS OF BLACK POWER

In this chapter I would like to examine some of the significant expressions of Black Power in America during the sixties,
particularly as reflected in the thought of Stokely Carmichael,
Floyd B. McKissick, Nathan Wright, Jr., and other spokesmen of
the movement. Here the purpose will be to analyze and compare
critically various aspects of the Black Power theme in order to
demonstrate:

1. that the integrationist and separatist tendencies
    of the black struggle are recurrent forces in our
    moral and social life;

2. that the Black Power movement, under the leadership
    of Carmichael, represented a strategic break with the
    traditional civil rights organizations and pointed
    toward a new direction for the black community; and

3. that there is a basic theological content in the
    corpus of Black Power thought which deserves careful
    attention and ethical analysis.

This frame of reference, I believe, will provide a way by
which we may test the presumption that Black Power played a
significant role in the development of Black Theology. Before
we investigate, however, the contemporary modes, it is important
to recognize that the evolutionary development of Black Power--
as expressed in the thought of Delany, Douglass, Garvey, and
DuBois--tended to set the stage for continuous Negro protest
during the late thirties, forties, and fifties.

During this period, there were a number of important events
that affected the status of black Americans in society. At the
community level, Adam Clayton Powell, who rose to prominence in
the middle thirties, was instrumental in leading a successful
campaign in New York City to open up jobs and end discrimination--
using the boycott as a strategy of protest.[1] At the political and
economic levels, A. Philip Randolph emerged as another prominent

81

leader during this period. As a social activist, A. Philip Randolph, who won his long fight in the late thirties to organize the Sleeping Car Porters, was an important force in the black man's struggle for equal opportunity and social justice.

As the United States became increasingly involved in World War II, black Americans began to raise the question as to what consideration would be given them, both in the armed services and in the manufacture of the materials of modern warfare.[2] Aware of discriminatory policies against Negroes in industry and housing, a group of outstanding Negroes--including A. Philip Randolph, Walter White, and T. Arnold Hill--submitted a seven-point program to President Roosevelt (in September 1940), outlining the minimum essentials in giving black Americans equal consideration in the defense program. According to Franklin, this group of community leaders " urged all available reserve officers be used to train recruits; that Negro recruits be given the same training as whites; that existing units in the army accept officers and men on the basis of ability and not race."[3]

Broadly speaking, the seven-point program advocated that equal job opportunity be given to blacks and that all discrimination be abolished in the armed forces. In the evolutionary development of Black Power, some historians such as John H. Franklin and Lerone Bennett have pointed out that World War II provided an occasion for change in race relations. Although the United States was concerned primarily during this period with the rise of totalitarianism, communism, and the possibility of nuclear war--the race issue was fastly emerging as a national problem. In January, 1941, A. Philip Randolph advanced the idea that one hundred thousand Negroes and other liberal forces would march on Washington unless the federal government initiate positive action to improve the social and economic status of black Americans. Randolph called off the march, but only after the President had assured him that positive action would be implemented.

Moreover, the threatened "March on Washington" by Randolph and other leaders forced President Roosevelt to issue an order prohibiting discrimination in employment in defense industries and in the federal government. It was in June, 1941, that President Roosevelt issued his famous Executive Order 8802, in which he said: "there shall be no discrimination in the employment of workers in defense industries or industries or Government because of race, creed, color, or national origin..."[4] President Roosevelt's Executive Order 8802 had important implications for blacks in matters related to equality of opportunity in employment.

During the forties, another important factor which increased our awareness of race as a national issue was the publication of Gunnar Myrdal's An American Dilemma. In this work, Myrdal depicted

the problem of the black man--in his struggle for equality and
social justice--as essentially a moral problem in the heart of
white America.[5] The so-called "American Dilemma" is defined by
Myrdal as a raging conflict between creed and deed, between the
democratic ideals, on the one hand, and the actual practices of
the American people, on the other. Myrdal's work dramatized that
the so-called "Negro Problem" is an integral part of a larger
whole.[6]

During the fifties and early sixties, black Americans
became more aggressive and militant in their struggle for freedom
and social justice. Civil rights organizations such as the
NAACP (National Association for the Advancement of Colored People)
and SCLC (Southern Christian Leadership Conference), launched a
series of attacks--in both public and private sectors of American
society--against patterns of discrimination and racial segregation. In December of 1955, the action of Mrs. Rosa Parks was
the decisive event that triggered the so-called "Montgomery Bus
Boycott" when she refused to obey a bus driver's order to give
up her seat to a white man. Thus a definite pattern of protest
was taking form during the fifties in the black man's struggle
against white oppression.

Moreover, this pattern continued into the sixties with the
"sit-ins" and "pray-ins"--starting first in 1960 in Greensboro,
North Carolina, where four Negro college students sat down in
places restricted to whites. The "sit-in" movement of 1960 and
the Interracial Freedom Rides of 1961 expressed the mood of an
era in protest. Perhaps the era of protest reached a zenith in
August of 1963, when some 250,000 citizens, black and white
together, marched on Washington in rebellion against social
injustice and oppression.[7] Thus the clamor for freedom, racial
justice, and human dignity on the part of the oppressed represented
a continuous refrain in the evolutionary development of Black
Power. In view of this social and historical context, we now turn
our attention to the contemporary emergence of Black Power on the
American scene.

THE EMERGENCE OF BLACK POWER: CURRENT MODES

The emergence of Black Power as a current force among black
Americans did not appear until the summer of 1966. It was in May
of the same year that Stokely Carmichael was in the process of
organizing the black people of Lowndes County in a voter registration drive, the result of which was the formation of an all-
black political party.[8] In the midst of these events, James
Meredith had started his one-man march through Mississippi to

encourage voter registration by blacks. Soon after Meredith began his long walk across the perilous terrain of Mississippi, he was gunned down by an assailant. Immediately, civil rights organizations rushed in marchers to complete the journey. It was during the so-called "Meredith March" that Stokely Carmichael electrified the nation by issuing his challenging call for Black Power![9]

The action of Carmichael reflected a strong reaction not only to the domineering attitude and exploitative practice of white power, but also to the traditional civil rights movement. The poignant cry for Black Power grew, in part, out of a syndrome of powerlessness--in view of the deferred dream of integration and social justice in an open society--on the part of black Americans. The promise of integration made by traditional civil rights organizations was never fulfilled, largely because the ruling whit e majority did not want it. The phrase "Black Power" emerged at a critical juncture in our society in which, says Washington, "the nation was no longer interested in civil rights" and had returned to the old attitude of blacks as "the Negro problem."[10] Thus, the inflammatory phrase, Black Power, struck a responsive chord in the hearts of many black Americans victimized by white prejudice and racial discrimination and disenchanted with the social, political, and economic state of affairs in white America.

In our discussion of Black Power, we recognize it to be a very complex phenomenon. It means many things to many people. When the infalmmatory phrase was uttered by Carmichael in 1966, it set into motion a series of debates among civil rights organizations--inside and outside the black community--that inevitably touched the whole of society. While it was embraced, on the one hand, by such rights organizations as SNCC and CORE; it was shunned, on the other hand, by the NAACP and the National Urban League.

Initially, the chief contemporary advocates of Black Power, beside Stokely Carmichael, were Floyd McKissick of CORE and H. Rap Brown, who in 1967 succeeded Carmichael as head of SNCC (the Student Nonviolent Coordinating Committee).[11] During the same year, among the chief spokesmen who stood in opposition to the use of the phrase "Black Power" as a civil rights slogan, were Roy Wilkins of the NAACP, Whitney Young of the National Urban League, Bayard Rustin and Martin Luther King of SCLC (the Southern Christian Leadership Conference). The feud between the various civil rights organizations is articulated by Carmichael in a speech delivered at the University of California in 1966. He asserted:

Now we are engaged in a psychological sturggle in this country and that struggle is whether or not black

84

people have the right to use the words they want to
use without white people giving their sanction to it.
We maintain whether they like it or not, we are gon'
use the word Black Power...we are not gonna wait for
white people to sanction Black Power.[12]

In the continuous debate over the use of the phrase "Black Power,"
Martin Luther King contended that he recognized the necessity
of power as a meaningful instrument in the struggle of black
people for freedom, but that he opposed the use of the slogan
because of its implications of black nationalism.[13] Roy Wilkins,
the Executive Director of the NAACP at that time, went even
further than King by suggesting that the slogan "Black Power" is
white racism in reverse, i.e., it reflected a doctrine of black
supremacy and separatism. For Wilkins, the slogan also implied
the exclusion of white liberals who had traditionally supported
the civil rights movement.

Bayard Rustin, in his article, "Black Power and Coalition
Politics," took a position similar to Wilkins' but apparently for
different reasons. He expressed disappointment over the use of
the slogan "Black Power" on the grounds that it threatened the
effectiveness of the whole movement:

I would content that "black power" not only lacks any
real value for the civil rights movement, but that its
propagation is positively harmful. It diverts the
movement from a meaningful debate over strategy and
tactics, it isolates the Negro community, and it encourages the growth of anti-Negro forces.[14]

Bayard Rustin, an influential intellectual leader of the civil
rights movement, spoke as a strategist, a pragmatist, one who
believed that the use of the term "Black Power" would divert the
movement and "encourage the growth of anti-Negro forces." As a
civil rights theorist, Rustin emphasized coalition politics,
i.e., the political strategy of seeking a coalition with white
liberals, trade unionists, and religious groups. Stokely
Carmichael, a chief exponent of Black Power, was in conflict with
Rustin and other civil rights spokesmen on the question of
coalition. The "advocates of Black Power do not eschew coalition; rather," says Carmichael, "we want to establish the
grounds on which we feel political coalition can be viable."[15]
As an advocate of Black Power, Carmichael identified what he
called "three myths or major fallacies" of coalition politics.

First was the current popular belief in the American society
that "the interests of black people were identical with the
interests of certain liberal, labor, and other reform groups."
The second major fallacy revolves around the "assumption that a

85

viable coalition can be sustained on a moral, friendly and
sentimental basis; by appeals to conscience."[16]

Critically speaking, Carmichael was suspicious of coalition
politics on the grounds that it tended to make the black community economically and politically dependent upon and subser-
vient to the white community. He felt that a basic restructuring
of social institutions in society was needed in order to organize
a sufficient power base within the black community which would
alleviate white oppression and exploitation. The dependent status
of the black community upon the white community contributed to
its own exploitation. In his book, *Stokely Speaks,* Carmichael
described the process of exploitation and victimization in this
way:

> The vast majority of Negroes in this country live in
> captive communities and must endure these conditions
> of oppression because...they are black and powerless.
> Without bothering to go into historic factors that
> contribute to this pattern...one can see that to cor-
> rect this pattern will require far-reaching changes
> in the power-relationships and the ingrained social
> patterns within the society.[17]

The skepticism of Carmichael regarding the viability of coalition
politics grew out of the conviction that the black people in the
American society would not be able to win true freedom and self-
respect unless they controlled their own community. For
Carmichael, the concept of community control is essential for a
free and responsible people. Community control means that the
vital resources of the black community must be controlled by the
people who live there and not by "outsiders." It means that the
black community must be politically, economically, and socially
unified in order to meet the needs of its people and to operate
from a base of strength rather than weakness. Carmichael felt
that coalition politics--as it was commonly understood in the
larger society--worked against the concept of community control
and encouraged exploitation and oppression of black people.[18]
While he regarded coalition politics as fallacious and maintained
that it contributed to the dependent status of the black community upon the larger white community, he did not, however, rule
out the possibility of political alliances. But the idea of
political alliance must be based on a quality of relationship
which gives oppressed blacks a sense of self-worth and adds to
the collective strength of the black community. Thus there are
grounds for viable coalitions between blacks and whites. In his
book, *Black Power: The Politics of Liberation in America,*
Carmichael asserts that viable coalitions stem from the following
preconditions:

86

(a)   the recognition by the parties involved of their
      respective self-interests;

(b)   the mutual belief that each party stands to
      benefit in terms of that self-interest from
      allying with the other or others;

(c)   the acceptance of the fact that each party has its
      own independent base of power and each does not
      depend for ultimate decision-making on a force
      outside itself; and

(d)   the realization that the coalition deals with
      specific and identifiable...goals.[19]

Here Carmichael makes the suggestion that he is not opposed to
political coalitions *per se* between blacks and whites; but those
based on myths or fallacies only contribute to the subordination
and exploitation of the black community. Black Power, whatever
else it may mean in the thought of Carmichael, seeks to correct
the approach used by traditional civil rights groups which
resulted in the subordination of the black community to the white
community.

According to Carmichael, the older leaders of the black
struggle at that time--such spokesmen as Roy Wilkins, Bayard
Rustin, and Whitney Young--understood the "concept of the civil
rights movement as a kind of liaison between the powerful white
community and the dependent black community."[20] Here the strategy
was one of accommodation to the larger white power structure.
Analytically speaking, Black Power represented a break with this
approach and pointed toward new directions for the poor and the
dispossessed: it suggested that black people must organize and
develop institutions of power within the black community in order
to win true freedom and self-respect.

Another important aspect of Black Power is the recognition
that it was not only a reaction against coalition politics but
also against the stance of traditional civil rights organizations.
Older civil rights groups, such as the NAACP and the National Urban
League, held in high esteem the goal of integration.

According to the advocates of integration, social justice
will be accomplished by integrating the Negro into the
mainstream institutions of the society from which he
has been traditionally excluded.[21]

This mode of thought reflects the ideal; but what is the meaning
behind the concept of integration? Is integration the real
solution to the so-called "Negro Dilemma"? In the thought of
Carmichael, Black Power seriously called into question the idea

87

of integration as the ultimate solution to the problem of the
black man in the American society.

The concept of integration, as understood in the larger
society, suggested the uncritical acceptance of the white man's
style, his religio-cultural value system, and his general
philosophical orientation to human existence.[22] The idea of
integration, as commonly understood, strongly implied that there
was nothing of worth or value within the black man's own religious
and social heritage; and he must therefore "integrate" into the
mainstream of the American life in order to be fully human.
Stokely Carmichael puts the matter this way:

> This concept of integration had to be based on the
> assumption that there was nothing of value in the Negro
> community, so the thing to do was to siphon off the
> "acceptable" Negroes in the surrounding middle class
> white community. It is true that the student demon-
> strations in the South during the early sixties...had
> a similar orientation. But...the overt symbols of
> white supremacy and the imposed limitations on the
> Negro community had to be destroyed. Now black people
> must look beyond these goals, to the issue of collective
> power.[23]

As an advocate of Black Power, Carmichael was concerned with the
preservation of the social, cultural, and religious life and
identity of the black community. Whereas the advocates of integration, on the other hand, wanted to "integrate" the whole black
community into the mainstream of American life, and such an
effort would destroy the social, cultural, and religious personality of the black community. "This is," wrote Carmichael, "the
essential difference between integration as it is currently
practiced and the concept of Black Power."[24]

With the growing disenchantment of the black community
coupled with the rising tide of white resistance to meaningful
social change, black Americans began to lose faith in the dream
of integration. Black people became increasingly aware that
integration--as currently practiced in the larger white society--
was nothing but a convenient rationalization for white domination
and control. They became increasingly aware that integration was
no more than a "subterfuge for white supremacy, i.e., as always
involving only a token number of Negroes integrated into white
institutions on the white man's terms."[25] As an advocate of
Black Power, Carmichael rejects this idea of integration as
being counter-productive and detrimental to the black community.
This type of integration meant tokenism and assimilation;
neither of which was accepted as a viable strategy in the black
man's quest for freedom and the right of self-determination.

Thus the call for Black Power on the part of the more militant blacks grew out of discontentment with the token achievements and accommodating tactics of the traditional civil rights groups. According to Nathan Wright, Black Power represented a "turnabout in both the mood and direction in the area once appropriately described as civil rights."[26]

In describing the shift in the movement from civil rights to the thrust toward Black Power, Killian, in *The Impossible Revolution?* makes a significant observation, as he quotes David Danzig's description of the shift on the part of blacks:

> What we have here, in effect, is a radical departure from the traditional conception of civil rights as the rights of individuals. This departure lies at the heart of the "Negro Revolution"...What is now perceived as the revolt of the Negro amounts to this: the solitary Negro seeking admission into the white world through unusual achievement has been replaced by the organized Negro insisting upon a legitimate share for his group of the goods of American Society.[27]

While the traditional civil rights movement asked for what was due the black man, the impetus toward Black Power symbolized a change in strategy by insisting upon a legitimate share of power for blacks in the American society. Danzig further observed that white liberals who traditionally supported civil rights, now found themselves confused and threatened--not by the so-called "solitary Negro"--but by "having to come to terms with an aggressive black community, seeking to enter the mainstream of society *en masse.*"[28]

In short, the emergence of the Black Power theme on the contemporary American scene did not take place in a vacuum; rather, it is reflective on the long, hard struggle by black people for political and economic justice, of the right to freedom and self-determination. The Black Power theme of the mid-sixties--in one sense--merely symbolized the continuation of the black struggle. In the mid-sixties, however, black Americans were becoming increasingly aware of the dominance of white power, the impact of white backlash, the declining momentum of the civil rights movement as an effective instrument for social change, and above all the growing sense of powerlessness and frustration by black Americans. These painful realities led disinherited blacks to chant a new battle cry: Black Power! This was the new battle cry--impregnated with meaningful expectation and creative hope--that replaced the "Freedom Now" slogan during the critical years of 1965 and 1966.[29]

Thus the emergence of Black Power on the contemporary

American scene was in large measure a spontaneous reaction by blacks to the dehumanizing force of white power. Danzig reminds us that Black Power also represented a radical departure from the traditional conception of civil rights to the extent that individual Negroes who sought admission into the white world through unusual achievements had now been replaced by the "organized Negro" insisting upon a legitimate share of power, and the goods of American society. In this sense, Black Power reflected a movement from "individual achievement" of the solitary Negro to a "collective focus" on the part of the black community in the struggle for equal justice and power.

A FUNCTIONAL DEFINITION OF BLACK POWER

Thus far in our examination of the concept of Black Power, we have attempted to suggest that it is a dynamic and controversial phenomenon--meaning many things to many people. It is not my intention to defend or attack the Black Power theme; but rather to explore its functional significance in the light of the social, cultural, political, and religious experience of black people in America. Carmichael reminds us that Black Power means "the coming together of black people to elect representatives and to force those representatives to speak to their needs."[30]

In our culturally pluralistic society, Black Power may also means economic and political self-determination. This particular mode of interpretation of Black Power is expressed in Washington's book, *Black and White Power Subreption*. Here he speaks of Black Power as an expression of "Black Self-Determination."[31] The concept refers to the political and economic organization of the black community for the purpose of gaining the necessary power to meet the diversified needs of black people. Black self-determination also expressed the desire of black Americans not only to have control of their communities, but to preserve group consciousness, integrity and pride.

Thus the phenomenon of Black Power, understood here as black self-determination, seems to be a functional prerequisite for black people, if they are to participate from a position of strength in a free and open society.[32] Proponents of Black Power such as Carmichael, Wright, and Washington suggest to us that the concept is functional because it works for the human betterment of oppressed blacks in our pluralistic society.

Therefore, an investigation of the literary sources of Black Power leads us to propose the following functional definition:

> Black Power is a symbolic strategy for social, political,
> economic, and religious self-determination on the part
> of black people in order to achieve euqality, social
> justice, and liberation from oppression in America
> and elsewhere in the world.

Functionally speaking, Black Power revolves around the ideas of black pride, self-determination, and the general improvement of the black condition. This is a rigorous definition of Black Power; but it will serve as a kind of general directive or norm in exploring its implications for Black Theology.

Its Symbolic Meaning: Rhetoric or Reality?

Thus far in our analysis we have suggested that the emergence of Black Power as a recurrent force on the American scene represented a break with traditional civil rights groups and pointed toward new directions for the black community. The Black Power movement--as a force in the life of the black community-- was an expression of the black man's desire to be free and to determine his own destiny. In this sense, Black Power represented a continuation of its historical evolutionary development. The exponents of Black Power, therefore, encouraged blacks to organize and develop institutions of power within the black community in order to operate from a base of political strength rather than weakness in the larger society. But from the perspective of methodology we may ask, Is Black Power a realistic goal for black people? Is it rhetoric or reality?

The legitimacy, or, for that matter, the illegitimacy of Black Power--as a viable force in the black community--depends on how we answer these questions. As we have indicated, Black Power means many things to many people. It is abhorrent to some; it is dynamic and revolutionary to others. On the one hand, the theme of Black Power has suggested the organization and development of political and economic power within the black community. This means that blacks must be developing institutions of power oriented around meeting the needs of the black community. On the other hand, the critics of the Black Power movement argue that it is divisive and disintegrative in the black struggle for freedom, justice, and social equality. Some critics have even suggested that Black Power represented "black nationalism" and that it is a mere subterfuge for "racism in reverse." How are we, then, to assess Black Power or plow through its rhetoric in order to discover its essential value for the black community?

According to Scott and Brockriede, in their book *The Rhetoric*

of Black Power, the theme of Black Power implies three fundamental ideas:

> An emphasis on black pride and on the black person's
> right to define and to structure the terms in which
> the struggle for racial equality is to be waged;
> a reinterpretation of integration as a need to
> assimilate black communities as groups into the larger
> society rather than to siphon off able black people...
> into that society; and a generally more militant
> insistence that ghetto conditions be improved now.[33]

It seems to me that the assumption on the part of Scott and
Brockriede--that Black Power, in its secular form, revolves
around the ideas of black pride, self-determination, and the
improvement of the black condition--is essentially correct.
These principal ideas, as expressed in the thought of Carmichael,
McKissick, and other spokesmen, have been the guiding force
behind the Black Power movement. But initially, the call for
Black Power by Carmichael was merely a slogan without content,
which tended to create more confusion than enlightenment within
the black community. For Carmichael, the new battle cry represented a rejection of the "old slogans and meaningless rhetoric
of previous years in the civil rights struggle."[34] The decisive
role of Carmichael, however, was one of a trumpeter; he shouted
in a thunderous voice, "We want Black Power!" And other militant
spokesmen such as McKissick, Wright, and Ron Karenga became the
real interpreters of Black Power.

Although Black Power had been initially expressed by
Carmichael as an instrument for the empowerment of black people,
there emerged in the public domain a great deal of confusion over
the use of the slogan. The news media added to the confusion.
Alvin F. Poussaint describes how the news media--largely white
controlled--distorted the Black Power slogan:

> In this country, these media are almost entirely white-
> controlled and are directed primarily to a white
> audience which ranges from avowed racial bigots to
> white liberals....White newsmen...often unconsciously
> slant and deliver news in such a way as to appeal to
> the sentiments of their readers. Thus newsmen not only
> influence but reflect the climate of race relations
> in American society.[35]

It is important to recognize that much of the confusion and
outrage surrounding the Black Power slogan was a creation of the
white press.[36] As we may recall, all of the major civil rights
organizations of the early sixties were oriented around the goal
of integration. The mood of the early sixties was one of

integration. "Integration defined the goal, determined the method, and established the tradition," says Chuck Stone.[37] The phenomenon of Black Power ruptured the liberal-integrationist tradition in its call for power and self-determination on the part of oppressed blacks.

However, many black and white Americans were frightened by the Black Power slogan. At the time, the white press even equated the slogan with racial violence and strongly suggested that it was responsible for the black rebellions in American cities during the mid-sixties.[38]

Analytically and methodologically speaking, the theme of Black Power symbolized a shift from a posture of radical-protest integrationism--not to nationalistic separatism--but to some intermediate position between separatism and radical integration.[39] As an advocate of Black Power, the alleged separatist or revolutionary posture of Carmichael turned out to be--upon closer examination--an intermediate position between pure separatism and radical integrationism. Concretely, the theoretical posture of Stokely Carmichael represented what Gayraud Wilmore calls "Provisional disengagement."[40] In terms of Black Power, the concept of provisional disengagement contains two basic ideas: first, it assumes that there can be no meaningful integration between unequals, i.e., between black and white Americans who share unequal political and economic power; secondly, it presupposes that Black Power is pragmatic to the extent that it represents a strategic retreat for the purpose of solidifying the social, political, and economic forces within the black community.

However, because of the frightening clamor of Black Power and journalistic irresponsibility, it is my contention that the two basic ideas underlying the "provisional disengagement approach" were never fully understood in the white or black communities of America. In addition to the offensive and retaliatory overtones of Black Power (i.e., the implied desire to strike back at "whitey" for having robbed the black man of his dignity), the verbalization of the slogan itself was perhaps strategically and politically unwise for at least three basic reasons.

First, the Black Power slogan--though dramatizing the issue of white racism and critically calling into question the virtues of integration--polarized the black freedom movement by forcing a bitter ideological debate between influential civil rights leaders at a time when *unity* was most desparately needed. At the time, prominent black leaders such as Whitney Young and Roy Wilkins were caught in a bitter feud over the directions of the black freedom movement. The result was one of polarization and massive confusion within the black community.

Secondly, the verbalization of Black Power, perhaps, proved to be strategically and politically unwise for more subtle reasons.[41] According to Chuck Stone, "Black Power broke an unwritten law of the democratic ethic. It did not disguise its ends in polite political rhetoric."[42] In observing the manner in which the American democratic system works with respect to the advancement of ethnic groups, Stone wrote:

> During the past hundred years, the Irish, the Italisns, the Jews, the Poles and other ethnic groups had painstakingly and almost surreptitiously built their ethnic power bases in politics and business. They had never publicly described their goal as the pursuit and acquisition of power. They simply went out and elected ethnic candidates...controlled political machines...and gathered enormous ethnic power on behalf of their respective groups. Rarely did these groups publicly create the impression that the unlovely scramble for power was that group's principal commitment in life.[43]

The basic American tradition is one which suggests that each rising ethnic group must devise and execute its own plan for economic and political advancement and self-determination. Ironically, the weakness of Black Power centers in its proclamation of what amounted to be an inflammatory slogan without a plan or program. Put another way, the symbolic verbalization of Black Power preceded the stage of concrete preparation for its realization among blacks within the American Society. The reverse should be the case.

Thirdly, the effectiveness of Black Power was impaired because of its *exclusive* appeal to blacks and blacks only. This exclucivism about Black Power tended to alienate not only the white liberal establishment but also black coalitionists who had worked long and hard in the cause of freedom and social justice for the poor and disinherited in this country. By openly and vigorously declaring its purpose--namely, the acquisition of power for the liberation of black people--Black Power became "the great spoiler of the American myth."[44] The great American myth is that of the "melting pot" theory, where each ethnic group in the American society is presumably given the same opportunity and freedom to carve out its own destiny. In this society, however, the only problem with the "melting pot" theory is the fact that the black man never really "melted" into the mainstream of American life. Charles Silberman, in his book, *Crisis in Black and White,* describes the real forces behind the famous "melting pot" theory:

> The crucial thing about the melting pot was that it did not happen: American politics and American social life are still dominated by the existence of sharply-

defined ethnic groups...these groups have been transformed
by several generations of life in America...And so if
Negroes are to assimilate, if they are to integrate with
the white American, the question has to be asked: with
which white American? With WASP? Or with the Irishman?
The Italian? The Slovak? The Jew?[45]

Black Power became the "great spoiler of the American myth" by
candidly declaring its purpose. "A psychologically powerless
people, unschooled in the subtleties of political machinations
and propaganda, are inclined toward a raw honesty when they
finally do decide to acquire power," wrote Stone.[46] While the
call for "Black Power" was a necessary first step, it still
proved to be strategically and politically unwise because it
promised more than it was able to deliver. To be sure, the initial
clamor for Black Power was more rhetoric than reality. While
Black Power represented an important response to the dominance of
white power and critically called into question the goals of
traditional civil rights groups, it seemed not to have had the
sufficient momentum or strength to transform the "structures of
oppression" in the larger society. "Although it struck a responsive chord among the majority of blacks who are militant," wrote
Washington, "Black Power failed because the ground for its
realization has yet to be prepared."[47]

In seeking to analyze and account for the initial failures
of Black Power as advocated by Carmichael and other exponents,
Scott and Brockriede, in their book *The Rhetoric of Black Power*,
observed three possible reasons.[48] First, there was the failure
on the part of the white press--i.e., journalistic irresponsibility--
in conveying to the general public only part of the message of
Black Power as articulated by Carmichael and other advocates.[49]
Secondly, Stokely Carmichael perhaps could have articulated more
concretely the meaning of Black Power to white liberals and
how they could become involved in a "new political coalition"
with blacks.[50] Third, the white liberal establishment must bear
a major share of the responsibility for reacting irrationally,
and sometimes fearfully, to the initial slogan of Black Power.
They failed to grasp the larger meaning and value as articulated
by its spokesmen.[51]

To summarize the positive as well as negative aspects of
Black Power, David Danzig makes the following critical observations. He wrote:

To the extent that "Black Power" expresses a determination to build a Negro community which would be more
than a euphemism for the ghetto, it is a valid and
necessary cry; to the extent that a despair of the
one-by-one absorption of "deserving" Negroes into the

general society and puts its faith instead in collective action aimed at dealing with a collective fate,
it is an intelligent response to the realities of
American life.[52]

In recognizing the ambiguities, contradictions, and sometimes the
exclusive conflicting claims of Black Power advocates, David
Danzig further observed:

> On the other side, however, "Black Power" is not by
> itself an adequate substitute for the coalition which
> provided the now obsolescent civil rights movement
> with its constituency, if only because Negroes as a
> minority will continue to need allies. A Negro move-
> ment based primarily on self-interest is a necessity, but
> a Negro movement based "exclusively" on self-interest
> is doomed to failure. The dilemma is real and cannot
> be escaped by blaming the Negro militants for alienating
> white supporters by their anti-white rhetoric.[53]

As for the rhetoric of Black Power, there is reason to believe that
a plausible solution to the "black problem" may lie in a new kind
of political coalition, where blacks and whites can participate
as equals: economically, socially, politically. This may take
the form of a *moral claim* on the part of the oppressed--as other
ethnic groups have done in the past--that Black Power is "good"
for the larger society because it contributes to the collective
strength of a significant segment of the American people: black
people. To be sure, there is a measure of truth in this *moral
claim*. It may provide a more genuine basis for dialogue between
black and white Americans.

BLACK POWER AND THEOLOGICAL PROMISE

Black Power is a concept impregnated with religious expectation and theological promise. Black Power seems to hold
theological promise and hope because it speaks to the black man's
fundamental sense of dignity and self-worth as a human being, or
as person-in-community seeking authentic human existence.

Theologically, the meaning of authentic human existence from
the black perspective tends to be reflective of two important
motifs in the phenomenon of Black Power, namely, the motif of
self-love and the motif of power. In examining the theological
elements implicit in Black Power, Professor Vincent Harding
observed that "it is likely that no element is so constant in
the gospel of blackness...as the necessity of self-love."[54]

96

Harding's perception of the theological implications of Black Power is highly suggestive. However, one must be aware that Harding writes as a Black Power religionist, whose intellectual interests lie outside organized Black religion and Black Theology.[55] John Oliver Killens, an intellectual and literary spokesman of the Black Power movement, also emphasizes the element of self-love in the black struggle. He asserts that Black Power

> does not teach hatred; it teaches love. But it teaches us that love, like charity, must begin at home; it must begin with ourselves, our beautiful black selves...it will settle for nothing short of love in return. Therefore, it does not advocate unrequited love....Most black folk have no need to love those who would spit on them or practice genocide against them....Profound love can only exist between equals.[56]

Killens believes that Black Power is calling for black self-love as a precondition to authentic human existence. The motif of self-love is a reflection of the individual's concern about the development of his inner powers. At the psychological level, this means that the individual must have a rational and healthy image of the self before he can enter into genuine relationships with others. Furthermore, Killens suggests that the motif of self-love as reflected in the Black Power theme demands nothing short of mutual love as a basis for meaningful inter-personal and communal relations between black and white Americans.

From a theological perspective, Major J. Jones, in his essay, "Black Awareness: Theological Implications of the Concept," makes a perspective observation. He reminds us that Jesus raised the question of self-love only in relation to our neighbor.[57] On the issue of self-love, Jones raises some pertinent questions: "Is it possible for the Negro to love himself, even as a group, and close out his white brother, without having something radically wrong happen to his self-loving process?" "Can human requirements be fully met by black people loving only black people?" On these critical questions, the writer concludes by suggesting that one cannot be fully sure that the motif of self-love can meet the ultimate test of achieving self-esteem and authentic black personhood which black awareness advocates.[58] However, Jones seems to be suggesting that while the black man must love and accept himself in the full sense of his blackness, the concept of self-love is a necessary but not a sufficient requirement for authentic black personhood. For a viable theological perspective, Jones argues that "true black awareness should make the black man more fit for the whole human context rather than the small arena of the black community."[59]

In contrast with Major Jones' position, Stokely Carmichael

takes a different stance on the issue of self-love. As an advocate of Black Power, Carmichael believes that the black community must perceive the idea of self-love as being both necessary and sufficient for authentic black existence. As for white people, they are not to be hated or scorned, but simply ignored. For Carmichael, Black Power means the building of a black community based on the principle of an undying love for black people only. On the other hand, Jones believes that self-love alone is not a sufficient base for authentic black existence. In the black man's quest for freedom and more hopeful future, he must move from the concept of self-love to one which embraces the whole of humanity. For Jones, the notion of self-love tends to function as a means toward a greater end--the creation of a truly humanistic community beyond racism.[60] In contrast, the notion of self-love in the thought of Carmichael tends to function as an end within itself--i.e., a love which creates black consciousness in the hearts of black people for each other and their community.[61] Thus Black Power, as an expression of self-love, is more *exclusive* in the thought of Carmichael, whereas for Jones, the phenomenon of Black Power is more inclusive.

Moreover, Carmichael believes that blacks for too long have been forced to love their white oppressors. For Carmichael, the love which Black Power advocates is essentially ethnocentric, i.e., a love "within the black community, the only American community where men call each other 'brother' when they meet." He further contends, "we can build a community of love only where we have the ability and power to do so: among blacks."[62]

In short, both Carmichael and Jones view the element of self-love as being vital for the liberation of the black community from the yoke of oppression and white racism in the American society; and both believe that the motif of self-love is a precondition for authentic black personhood. These are the main similarities and dissimilarities in their thought.

Another element implicit in the Black Power theme, which may offer theological promise, is the element of power. The meaning of Black Power in theological perspective implies that in order for the black man to realize his potentiality as a human being, he must have power. All men need the power of being as well as the power to become. "Indeed, the Greek words for power (bia) and life (bios) reflect the essential interrelationship of power and life," says Nathan Wright. He further argues that "power is basic to life. Without power, life cannot become what it must be."[63] Therefore, the motif of power--in addition to a healthy and loving image of the self--is essential to the life of black people if they are to have true freedom and the right of self-determination.

Furthermore, proponents of the Black Power theme suggest to us that if God's noble design in human creation is to be fulfilled, all men must have power.[64] The issue of power is a crucial one for black people. This seems to be true primarily because many black Americans consider it to be important for authentic black existence. A group of black churchmen--concerned with the ethical problems of power in America--in 1966 published a full-page advertisement in the *New York Times* which said, in part, that "the fundamental distortion facing us in the controversy about 'black power' is rooted in a gross imbalance of power and conscience between Negroes and white Americans."[65] It seems to me that the real theological promise of the phenomenon of Black Power stems precisely from the unrelenting struggle on the part of concerned black Americans to call morally into question the "power structures" of the American society with respect to social justice and responsibility. For it is these "power structures" which tend to dominate and continuously exploit black life. In short, Black Power--in terms of its theological promise--is a moral call for radical change in the structures of society through a redistribution of political and economic power.

Some Presuppositions of Black Theology

We shall now consider some of the presuppositions of Black Theology. This inquiry, however, makes no claim to treat all presuppositions of Black Theology, but only those which we may consider important and indispensible for reflection. Analytically speaking, the presuppositions are:

1. that Black Theology requires a historical approach;

2. that there is a dialectical relationship between the black experience and Black Theology; each must be interpreted in terms of the other; and even the Christian faith is interpreted--or reinterpreted-- in the light of black experience and theology;

3. that Black Theology is a theology of liberation;

4. that Black Theology is a theology of involvement; and

5. that Black Theology is a theology of revolution.

These presuppositions are implicit in the corpus of Black Theology.

The first presupposition of Black Theology is the contention

99

that it must speak to the historical experience of black people in American society. A sense of history runs through the whole of Black Theology. Gayraud S. Wilmore's recent work, *Black Religion and Black Radicalism,* is an illustration of this approach, seeking to explore the historical roots of black religious phenomena.[66] Retrospectively, black theologians recall the importation of our black forefathers from their African soil, the agonizing system of chattel slavery, and the demeaning conditions under which black slaves struggled for survival. They also recall the oppression perpetrated upon blacks at the founding of the Republic, at the political and social events that preceded the Civil War, when blacks of African descent were designated as "subhuman beings" and denied constitutional rights by white society.[67]

At every historical juncture, black theologians are compelled to reflect critically on the black experience and interpret this experience in light of the Christian faith, so as to find meaning and purpose in black experience. In retrospect, black theologians find themselves reflecting on the historic role of the Black Church as a voice of protest, freedom, and eschatological hope for disinherited blacks. The significance of the role of the Black Church before the Civil War is documented by James H. Cone in his book, *Black Theology and Black Power.* He argues:

> The black church was born in protest. In this sense, it is the precursor of Black Power. Unlike the white church, its reality stemmed from the eschatological recognition that freedom and equality are the essence of humanity, and thus segregation and slavery are diametrically opposed to Christianity. Freedom and equality made up the central theme of the black church; and protest and action were the early marks of its uniqueness.[68]

A second presupposition which we may consider stems from the recognition that there is a dialectical relationship between Black Theology and black experience; each must be interpreted in terms of the other. Furthermore, Black Theology arises from an identification with the oppressed blacks of America, seeking to interpret the Christian faith in light of the black condition.[69] This means that there is a continuous dialectical relationship between Black Theology and black experience on the one hand, and Christian theology on the other.

Moreover, Black Theology does not negate Christian theology in light of the struggle of black people for liberation, equal justice, and human dignity in a society of racial prejudice and dehumanization. Cone argues that Black Theology is an authentic expression of Christian theology, citing two reasons:

100

> First, there can be no theology of the gospel which
> does not arise from an oppressed community....Secondly,
> Black Theology is Christian theology because it centers
> on Jesus Christ.[70]

Here Cone's presupposition that Black Theology is Christ-
centered grows out of his conviction that white religionists
have failed to relate the gospel message of Jesus to the dehumanization suffered by black people in a white racist society.
Thus Jesus is conceptualized as the Holy One who liberates black
humanity from the iron claw of white oppression.

A third presupposition, which seems to be at the heart of
Black Theology, is the theme of liberation. Proponents of Black
Theology, in spite of their philosophical differences, tend
to affirm that it is a theology of liberation. This important
point is made explicit in an article written by Joseph A.
Johnson, Jr., entitled: "Jesus, the Liberator." Dr. Johnson,
Presiding Bishop of the Christian Methodist Episcopal Church in
Shreveport, Louisiana, articulates his position concerning Jesus:

> Jesus is the Liberator. He is the revelation of
> wisdom, the power, and the love of God. This was the
> message which the early Christian preachers were com-
> missioned to proclaim. This message was called the
> Kerygma...at the heart of the Kerygma lies this funda-
> mental Christological affirmation: Jesus is the
> Liberator! Jesus is the Emancipator![71]

The theological affirmation that "Jesus is Liberator" is perhaps
the most fundamental presupposition of Black Theology. It is
a presupposition implicitly expressed in the thought of most
black theologians. However, the basic premise that "Jesus is
Liberator" is not alien to Christian theology; it is a recurring
theme woven into the texture of Christian church history,
especially where religious sectarian or minority groups have
experienced oppression in the larger society. Comparatively, what
seems to be relatively unique about Black Theology--in its
relationship to the corpus of Christian theology--is its unrelenting and perennial emphasis on the liberation motif of the
gospel message and its relevance to the black condition.

A fourth presupposition implicit in Black Theology is the
contention that it must be a "theology of involvement."[72]
Traditional, philosophical and metaphysical statements concerning
the nature of God--i.e., theological debates over the immanence
versus the transcendence of God--are important for black theologians.
In a biblical sense, black theologians suggest that the relationship between God's immanence and his transcendence is paradoxical;
each must be understood in terms of the other.[73] However, the

101

immediate concern of black theologians seems to revolve more
around the awesome task of interpreting the meaning of the
Christian faith to an oppressed people whose daily experience is
one of misery, suffering, and exploitation. In speaking of the
task of Black Theology, James Cone puts it this way:

> The task of Black Theology...is to analyze the black
> man's condition in light of God's revelation in Jesus
> Christ with the purpose of creating a new under-
> standing of black dignity among black people, and
> providing the necessary soul in that people to destroy
> racism.[74]

Black theologians assume that part of their theoretical task is
to explore the meaning of the Christian faith in terms of its
relevance to the condition of blackness: a condition of
oppression, suffering, and dehumanization in white America.
Through God's liberating power, however, the condition of the
black man is transformed; he is set free for freedom, i.e., the
freedom to live and respond, and freedom to be involved in
creating a community where each person would have self-respect.

Black Theology, as a theology of involvement, not only
attempts to speak to the existential experience of black people
in the American society, it also seeks to transform an unloving
relationship based on racism into a loving relationship based on
equal justice and social equality. Since some form of dehumanization is a daily experience in the lives of most black people in
white America, Black Theology dares to raise--in the words of
Roberts--the poignant questions: "Does God care?" Is God just,
loving, and merciful? Is God all-powerful? Why does her permit
undeserved suffering? Is God near? Does he watch over all
men?"[75]

To be sure, there are pertinent and serious questions for
Black Theology that deserve thoughtful analysis and interpretation. If Black Theology is to be relevant in the struggle for
black liberation and self-determination, satisfactory answers
must be found to these and other pivotal questions. In this sense,
Black Theology must be what Roberts calls an "answering
theology."[76]

Finally, Black Theology presupposes the motif of revolution.
The radicalism of Black Theology centers in its call for revolution. We define the term "revolution" to refer to any "sudden
change in the societal structure, or in some important feature
of it."[77] Revolution is "a form of social change distinguished
by its scope and speed. It may, or may not, be accompanied by
violence and temporary social disorganization...the essence of
revolution is the sudden change, not the violent upheaval which

frequently accompanies it."[78] Therefore, the presupposition of revolution inherent in Black Theology is a call for change in the structures of society which tend to oppress and exploit the poor, the weak, and the helpless among us.

Joseph Washington speaks cogently of this revolutionary presupposition underlying Black Theology in his book, *Black and White Power Subreption*. He holds that it is the responsibility of black theologians to develop a theology of revolution for at least three reasons:

> First, black people have as their unique function in this world the vocation for revolution, whereby all people through them become human and attain their manhood. The second reason that black theologians ought to develop a revolutionary theology is not only as pre- paration in the event it becomes necessary but as their now special achievement. That is, Black Power is the creation of black people. So far, black theologians have followed its lead in terms of taking up and supporting the themes of pride, mutual support, organi- zation, etc....The third reason black theologians should develop a theology of revolution is a realistic appraisal of the situation.[79]

Here we note that Washington's emphasis on the element of revo- lution as an undergirding presupposition of Black Theology is, in essence, a formulation of what we might call a "Black Power theology of revolution." The Black Power theme, in the thinking of black theologians, gives real impetus and direction to Black Theology by stressing the motifs of freedom, self-identity, black pride and manhood. Black Theology identifies God's redemptive work as the work of revolution. It seeks to affirm that God is not only working in the communities of the oppressed--liberating and reconciling broken humanity--but that God's redemptive power, through Jesus Christ, is ushering in a new social order.

To summarize, we have suggested that there are at least five implicit presuppositions underlying Black Theology. These may be stated as the following:

1. Black Theology requires an historical approach.

2. There is a dialectical relationship between Black Theology and black experience; each must be inter- preted in terms of the other. While the black experience is a source of Black Theology, the latter also bears a dialectical relationship to Christian theology.

103

3. Black Theology is a theology of liberation.

4. Black Theology is a theology of involvement.

5. Black Theology is a theology of revolution.

Critically and analytically speaking, there is a structure of interrelationship between these presuppositions of Black Theology.
But theological ambiguity is also present. On the one hand, the
structure of interrelationship between the five implicit canons
of Black Theology is dynamic, while on the other hand, it is
polemical and problematic.

The most casual observation suggests that there are divergent
and even contradictory emphases in Black Theology. If the themes
of liberation and involvement are unifying threads of Black
Theology--which seems to be the case with some black theologians--
in what sense, then, may we speak of Black Theology as revolutionary? For instance, Joseph Washington declares that black
theologians ought to be developing a "Black Power theology" of
revolution. However, I take issue with Washington's position for
two primary reasons: first, it is not altogether clear if it
is either desirable or possible to carve out of the corpus of
Black Power a "theology of revolution" without adequately evaluating the built-in moral dilemmas and philosophical contradictions of Black Power itself. Second, Washington's position
seems to be ethically ambiguous on the intention of a Black
Theology of revolution. At one point, he equates a Black Theology
of revolution with the possibility of violent conflict; at
another point, he equates it with the creation of a new social
order in the American society.[80] It seems to me that a quali-
fication must be made between "revolution" as referring to the
moral force of constructive social change and "revolution" as
violent struggle or conflict between blacks and whites in America.
The former position, I accept; the latter stance, I find untenable
because of its incompatibility with the essentials of Christian
theology. After all, Black Theology does not negate Christian
theology; but rather it seeks to interpret its basic truths in the
light of the black man's struggle for genuine freedom, human dignity and manhood.

Thus the element of revolution is a valid presupposition of
Black Theology to the extent that it declares war against racism,
injustice, and all dysfunctional structures which inhibit the
realization of human personhood. In short, the relationship
between the five implicit canons of Black Theology is both dynamic
and polemical-problematic. While Black Theology is, in part, a
reflection of the black experience, its roots also emanate from
the well-spring of Biblical faith. In this sense, Black Theology

104

expresses the eschatological hope that--through God's redemptive love and power--a new social order will be born.

The focus of the last chapter will give more critical attention to the problem of Black Theology and Christian ethics today. We turn now to the ethico-theological system of Martin Luther King, Jr.

Questions for Additional Study

1. Why was the emergence of Black Power necessary since the long-awaited era of "integration" had finally come to blacks during the early sixties?

2. Why did the initial articulation of the slogan "black power" lead to so much confusion among civil rights leaders and white liberal supporters of the Black Cause?

3. Is there a burning need for a new ethics of Black Power today? If so, what form should it take as the black community grapples with the problems of unemployment, black-on-black crime, youth unrest, and the crisis of affirmative action programs in American society?

4. Theologically and ethically speaking, how can the black community begin to move from the rhetoric of disciplined reflection and *reaction* to the posture of moral action and *aggressive involvement* to eliminate all vestiges of racial injustice?

5. From a biblical viewpoint, what specific exegetical problems arise by virtue of the claim on the part of some scholars that Black Power is an expression of God's revolutionary message of liberation to 20th century man?

6. In the light of the apparent shift in focus today from Black Theology to African and other third world theologies, what particular dilemmas does this pose for the black Christian who operates essentially out of the American context?

7. What comparisons and contrasts can be found between Black Theology and other so-called third world theologies?

8. What is the relationship of Black Theology to the ongoing life, mission, and purpose of the Black church in contemporary society?

Related Readings

Boesak, Allan A., *Farewell to Innocence: A Socio-Ethical Study on Black Theology and Power.* Maryknoll, New York: Orbis Books, 1977.

Cleage, Albert B., *Black Christian Nationalism.* New York: Sheed and Ward, 1972.

Cone, James H., *Black Theology and Black Power.* New York: The Seabury Press, 1969.

Cullmann, Oscar, *Jesus and the Revolutionaries.* New York: Harper and Row, Publishers, 1970.

DuBois, W. E. B., ed., *Some Efforts of American Negroes for Their Own Betterment.* Atlanta, Ga.: Atlanta University Press, 1898.

Edwards, George R., *Jesus and the Politics of Violence.* New York: Harper and Row, Publishers, 1972.

Fanon, Frantz, *The Wretched of the Earth.* New York: Grove Press, 1966.

Goldston, Robert, *The Negro Revolution.* New York: The Macmillan Co., 1968.

King, Martin Luther, Jr., *Where Do We Go from Here: Chaos or Community?* New York: Harper and Row, Publishers, 1967.

Lincoln, C. Eric, *Sounds of Struggle: Persons and Perspectives in Civil Rights.* New York: Friendship Press, 1967.

Muse, Benjamin, *The American Negro Revolution: From Non-violence to Black Power.* New York: Citadel Press, 1968.

Powdermaker, Hortense, *After Freedom.* New York: The Viking Press, Inc., 1939.

Spear, Allan H., *The Making of a Ghetto.* Chicago: University of Chicago Press, 1967.

Ward, Hiley H., *Prophet of the Black Nation.* Philadelphia: Pilgrim Press, 1969.

CHAPTER VI
MARTIN LUTHER KING, JR.:
LIBERATION ETHICS IN A CHRISTIAN CONTEXT

Increasingly, there is a persistent concern among community leaders, educators, theologians and social ethicists alike of the necessity to re-examine the thought of Martin Luther King, Jr. The difficulty in rational reflection upon any one phase of King's thought lies in the fact that so much has been written *about* his philosophy and theology and his contribution to the non-violent freedom movement of the last two decades. It is never easy to find one's way into another side or dimension of a person's thought. Yet as we attempt to discover more "promising moral indicators" for the future, we are compelled by the sway of events to investigate, critically and appreciatively, the ethical dimension of the thought of King.

From my own vantage point in ethics, the most significant singular contribution of King to our understanding of the moral life, in a Christian context, is perhaps the growing awareness that he--more than any of his contemporaries, black or white-- dared to believe the American Dream of "freedom, equality, and justice for all" by deliberately internalizing those *same* values into his own personal life as the archsymobl of ethical conduct.

For the black Christian the meaning of ethics, as a critical tool of self-reflection, must be concrete and *contextual*. The point of departure for black Christian ethics is the community in which black people find themselves and what they believe about Jesus Christ in their struggle to make sense out of the American experience. Thus our reflection upon the ethics of King must necessarily begin with Christian beliefs and the appropriation of the ethical teachings of Jesus to the moral life in black. For the black Christian, therefore, one's ethics must be avowedly Christian ethics. Otherwise, the agent's engagement in "ethical talk" about the Christian faith, and its relevance for social change, is senseless.

In any event, to speak of the ethical side of King's thought will involve an attempt to delineate his social ethics as the major focus of critical reflection. However, I may point out that

this writer is also cognizant of the fact that one of the corol-
laries in King's though is the inseparability of Christian
theology and ethics, on the one hand, and the implications of
ethical principles for involvement in social action, on the
other. So then, the fundamental thesis of this chapter is the
position that the ethics of Martin Luther King, Jr.--viewed
largely as an expression of liberation ethics *par excellence*--
cannot be adequately understood apart from a Christian *context*
and those forces which gave rise to the civil rights revolution.

Obviously, the ethical thought of King provides the occasion
for sober reflection. For the black Christian ethicist and
theologian, it invites one to participate in a challenging and
yet difficult task. The seriousness of the ethical task involves
nothing less than what Professor Herbert O. Edwards calls "telling
the truth" about the black experience in white America. It seems
to me that the ethics of King is also important to come to grips
with because it enables the agent to more cogently identify the
theological and normative basis for "digging into the funky facts"
of black life in one's quest for truth and human liberation. Here
our reflection shall be limited to four primary moral considerations in our discussion of the social ethics of Dr. Martin Luther
King, Jr., namely:

1. the dilemma of powerless morality versus immoral power;
2. the principle of love-monism;
3. the motifs of justice, faith, and forgiveness as a new
   basis for the social order; and
4. the concept of the "beloved community" as a formable
   paradigm in the achievement of liberation in black-white
   relations.

THE DILEMMA OF POWERLESS MORALITY
VERSUS IMMORAL POWER

In his book, *The Trumpet of Conscience,* King identified two
significant phases of the civil rights movement, namely, the
phase of aggressive nonviolent resistance, (the period 1955-1965),
and the phase of white resistance or white backlash (the period
1965--).[1] These phases are important in our perspective on some
of the moral and social dilemmas of black Americans to the extent
that they help us to understand the frustrations, anxieties,
and exploitation suffered by black people in America. Compelled
by forces of racial bigotry, discrimination, and poverty, black
Americans remain still on the periphery of society--seemingly
condemned to a life of misery, alienation, and economic insecurity.[2]

110

In phase one of the civil rights movement, one of the dilemmas faces by black Americans was essentially legal in character. According to King, the struggle for civil rights during this period took many forms and has involved such organizations as the NAACP (National Association for the Advancement of Colored People), CORE (Congress of Racial Equality), and the National Urban League. These national organizations have been in the forefront of the battle for civil rights and equal justice on the part of the poor and disadvantaged by rigorously contesting in the high courts of the land the black man's legal rights to public accommodation in a supposedly free and democratic society.

Charles F. Sleeper, in his volume *Black Power and Christian Responsibility*, observes the following characteristics of the civil rights movement during phase one of the black liberation struggle: first, the black freedom movement was to a large degree a middle class movement; second, the movement in terms of strategy focused its energies primarily on the goal of desegregation of public facilities; third, coalition with liberals and other sympathetic persons to the black cause; and fourth, the movement was to a large extent non-violent.[3] By making use of the strategy of aggressive non-violent resistance in light of the condition, the movement--under Dr. King's moral leadership-- was able to score impressive victories throughout the South. The North, however, was a different matter. The Chicago disturbance of 1965 is a case in point. The effectiveness of the civil rights movement in the South--in terms of meaningful social change in black-white relations--met with frustration and disappointment in many northern cities. According to David L. Lewis, King soon discovered that the political and social climate of Selma, for instance, was quite different from Chicago; and that the methods of Selma were not easily transferable to the complex urban metropolis of Chicago.[4] Beneath the surface of the movement was a growing restlessness, in both the North and South, that white society was not genuinely committed to the full realization of freedom, equality, and justice for black Americans. Commenting on the transition from phase one to phase two of the movement, King wrote:

> Negroes were outraged by inequality; their ultimate
> goal was freedom. Most of the white majority were
> outraged by brutality; their goal was improvement, not
> freedom nor equality. When Negroes assertively
> moved on to ascend the second rung of the ladder,
> a firm resistance from the white community developed.
> This resistance characterized the second phase....In
> some quarters it was a courteous rejection, in
> others it was a stinging white backlash. In all
> quarters unmistakably it was outright resistance.[5]

111

Theoretically, we may say that a dilemma exists when there is a situation involving choice between equally unsatisfactory alternatives.[6] When alternatives are plain and there are clear-cut choices between right and wrong in human situations, there is no dilemma. A dilemma exists, however, in those human situations where there is moral ambiguity or obscurity. Thus the dilemma of phase two, in contrast to phase one of the civil rights movement, is essentially a dilemma of power. Viewed in its larger context, "the new American dilemma is one of power," says Kenneth B. Clark. He goes on to assert that "the dilemma is a confrontation between those forces which impel a society to change and those which seek to maintain the past."[7] Comparatively speaking, Dr. Martin Luther King conceptualizes the dilemma in a similar fashion but from an ethico-theological perspective.

In his perceptive work, *Where Do We Go From Here: Chaos or Community?*, King attempts to articulate the nature of this dilemma as a response, in part, to the phenomenon of Black Power and in light of the social, political, and economic power structures of the American society. He asserts:

> There is nothing essentially wrong with power. The problem is that in America power is unequally distributed. This has led Negro Americans in the past to seek their goals through love and moral suasion devoid of power and white Americans to seek their goals through power devoid of love and conscience....It is precisely this collision of immoral power with powerless morality which constitutes the major crisis of our times.[8]

Martin Luther King's cogently relevant perception of the crucial dilemma of our times, i.e., the dilemma of "powerless morality versus immoral power," raises for the ethically sensitive person many difficult questions. For example, what is the nature and role of power in human community? Can the oppressed black man in America achieve full manhood or a sense of "being somebody" without power? What is the ethical responsibility of those who hold power with respect to the powerless and dispossessed? What is the ethical relationship of love, power, and justice? In light of King's ethico-theological perspective, can one speak authentically of a "powerless morality," if love is in fact an integral part of the moral ethos of the black community as well as the controlling norm for social action? Can love *really* make a difference in the community of oppressed blacks? To be sure, there are some critical questions which may help to give greater shape and form to our discussion of the social ethics of Martin Luther King, Jr., especially in the light of his apparent emphasis upon the ethical principle of love in human relations.

THE PRINCIPLE OF LOVE-MONISM

Thus far we have already observed that the civil rights movement was one of the foundational touchstones in our understanding
of the structure of King's ethical system. Although Martin
Luther King was trained as a theologian, he was primarily concerned with the business of Christian social ethics,[9] particularly
in light of his struggle to resolve one of the most perplexing
moral problems to needle the American conscience: race. In
varying degrees, his ethics arises out of his theology; indeed,
there is a sense in which his theology exercises nominalistic
control over his social ethics. However, the process is not a
static-deductive relation but a dynamic interplay between his
ethics and theology as he sought to respond to the pull of contemporary events.

Concretely, I believe that the essential structure of King's
ethics is expressed, at least at the beginning, primarily in his
volume *Strength to Love*. It appears that the basic ethical
theme permeating the whole of this classic book of sermons,
Strength to Love, is the principle of agapeistic love. In fact,
the love ethic seems to be at the center of his social thought.
As we reflect here upon the ethics of King there are at least two
critical questions that must be posed. First of all, the fundamental theoretical question from a contextualist's viewpoint is
not what is love, but rather what does love require in the
situation of oppression? Secondly, what does love do in light
of the struggle on the part of black folk for liberation?

The principle of love in Dr. King's social ethics is fairly
consistent as the key integrative criterion for involvement in
social action. I believe, however, that evidence would suggest
that the norm of love appears to be far more visible and functional during the early stages in the development of the civil
rights movement than the latter ones. Analytically speaking,
one of the problematics with the ethics of King, especially in
terms of its contextual relation to the Christian faith, is the
traditional manner in which he begins by telling the reader or
explicating, theologically and philosophically, about what love
is rather than about what love *requires* on the part of the agent.
In other words, one cannot readily discern, at first glance, the
implications of what may be called the "contextualization of the
ethical act" in light of the existential and historical realities
of black oppression in white America. Here the so-called
"ethical act" of which I refer is the act of love manifested in
the context of the community of faith and trust. For example,
Dr. Martin Luther King, in *Strength to Love*, outlines three basic
ideas on the concept of love--following essentially Nygren's
ethico-theological interpreation. In reflecting upon the Greek

113

New Testament analysis of the term "love," King writes:

> Love is something much deeper than emotional bosh....
> The word *eros* is a sort of aesthetic or romantic
> love. In Platonic dialogues *eros* is a yearning of
> the soul for the realm of the divine. The second word
> is *philia*, a reciprocal love and the intimate
> affection and friendship between friends...The third
> word is *agape,* understanding and creative, redemptive
> goodwill for all men....Agape is the love of God
> operating in the human heart. At this level, we love
> everybody because God loves him....[10]

To be sure, Dr. King internalized the concept of love as a basic
principle for both his ethics and Christian theology. In his last
book, *Trumpet of Conscience,* King speaks of the principle of love
as cognate to his theology and moral philosophy as well as to his
basic understanding of man in human society. Since human dignity
is viewed as one's birthright in the ethico-theological thought
of King, every person is a child of God with equal value and
worth. For King, the importance of agapeistic love for the
moral life is dramatized when it operates in the human heart.
"When you rise to this level," says King, "you love all men not
because you like them, not because their ways appeal to you, but
you love them because God loves them."[11] Here the social ethics
of King remind us that love is much greater than liking; it is
constructive in human community and universal in character.

Critically discerned, there are perhaps two serious theoretical problematics in his ethical thought thus far. First, the
sensitive student of Christian social ethics would, undoubtedly,
observe the *prima facie* difficulty, I think, with King's over-
whelming emphasis on the norm of love--resembling a kind of "love
monism"--in his particular mode of ethical delineation. His
formal point of departure, as we have already observed, attempts
to outline what love *is* without equally, though inadvertently,
identifying with sufficient clarity what love requires for both
the oppressor and the oppressed.

In recalling the crisis that plagued the civil rights movement during the mid-sixties, Vincent Harding, a perceptive interpreter of the black experience, reports hearing a Black Power
advocate saying--in terms of King's dramatic emphasis on the love
ethic in race relations--that "Martin Luther King was trying to
get us to love white folks before we learned to love ourselves,
and that ain't no good."[12]

Whether this report is a mere expression of candid anger
uttered by one disillusioned black man is not the point. What
seems to be important here is a failure of perspective to clearly

114

delineate what love demands in a society where the oppressed black man has been forced, historically and to a degree contemporarily, to look up to his oppressor as the "Great White Father," as the "Great White Hope." To be sure, I am not implying here that Dr. King's social ethics does not radically repudiate the superordination/subordination syndrome traditionally characteristic in black-white relations. It does, without doubt. Neither am I suggesting that King does not relate love and justice as a historical possibility for corrupted man. Ultimately, both love and justice are inseparable in his ethico-theological thought.

What I am suggesting, to begin with, is a somewhat uneasy feeling that King's ethics reflect an overcommitment to agapeistic love as the ultimate norm--without giving equal attention to other vital normative concepts of the Christian faith relative to the black man's quest for freedom and first-class citizenship in America. I think that J. Deotis Roberts is essentially correct in his observation that "Dr. King built his theological ethic mainly on his examination of the concept of love."[13]

The second theoretical difficulty here in our analysis is in part derivative from the first. That is to say, Dr. King's stress upon agapeistic love as redemptive goodwill, at least sociologically considered, tends to be obscured when applied to the funky facts of life in a white-dominated society. On the one hand, the love-ethic places, perhaps, an unrealistic ethical burden upon oppressed blacks to "love your enemy"; while on the other hand, the oppressor is apparently left, if hindsight is any indicator of future socio-ethical patterns between blacks and whites, to interpret love as "sentimentality" as he continues to operate with racist attitudes--often disguised under the cloak of goodwill and universal brotherhood! In terms of black-white relations, there is a growing awareness among some people of the black community that the love-ethic is, perhaps, too lopsided--a sort of burden the new black man is apparently no longer willing to bear. Many blacks feel today that they have already over-emptied themselves, have already gone the second mile of the way, have already been for too long the doormat and ashtray of white abuse and bigotry; that there must be a process of reciprocity in the areas of human and moral relations between blacks and whites, if we are to have a viable society.

Again, we must return to the basic question, "What does love require in a situation of oppression?" In one's attempt to respond, creatively, to the ethical requisites of love, there are perhaps three primary considerations that claim attention in our assessment of King's ethics as reflective of a kind of "agapeistic love-monism." Accordingly, the principle of love manifested in the ethical thought of King requires--clearly and unmistakably--justice, faith, and forgiveness as minimum preconditions for the

115

moral life as well as for the construction of a new social order
where each person can meaningfully participate and contribute
based on his ability and interest.

THE RELEVANCE OF JUSTICE, FAITH, AND FORGIVENESS

In the first place, love requires justice as a relevant
instrument in dealing with complex social structures; justice is
rudimentary and elemental in any viable system of Christian
ethics in a black context. Obviously, a number of social ethicists
in the long history and tradition of the Christian faith have
spoken of the relationship of love to justice in terms of polar
tensions. For example, Reinhold Niebuhr, one of King's intellectual mentors, speaks of love as the ultimate fulfillment of
justice, but never a substitute for justice.

Concretely, the concept of justice in the ethico-theological
thought of King, though not clearly defined, appears to be
deeply rooted in Biblical faith. Apparently, the historical
Biblical faith informs King's social ethics as he attempts to make
sense out of the reality of black suffering in white America.
For King, the idea of justice is partially contained in the
idiomatic symbol of the prophet Amos. In poetic language
Dr. King emphatically proclaims:

>...I still have a dream today that one day justice
>will roll down like water, and righteousness like
>a mighty stream. I still have a dream today that in
>all of our state houses and city halls men will be
>elected to go there who will do justly and love mercy
>and walk humbly with their God....[14]

While the eschatological motif of hope is ever present in the
thinking of Dr. King the accent falls on "justice" as the righteousness of God, penetrating the political, socio-economic and
religious structures of history. Ultimately, King's ethics and
theology seem to suggest that God would make right what men have
made wrong because "the arch of the moral universe is long but
it bends toward justice." As an instrument of love, justice
means--in the classic sense--giving to each man his due. In
human society where rational men must adjudicate the merits and
demerits of conflicting claims between social groups, the rightful
"due" of each person is equality, (more about this ethical
stance later).

In any event, the divine love of God as understood in the
thinking of King includes a passionate concern for social justice

116

embodied in human institutions of society. Thus justice is not only an instrument of love, it is also the end goal of racial struggle.[15] As a Christian social ethicist, Dr. King, in his volume *Why We Can't Wait,* affirms the interrelated character of love and justice in a crisis-packed society of prejudice and cultural racism. Dr. King believed that too long had the white establishment insisted that black people "wait" for their civil rights--as on some sort of installment plan--while other social groups enjoyed the full "moral blessings" of the Declaration of Independence.[16] Here it seems to me that King's social ethics is a piquant reminder to the nation and world communities that "justice too long delayed is justice denied."[17] In a society where people of color are penalized and oppressed because of their ethnicity, the norm of justice must be one of the key integrative norms undergirding our basic social institutions.

Perhaps the influence of Reinhold Niebuhr may be more critically assessed here with reference to the principle of justice as a moral requisite of love in the thinking of King. Professor Niebuhr advocates that justice is a possible attainable goal for human society and an approximation of love. Niebuhr writes:

> The social justice which Amos demanded represented
> a possible ideal for society. Jesus conception of
> pure love is related to the idea of justice, as the
> holiness of God is related to the goodness of men. Pure
> love and holiness transcend the possible and historical.[18]

I believe that it is important to point out that Niebuhr's understanding of justice and love is a dialectical one. Because of the universal human condition of sin, Niebuhr holds that the logical ideal synthesis of love and justice is never completely actualized in history. In dealing with the economic, social and political realities of his day, Niebuhr passionately criticized the illusions which often underlined liberal protestantism and moral idealism concerning the nature of man and his capacity to create a society based totally upon the ethical principles of love, peace, and brotherhood. From a historical perspective, Reinhold Niebuhr's classic work, *Moral Man and Immoral Society* (1932), was a powerful rejection and redefinition of the social gospel, with its faith in the politics of love and reason. It would seem that Martin Luther King, along with Niebuhr, believed that scientific intelligence and moral piety alone could not eradicate the social conflict brought on by the situation of racism in American society; and that those who would stake all on purely moral or rationalistic methods ignore the limitations in human nature as well as the apparent incapacity of social groups to operate solely on the basis of a love ethic. For both King and Niebuhr, the idea of justice appears to be a more ethically relevant norm for the social order; although King's ethical stance is not so clearly articulated. Yet in terms of the realization of an American social order based essentially upon "absolute justice" and "perfect love," I believe that Niebuhr's famous dictum is a sober reminder to the utopian dreamer that: "Man's capacity for justice makes democracy possible; but man's inclination to injustice makes democracy necessary."[19]

We may further observe that in the ethico-theological thought of both King and Niebuhr, the idea of justice is deeply connected or interwoven with the notion of equality. Normatively, Niebuhr contends that the regulative norm of justice is clearly equality. That part of what it means to do justice with reference to the poor and oppressed is implied in the concept of equality; that the due of each man ethically is equal treatment within the social system. For the disinherited black community, it may well be that the regulative principle of equality is the "middle-ground" between absolute love and absolute justice. "Equality as a pinnacle of the ideal of justice implicitly points towards love as the final norm of justice...under the conditions of sin. A higher justice," says Niebuhr, "always means a more equal justice."[20] Thus it would seem that Martin Luther King not only drew upon Niebuhr's understanding of justice, but even went a step further to demonstrate how justice and equality must function hand-in-hand in this nation, especially on behalf of the poor and disadvantaged.

In any event, the idea of justice in the ethical thought of King means that it cannot be redically separated from love as one of the crucibles of the moral life. In a practical way, King often spoke of the "power of love" in terms of its capacity to raise the political, social, and moral conscience of the entire nation with regard to the collective struggle of the black man to achieve genuine freedom and manhood. As an instrument of love, justice must function, I believe, as a sort of *centrifugal* force which radiates the whole human society, on the one hand, and as a kind of *centripetal* force in the humanization of the social order with all of its divergent elements, on the other. In essence, King believed that the moral relationships between men in society, between black men and white men, between individuals and social groups cannot be adequately established apart from the ethical importance of justice. All in all, justice is a minimum pre-condition for meaningful dialogue between the oppressed black man and the white oppressor; and where there is no justice, as the basic moral rule for human conduct, the norm of love becomes abortive.

We now come to the principle of faith in our discussion of the ethical system of Dr. Martin Luther King, Jr. In the second place, we may note that love requires faith. For King, the Sermon on the Mount is the central normative paradigm for the moral

life in human community. The admonition to love one's neighbor--
by perceiving the human need--also implies an abiding faith in
one's neighbor. Here a few questions seem appropriate to raise,
namely, What does it mean to have faith in one's neighbor? Faith
in God? Faith in the possibility of human community? The ethics
of King suggest that the meaning of Christian morality in the
area of neighbor relations cannot be authentic outside the
establishment of a real fellowship of trust and confidence
between men of goodwill. Further, it is reasonable to assume that
the motif of faith as reflected in the ethico-theological thought
of King arises out of his basic conviction concerning the nature
of God.

Paradoxically, the believer's perception of the love of God
is somehow incomplete and ethically misguided without the mutual
requirement of faith in God as expressed in one's neighbor. For
King, faith and love are inseparable because they are theologically
rooted in the believer's understanding of God--a God who is
deeply concerned about the poor and oppressed of the land. This
particular ingredient is expressed by Dr. King's declaration
that "...faith will sustain us in our struggle to escape from the
bondage of every evil Egypt. This faith will be a lamp unto our
weary feet and a light unto our meandering path. Without such
faith, man's highest dreams will pass silently to dust."[21] The
important thing here is the recognition that faith provides the
oppressed with the moral impetus to change the conditions of
their lives--especially the faith we discover in ourselves which
leads to self-respect.

In short, the ethics and theology of King seem to indicate
that faith itself is action-oriented; it is not passive submission
to the yoke of oppression as the black man's lot in the modern
world or based on some prefabricated moral standard external to
the black experience. For King, faith is trust and reliance upon
God which manifests itself in a kind of belief in the basic
integrity of the neighbor because it wills the neighbor's good.
Theologically, faith is the inner assurance of knowing that "as
we struggle to defeat the forces of evil," writes King, "the God
of the universe struggles with us. Evil dies on the seashore,
not merely because of man's endless struggle against it, but
because of God's power to defeat it."[22] So then, the element of
faith as trust is both a requirement of love as well as a moral
requisite for human life.

Thirdly, the expression of forgiveness is relevant and
important in terms of our understanding of Dr. King's social ethics
in a Christian context. Forgiveness is the fruit of divine love
in the heart of the faithful believer. Ethically, King is suggesting that anyone who takes the Christian gospel of liberation
seriously must be open to forgiveness which leads to the possibility

119

of reconciliation between blacks and whites in America. Forgiveness, however, is contingent upon repentace which involves a change in mind and intention. Obviously, the critical question in black-white relations for a number of observers is simply this: "Can the white man repent of his racism and the demoralization of the oppressed black man?" And since the wounds or marks of oppression are so deeply carved into the black man's soul, can he find existentially and spiritually the courage to forgive?

I think that the virtue of forgiveness, in a Christian con-text, is perhaps the highest virtue of agapeistic love--if for no other reason than human fragility and man's tendency toward self-centeredness. We find it "hard" existentially and ethically to forgive the enemy, and even much less to *love* one's enemy. Yet it is a requirement of the moral life--in light of the black religious experience--if we are to take the Christian norm of love, as reflected in the thought of King, seriously. Furthermore, it would appear that King's particular expression of the meaning of Christian social ethics in a black context demands that we for-give because God forgives. We are to love because God's love is impartial. Moreover, he felt that forgiveness, as a fruit of love, is initiated by God. "Man is a sinner in need of God's for-giving grace," writes King. "This is not deadening pessimism; it is Christian realism...God's unbroken hold on us is something that will never permit us to feel right when we do wrong or feel natural when we do the unnatural."[23] To be sure, the motif of forgiveness as a value in the ethical thought of King is indis-pensible because it incorporates the spirit of reconciliation; it anticipates the establishment of community. Here we shall turn to perhaps the central eschatological, normative goal in King's ethics: the achievement of the beloved community, the true home of liberation.

THE BELOVED COMMUNITY:
LIBERATION IN A CHRISTIAN CONTEXT

In treating King's ethical thought as informed by his writings, the notion of the "beloved community" is, undoubtedly, a dominant eschatological paradigm. The compelling dream implicit throughout the thought of King, both for America and the world, was the dream of the beloved community. Thus far in our analysis we have explicated the position that the principle of love requires justice, faith, and forgiveness as minimum requisites for the moral life. Now it seems appropriate that we consider here the key question, "What does love demand that we do" in our evaluation of King's social ethics in a Christian context.

120

First of all, King believes that love is not passive and submissive but active and regenerative. Love serves as the motivating force in creating the basis for the realization of the beloved community; the power of love is the only human force that has the capacity to bring community into existence. Kenneth L. Smith and Ira G. Zepp, in their book *Search for the Beloved Community*, illustrate this particular viewpoint concerning the ethical thinking of Martin Luther King, Jr.[24] From a theological and ethical perspective, King's vision of the beloved community is in part symbolized in the cross which brings hope and new life to all, especially the poor and outcast. He asserts:

> The cross is eternal expression of the length to which God will go in order to restore broken community. The resurrection is a symbol of God's triumph over all the forces that seek to block community. The Holy Spirit is the continuing community creating reality that moves through history.[25]

Secondly, the principle of love in King's social ethics has what may be called a "transformative-creative character" of its own with reference to individual and social structures. "Love is the most durable power in the world. This creative force, so beautifully exemplified in the life of our Christ, is the most potent instrument available in mankind's quest for peace and security,"[26] writes King.

Thirdly, the essence of the moral life in the beloved community is primarily informed by love--a type of love that liberates and reconciles. There is a peculiar manner, in one's reflections upon race relations in America, in which King spoke of liberation (i.e., authentic freedom), reconciliation, and the love-ethic as a phenomenon intricately related to the concept of the beloved community. He wrote:

> Love may well be the salvation of our civilization....It is true that as we struggle for freedom in America, we will have to boycott at times. But we must remember... that a boycott is not an end in itself....But the end is reconciliation; the end is redemption; the end is the creation of the beloved community. It is this type of spirit and this type of love that can transform opponents into friends. It is this type of understanding good will that will transform the deep gloom of the old age into the exuberant gladness of the new age.[27]

Here we may discern that Dr. King's conception of the beloved community is the vision of the "new age"--the age of liberation for all oppressed people. Ethically, the so-called "new age" is a social vision of the new society; one in which racial hatred is rejected and brotherly love--in the generic sense of the term-- radically affirmed. King held the moral conviction that it is only by projecting the ethics of love to the center of our lives that we will be able to "cut off the chain of hate." Perhaps his perception here of agapeistic love reveals a higher ethical good implicit in the term liberation than traditionally ascribed by many contemporary black theologians in their theological analysis of the black religious experience. It may well disclose a type of liberation *par excellence,* because its essential nature characterizes what he calls disinterested love--completely self- giving, expecting nothing in return. For King, it is this type of love that represents the genuine source of human liberation. *Agape* as disinterested love seeks to restore and renew broken relationships in human community. In his work, *Stride Toward Freedom,* King put it this way:

> *Agape* is love seeking to preserve and create community.
> It is insistence on community even when one seeks to
> break it. *Agape* is a willingness to go to any length
> to restore community....it is a willingness to forgive,
> not seven times, but seventy times seven to restore
> community.[28]

Undoubtedly, the concept of agapeistic love, in the ethics and theology of King, is envisaged as that force which moves us toward the creation and development of the beloved community. Agape is that type of love which cements broken relationships and restores a sense of community among the children of God. In short, King makes no radical ethical distinction between friend and enemy in terms of the purposive thrust of love; agape is directed toward both.

This brings us to a rather critical juncture in our analysis of the concept of the beloved community, namely, the indispensi- bility of the principle of reconciliation in dealing with the race question in America. Evidence suggests that King did not develop-- in any systematic way--a doctrine of reconciliation. But if one takes seriously King's ideal of Christian brotherhood and his vision of the beloved community beyond racism, oppression and in- justice, then it would seem that reconciliation between blacks and whites is perhaps a logical byproduct of genuine liberation; it is a moral correlative. King's view of reconciliation is informed by the Judeo-Christian faith, particularly the radicalizing of the ethics of Jesus, which stressed, in large measure, the gospel of liberation for the poor under the Fatherhood of God and the Lordship of Christ.

Theologically and ethically, universalism is an ever-present strand in the thought of King. As a prophetic voice in the cause of freedom, social justice, and brotherhood, King declared:

...now the judgment of God is upon us, and we must either
learn to live together as brothers or we are all going to
perish together as fools.[29]

In the black man's struggle for racial justice in American
society, Dr. King held the moral conviction that ultimately our
loyalties must transcend the narrow confines of race, class, and
nation. In striking a universal note, he suggested that people
of conscience must be concerned about developing a "world perspective" in the cause of freedom, justice and love--the genuine
hallmarks of the beloved community. In the final analysis, it
would appear that Dr. King believed that the basic truth undergirding the development of a "world perspective" stems from the
claim, ethically and theologically, that all life is interdependent. No individual or nation can live alone. With a moral-
philosophical ring, King struck the chord of reconciliation in his
vision of the beloved community when he said to America:

It really boils down to this: that all life is interrelated. We are caught in an inescapable network of
mutuality, tied into a single garmet of destiny.
Whatever affects one directly affects all indirectly.
We are made to live together because of the interrelated structure of reality.[30]

Questions for Additional Study

1. What current risks are involved for the black Christian community in King's ethical proclamation, "love your enemy"?

2. Given the radical demands for social justice and the subsequent eclipse of "white liberal moral consciousness," can blacks and whites live together in the future?

3. What are the ethical tasks of the church in response to the blatant resurgence of white racism, particularly in education and in employment today?

4. Ethically speaking, to what extent is non-violence operative--given the perennial situation of black-white oppression--as a strategy for social change and liberation?

5. Is there a sort of moral danger or the possibility of "over-commitment" to non-violence as the *only* strategy in the black liberation struggle?

6. Theologically and ethically, can there be any real basis for mutual love between the ex-slave and ex-slave master since both have, apparently, different objectives in the world?

7. What is the relationship between King's social ethics and the ethics of the Black church?

8. The ethical question, "What ought I to do?" has a technical kind of relevance for many in church and society today. Does it not have to be raised in a different *structural context* in order to do justice to the particularity of black oppression?

9. Since the reality of oppression of blacks by whites is not merely individual but *social*, the critical ethical question is: What ought *we* to do?

Related Readings

Bowker, John, *Problems of Suffering in Religions of the World.*
London: Cambridge University Press, 1970.

Buswell, James O., III, *Slavery, Segregation and Scripture.*
Grand Rapids: Wm. B. Eerdmans Publishing Co., 1963.

Fredrickson, George M., *The Black Image in the White Mind.*
New York: Harper and Row, Publishers, 1971.

Kelsey, George D., *Racism and the Christian Understanding of Man.*
New York: Charles Scribner's Sons, 1965.

_____. *Social Ethics Among Southern Baptists, 1917-1969.*
The Scarecrow Press, Inc., 1972.

Lincoln, C. Eric, *The Black Muslims in America,* rev. ed., Boston:
Beacon Press, 1973.

Jones, Major J., *Christian Ethics for Black Theology.* Nashville:
Abingdon Press, 1974.

Niebuhr, Reinhold, *Moral Man and Immoral Society.* New York:
Charles Scribner's Sons, 1932.

Pettigrew, Thomas F., *Racially Separate or Together?* New York:
McGraw-Hill Book Co., 1971.

Roberts, J. Deotis, *Liberation and Reconciliation: A Black
Theology.* Philadelphia: The Westminster Press, 1971.

Smith, H. Shelton, *In His Image, But: Racism in Southern
Religion, 1780-1910.* Durham: Duke University Press, 1972.

Thomas, Latta R., *Biblical Faith and the Black American.* Valley
Forge: Judson Press, 1976.

Wyne, Marvin, et. al., *The Black Self.* Englewood Cliffs,
New Jersey: Prentice-Hall, Inc., 1974.

CHAPTER VII

SOUNDS OF ETHICS AND BLACK THEOLOGY

The central problem of our current discussion is an attempt
in part to find a viable answer to one of the crucial questions
which appears to be on the hearts of many blacks these days, namely,
"What ought we, as a community victimized by racial oppression
and believers in the Christian faith, to do?" Obviously, the
answer we give will affect, especially, the quality of our religious
and spiritual lives as well as the kind of world we live in. Since
our oppression in white society, largely speaking, has been
unrepentantly dished out not primarily as individual black men and
women, but as a social group, it would seem to me that "What ought
we to do?" is a logical prior question to the classical ethical
question, "What ought I to do?" or to turn it about in the indicative mood, "What am I to do?"

It is my basic thesis here that the "sounds of ethics" in
relation to black theological discourse must be the kind of *sounds*
which can best fashion an appropriate response to the reality of
oppression, if we are to have a viable future for blacks and other
oppressed peoples who seek freedom, justice and self-determination
in modern society. In one sense, I contend that the *sounds* of
ethics in the liberation struggle worldwide are, in some respect,
similar to the religio-cultural matrix of Black Social Christianity
itself; they are, perhaps, first and foremost symbolic of the new
moral agent; they form a new symbolic way in which the black man
as agent can perceive his own worth not only as a person, but as an
ethical participant in shaping a different set of values for his
social existence. As Lerone Bennett has pointed out so aptly concerning this new black man:

> ...to accept himself, to accept the color of his skin
> and the ambiguity and lessons of his experience; to see
> with his own eyes and hear with his own ears and to
> find new language and new forms to express what he
> sees and hears; to see Negro experience within a wider
> context, to relate that experience to the great human
> themes of liberation and oppression, struggle and
> growth, victory and defeat; to express himself
> directly, openly, honestly, and if necessary, brutally,
> without a prior check with the white Other..."[1]

127

I believe that such an expressive and moral mood is in fact implicitly disclosed in the terminology of "sounds." In another sense, we may say that Ray Charles, for instance, the famous rhythm and blues singer/composer, expresses in a very profound way the sounds of black religious experience. He exhibits the capacity to "see" or "discern" aspects of the human condition, perhaps, far more critically than those of us who have the good fortune of full physical vision. The ethically sensitive individual knows that the sounds of "soul"[2] run deep, so very deep, into the auspicative or acoustic membrance of the American social conscience. To be sure, the "sounds of ethics" today are reflective of the cries of the man from the bottom. Theologically, they are the "sounds" of the oppressed in every hamlet and village of the world community: sounds or cries for radical social change, for economic justice in the marketplace; at the deeper spiritual and moral levels, they are cries for respect and recognition, for response and love in human community. Though painfully discomforting for the social system, could these be "sounds" the larger society no longer wants to hear? Can America or the Christian Church, at whose hand so much racial hypocrisy has been wrought, afford to ignore these prophetic sounds from the man at the bottom? It would seem to me, particularly in the case of the ex-slave oppressed black man, that the wider society no longer wants to listen.

Perhaps this is true, as some Black theologians and social critics would argue, not primarily because the black man has been cursed, feared, or to a greater or lesser degree morally abused by the larger white society. Rather, it is because of, as I see it, the fact that his soul is no longer on *ice*. Paradoxically, he must still be listened to; he still must be reckoned with. The ethical sounds we hear from the man at the bottom are crystal in their implications: America must make way for his new identity, for his cultural contributions, art, and literature; for his religious and theological heritage.

In this chapter, however, I wish to engage our thinking relative to the following ethico-theological issues and concerns:

1. the Moral way and Ethical way;
2. the problem of Christian ethics and Black Theology;
3. a constructive statement on the agent's quest for a Black Christian Social Ethic;
4. an unstructured ethic of responsibility; and
5. the idea of a unified theory of freedom in the future of Black Theology.

THE MORAL WAY AND ETHICAL WAY IN BLACK LIFE

I wish to elaborate and give credence to the view that there is, at least analytically speaking and not at the expense of bifurcating the whole, a "moral way" and an "ethical way" in black life. That in the agent's attempt to provide conceptual and theoretical clarity between ethics and Black Theology such a delineation is undoubtedly needed. In black theological discourse these two perspectives, in our ethical inquiry into the Black experience, are not mutually exclusive but interdependent in character. I believe that it is appropriate, however, that we begin here by raising the crucial theoretical question, "What is the moral and the ethical?" in order to provide optimum clarification to our investigation of the black religious experience, particularly for the serious student of Christian social ethics and Black Theology.

The terms "moral" and "ethical" are often used as equivalent to "right" and "good," and as opposed to "immoral" and "unethical."[3] In dealing with the complexity of social behavior in society, we often make reference to standards of the moral life, moral leadership, moral consciousness, or the moral point of view. While this type of reflection may very well be intellectually proper and fitting, it does little to tell us about the nature of the ethical. To be ethical does not mean necessarily that an individual person, given the complexity of his religio-cultural ethos, or by virtue of his theological perspective, is morally right or morally good. Although the ethical is related to, or, pertaining to morality. For example, there is a marked difference, so to speak, in the implications between the two statements: "Say, Brother, I got a moral problem!" and "Say, Brother, I got a problem that's ethical"; or, for that matter, between the two questions, "What is the *ethical* thing to do?" vis-a-vis "What is the *moral* thing that I must do?"

Perhaps in some respects, the stereotype of the "traditional" Black preacher is an interesting case in point. The preacher of the black community, for instance, may feel the need to wear, in terms of conventional religious dress codes, an old-fashioned dark suit while engaging in his regular pastoral functions of the institutional church. On the one hand, he may be consciously adhering to an unarticulated standard of conduct based on his perception of the congregation's expectation of him in the ministerial-pastoral role. Here the particular mode of conduct constitutes what may be said to reflect a "moral" pattern because it is behavior in accordance with acceptable standards or representative norms of a given religious community. On the other hand, the precise moment, however, the black preacher calls into question a given mode of conduct or raises the critical question, "Why must I conform?" or "Why should I behave in his manner?", then and only then is the

129

structure of the "ethical" set in appropriate relational perspective. Why should slaves, for instance, behave as slaves? Why
not as free men? It seems to me that it is only when one attempts
to plow through, indeed, to struggle with some of the bedrock
assumptions undergirding social behavior, can the person as moral
agent begin to understand his value system and maintain his integrity in human community. To be sure, one's integrity is interwoven
and bound up with our understanding of social behavior on the
part of the moral agent. Eliseo Vivas, in the book *The Moral Life
and the Ethical Life,* describes this pattern of ethical awareness
by contending that

> The nature of the moral person has not been explained
> when it is suggested...that integrity concerns the
> preservation of a value system against intrusion of
> unassimilable values. Integrity does indeed involve
> preservation; but it also involves the preservation
> of a man's or a people's status as person, as moral
> agents. A moral agent is concerned with acting morally;
> and the concern leads him to respond to moral demands
> made of him in the spirit in which they are made as
> much as it leads him to wish to protect his moral
> system from destructive alien values.[4]

Now in contrast to the idea of the "ethical"--a notion which we
shall return to later--the term "moral" for many students of
ethics is used to connote social convention. Sociologically considered, it is the product, or more concretely the by-product, of
the religious and cultural institutions of society; it is an
instrument of the culture. Thus the term "moral" or "morality" in
a broader context functions as a regulatory agent with respect
to the way we actually behave in accordance to certain accepted
rules of a given community. "The morality of a community," says
C. H. Whiteley, "consists of those ways of behavior which each
member of the community is taught, bidden and encouraged to
adopt by other members."[5] Against this descriptive and theoretical background, it seems logical to assert therefore that the
moral way refers, in varying degrees, to the *actual historical
existence of black folks in America.* Descriptively, it is indicative of those patterns of conduct which take their essential
clues from the norms and values implicitly and explicitly manifested in the totality of Black experience, particularly the
religious and moral assumptions emmanating from the Black Church.

In many respects, however, the "moral way" of black life
appears to be almost tantamount to economic repression, injustice,
and exploitation of the weak and helpless by the larger society.
Historically, Black theologians would have us to remember that
the peculiar elemental factors of pain, suffering, and a common
eschatological hope really constitute those critical ingredients

of the "moral way" of black existence. These strange factors helped to shape and give form to the black person's moral identity. Notwithstanding, I think that a closer view of the structure of our typology is needed at this time.

In the first place, it is my contention that the moral way is indicative of the dialectics of social experience in which the oppressed dehumanized black man has actually undergone, largely speaking, as part and parcel of the American cultural system. For example, Elliot Liebou's volume, *Talley's Corner*, describes in large measure the moral way of black life in urban America. *Talley's Corner* is a microscopic view and penetrating analysis of the ups and downs, ins and outs of alienated black males who have been abused and misused by society at large. It portrays the complex pattern of social behavior of street corner men who are caught up in the "dialectics of survival," playing the game of life by moral rules not fully of their own making--but nonetheless, playing as best they can. In a rather strange ethical manner, *Talley's Corner* goes a long way, I believe, in helping us to understand the so-called "winners" and "losers" of the street corners who dared to assert their humanity in the pursuit--not necessarily of fortune and fame--but perhaps even more real and true the ordinary virtues of life. Concerning the actual moral life of this marginal sub-culture within the larger social system, Liebow writes:

> The streetcorner is, among other things, a sanctuary for those who can no longer endure the experience or prospect of failure. There, on the streetcorner, public fictions support a system of values which, together with the value system of society at large, make for a world of ambivalence, contradiction, and paradox, where failures are rationalized into phantom successes and weaknesses magically transformed into strengths.[6]

Secondly, it is important to note at least descriptively, and to a certain degree existentially, that the moral way of black life is also a reflection of what may well be a deeper psychosocial dilemma of the wider society. Sociologically, I believe, it reveals something about the pain and moral dilemma of being "black" in a white racist cultural system; where the norms and standards of morality tend to be determined by others; and where one's very identity--as a human being who so happens to be black-- is often looked upon with a kind of suspicion, disdain, and distrust. The provocative book, *Confessions of a White Racist* by larry L. King, reveals, in a rather candid way, the moral dilemma inherent in the white American psychic as it relates to attitudinal perceptions of blacks by many "good," "law-abiding," "God-fearing" white folks.

Larry L. King, ethically speaking, is an interesting case in point. His analysis of black-white relations in America is one which I found to be intriguing because he reminds the nation of what some white theologians, Christian ethicists, and liberal politicians would have us to forget: namely, that the reality of racial prejudice still constitutes a *peculiar moral dilemma* for the Christian church and white America. In *Confessions of a White Racist,* King tells us how he as a young white youth began, almost subconsciously, to acquire and internalize certain "morally wrong" attitudes about people of color. He recalls:

> Quite without knowing how I came by the gift, and in a complete absence of even the slightest contact with black people, I assimilated certain absolutes: the Negro would steal anything lying around loose and a high percentage of all that was bolted down; you couldn't hurt him if you hit him on the head with a tire tool; he revered watermelon above all other fruits of the vine; he had a mule's determination not to work unless driven or led to it; he would screw a snake if somebody would hold its head.[7]

It seems to me that one of the observations to be made here, though powerfully inflammatory and stereotypical in nature, is not only the rather obvious overt intensity of prejudice against blacks but the cultural modes by which certain "peculiar attitudes," morally abhorrent to be sure, are nevertheless transmitted by the social system; and how each affects the quality of the moral life in black. And how, in turn, these peculiar attitudes acquired by whites influence their social, religious, and ethico-theological perspective, when it comes down to the gut level of black-white relations in this country.

Thus we are called upon to recognize that the "existential-otherness" of the moral way, (i.e., the negative impact of a white racist value system on black life), is a matter that the ethically sensitive Christian must take seriously in both black and white communities. Further, Larry King illuminates our collective awareness through the illustration of how reasonable men and the normative culture have justified--theologically considered--their economic domination and exploitation of blacks. "God's all-seeing eyes had been so displeased," write Larry King, "that his book (the Bible) consigned blacks to be, 'hewers of wood, and drawers of water,' 'a servant's servant' happiest when waiting tables, playing banjo, or riding in the back of the bus."[8] In essence, there is, I think, a striking truth--as the noted anthropologist Ashley Montagu observed--that "racism is man's most dangerous myth."

Thirdly, the moral way in the formal structures of black

132

theological/philosophical and socio-historical thought is the way
of *blackness*.[9] Our explication and emphasis upon the moral way
indicates something about the very nature of white America which
black America has known all along, i.e., that the ethical reality
of *blackness* is often surrepticiously construed by the over-
whelming majority of white Americans to be a "negative vice"
rather than a "positive virtue." Some liberals of enlightened
moral persuasion put forth the argument that if blacks would just
give up, or substantially modify at least for a while, their
stress on "blackness" a more progressive pattern of equal justice
and cooperation could be realized. Indeed, some would argue that
the very structure of the ethics of blackness constitutes nothing
less than racism in reverse. Other white theologians and a few
liberal churchmen would have us believe that an integrated America
could, undoubtedly, be achieved were it not for our blackness.
Our Blackness! Our Blackness! Our Blackness! Any measure of
moral logic would suggest, however, that people of the black community have long since realized how the reality of cultural
racism can give rise to a moral dilemma which inhibits whites from
seeing blacks as human beings of equal status before God and man--
regardless of personal achievements. Furthermore, I think that
R. S. Browne is essentially correct in the observation:

> Even with a Ph.D., a Nobel prize, a Congressional Medal
> of Honor or a vast fortune, a Negro is still a "nigger"
> to many (most?) white Americans and the society does not
> let him forget it for very long. Nor does the sensitive
> Negro really want to forget it; he wants to change it.[10]

It is quite apparent that black folks and all ethically sensitive
persons must begin to move, in a pragmatic way, to declare war
on any and all forms of racial bigotry and economic-political
repression, if we are to ascertain a higher level of religious
and moral consciousness.

We have, thus far, attempted to delineate some of the salient
dimensions in our theoretical construct of the "moral way" of
black life. Suggestive as these are, there is a further need,
I think, to say a word about the structure of the "ethical" in
the life of oppressed blacks. It should be pointed out, however,
in the view of this writer, that the distinction between the
"moral way" and "ethical way" is purely a theoretical matter--
oriented in varying degrees around achieving optimum clarifi-
cation--for in the context of the black religious experience, life
itself tends to be perceived wholistically.

Theoretically speaking, we may describe in part the "ethical
way," with reference to the black Christian community in America,
as the way of self-critical ethical discourse. In a formal sense,
the black theologian believes that it begins essentially with,

or more appropriately, must begin with a basic praxeological-constructive analysis of the black condition--a reality that is still marred, unfortunately, by the oppressive domination of white culture over black life. In the life of the black Christian community, however, ethical discourse in contrast to moral discourse or the moral way, refers to that pattern of normative reflection which enables the agent to change; this is true not primarily because the black theologian and moral philosopher share in the common task of critical reflection, but because the gospel of Jesus Christ demands ethical change if we are to become what God created us to be: free and responsible human beings.

Theologically, the religious practitioner and black theologian alike believe that the "ethical way" begins with the affirmation of Jesus Christ, and loyalty to his rule, as constituting the central norm for the life of the oppressed. In my opinion, it is apparent that the validity of this claim arises out of the black man's awareness that the "ethical way" itself is, perhaps, best symbolized in the Oppressed One who says to the dispossessed, "I am the way, the truth, and the life..." (Jn. 14:6).

Furthermore, it is reasonable to assume that if, in fact, the ethical way is partially defined as the way of ethical discourse, then the human agent cannot truly understand the "nitty-gritty" stuff of black life without discerning the burden of the ethical. Paradoxically, one can be *moralistic* about the religious experience in black without being ethical; but one cannot be ethical in his assessment of the human condition without, at the same time, being moral. The discernment of the ethical implies something more. In his classic work, *Either/Or,* Kierkegaard's careful treatment of the nature of the ethical is instructive and relevant in our reflection upon the black religious experience in America. Kierkegaard holds that "the ethical always consists in the consciousness of wanting to do the good."[11] For the Christian, the ethical life is the life that counts; the ethical seeks the "good" and the "right" because it always indicates self-conscious involvement and participation in the totality of man's being-- the material, the spiritual, and the eternal. Kierkegaard put the matter this way:

> ...the energy with which I become ethically conscious
> is therefore the thing that counts or rather I cannot
> become ethically conscious without energy. I can
> therefore never become ethically conscious without
> becoming conscious of my eternal nature.[12]

In his analysis of the ethical life, Kierkegaard concludes by suggesting that it is only when individual persons begin to view life ethically, can we, then, begin to reflect the beauty of the whole of human existence.

There are two or three fundamental observations which seem appropriate, more or less, in summarizing our discussion of the concreteness of the ethical relative to the black religious experience in American society. First, the ethical is not merely an abstract reflective tool of theological analysis or a relevant component of empirical inquiry. For the oppressed black community, I believe that its purposive focus must be far more penetrating. The ethical is the growing cutting edge of historical existential experience. It is the uneven, radicalized leaven that helps to inspire and regenerate the downtrodden; a mode of reflection that commands the whole being of the agent in the struggle for social, cultural, and political liberation of the black community. To be sure, there can be no lasting creative self-critical consciousness, as I see it, neither in the Black Church as a social institution, nor in the black community at large--with all of its complex components--at the exclusion and neglect of the ethical.

Secondly, I believe that the "ethical way" or the discernment of the ethical consciously seeks to locate the "good," the "right," and the "just" in every historical period. For the black Christian community today, this can only mean--from my own vantage point--that the ethical is dynamic and fluent; especially in the sense that it attempts to use the oppressed's *location in history* as a key moral indicator of what one or a given minority group ought to do. Perhaps in this light, the ethical persistently struggles to avoid a purely metaphysical-theoretical abstractionism. In this way, I think that the ethical is never far from the pulse and heartbeat of the liberation struggle itself, particularly in light of the black man's attempt to constructively delineate his own moral, spiritual, and religious values. Thus in ethical discourse one is concerned with both the internal and external struggles of black people in America relative to one's understanding of what is right and wrong.

Thirdly, the ethical does not search for, either deliberately or forthrightly, the road of socio-moral consensus for its own existence. Rather, as we have seen, the ethical seeks self-critical analysis of social consensus in the community; it probes the nature of the "good" and the "right" by relating its essence to what God has done for men, particularly the poor and oppressed, and what God will continue to do for man,[13] and what he requires of him to do for himself--namely, to take moral responsibility for his own freedom and historical existence in the world. For Black Theology, the ethical here can only mean the realization that God wills freedom on behalf of the oppressed; that God wills for man a purposive moral and ethical life as best we can determine through the Scriptures. Thus it is God who establishes what the requirements, ultimately, of the moral and ethical life should be in the community of the oppressed.

CHRISTIAN ETHICS AND BLACK THEOLOGY IN DIALOGUE

The basic contention of our discussion here is the recognition
that there can be no viable Black Theology without ethical foundations. It is obvious, I believe, that the need for meaningful
dialogue between ethics and Black Theology is imperative. If
Black Theology decides, unwittingly to remove itself from the
ethical domains and moral considerations of the Christian faith,
it then ceases to be the *elan vital* (i.e., the living force or
vital principle.) and thereby loses its validity, eschatological
and prophetic vision, as well as its historical relevance to the
black struggle. The words of Professor Roger L. Shinn may well
be appropriate in this context in terms of our reflection upon
the relational character of Christian ethics and Black Theology.
In an article entitled, "Some Ethical Foundations of Christian
Theology," Professor Shinn states:

> Theology exists for the Gospel, not the Gospel for
> theology. And the Gospel--the good news of God's king-
> dom and his gracious deed in Christ--is social...and
> ethics is basic to theology. Just as there can be no
> Christian ethics without theological foundations, so
> there can be no theology without ethical foundations.[14]

In his book *The Groundwork of Christian Ethics*, N. H. G.
Robinson appears to be right on target when he says that Christian
ethics and Christian theology or dogmatics cannot be radically
separated into watertight compartments, that Christian ethics
as a normative science must be understood within the boundaries
of theology.[15] Furthermore, the discipline of Christian ethics--
in varying degrees, regardless of the normative postulates which
may or may not borrow from the social sciences and the wider cul-
ture--tends to naturally emanate from Christian theology. Thus
Christian ethics in a manner of speaking draws its suppositions
from the practical principles, religious beliefs, and moral truths
inherent in Christian theology. Accordingly, the Christian ethic
at the practical level is not, in the first place, primarily an
abstract principle by which we can understand the moral order of
the universe; or a metaphysical principle which enables the
agent to rationally discern the being of God as the Creator,
Redeemer, and Sustainer of human existence.[16] Rather, the
Christian ethic is a pattern for the moral life; it is a particular
way in which the Christian believer, black or white, thinks about
the meaning of the Christian faith as it relates to his own
behavior, experience, and conscience in human society.

Once the Christian ethic, from a black frame of reference,
loses touch with the ethical reality--with the ups and downs of
the poor and oppressed in their struggle for meaning, human

dignity, freedom, and wholeness--it ceases to be, at that very existential moment, a viable ethic. Moreover, it seems to me that Christian ethics loses its tenability and forceful claim at the precise moment it becomes, unwittingly, preoccupied primarily with rigid intellectual and scholarly debate over "proper" Christian standards for human conduct watered down by methodological schematisms; and thereby it becomes only indirectly concerned with the living faith and the cries of the needy in this life. "Just as the Christian faith is not merely an intellectual system or propositions which have no immediate connection with life," says Robinson, "so the Christian life cannot be understood apart from the faith by which it lives."[17] Further, he goes on to point out that:

> if...the Christian life is essentially a life of faith, then Christian ethics can never properly be divorced from Christian dogmatics, and the separation between them is no more than a methodological device for the sake of orderly and systematic study.[18]

To be sure, Christian ethics engages Black Theology in the sense that it compels us to reflect upon the normative use of the term "Christian" in a black context. Whatever else we may say about the terminology "ethics," the accent certainly falls upon the former as an axiomatic indicator. "It sets itself the task of giving a systematic account of the life that Christians ought to live, of the claim that God in Christ makes upon them," declares Robinson.[19]

All of this, thus far, sounds well and good. There is a growing awareness in some theological circles, however, that Christian ethics is problematic at a number of points, particularly in terms of the manner in which some white theologians interpret its import as a response to black ethnicity and the revolutionary cries of the oppressed for human justice. First of all, it would appear that far too many theologians and moral philosophers on the contemporary American scene identify, though perhaps some inadvertently, Christian ethics with the maintenance of the status quo. This peculiar irony occurs, I believe, in spite of the fact that American writers in Christian ethics of recent decades have been fundamentally concerned about moral action and social issues.[20] Such an identification in the thinking of a number of black theologians has inhibited, in one way or another, genuine and creative dialogue between blacks and whites, and their apparent desire to map out territories of mutual concern and common moral interest. I think that James Cone is essentially correct in the observation, as expressed in his recent book, *God of the Oppressed*, concerning theoretical-conceptual modes in which the Christian ethic is often cast:

137

Theologians of the Christian Church have not interpreted Christian ethics as an act for the liberation
of the oppressed because their views of divine
revelation were defined by philosophy and other
cultural values rather than by the biblical theme of
God as the Liberator of the oppressed.[21]

In a similar manner, Professor Cone goes on to further identify
this conceptual problematic in the body politic of white ethico-
theological thought by asserting:

If American theologians and ethicists had read the
Scripture through the eyes of black slaves and their
preachers, then they would have created a different
set of ethical theories of the "Good." For it is
impossible truly to hear the biblical story as told
in the songs and sermons of black people without also
seeing God as the divine power in the lives of the
oppressed, moving them toward the fullness of their
humanity. Any ethic derived from this God, then,
must be defined according to the historical struggle
of freedom. It cannot be identified with the status
quo.[22]

Secondly, it would seem that Christian ethics, as it is done
by a number of theologians and ethicists, is problematic--in
terms of a meaningful dialogue with Black Theology--not only
because of its tendency to sanction the status quo, but also
because of its unholy alliance with mainstream American capitalism,
particularly as reflected in the ethic of bourgeois "rugged
individualism." Too often, the result of the latter is an ethic
that rewards the rich for being rich, regardless of what that
means; and it punishes the poor for being poor, regardless of
what social or cultural condition. Despite the fact that the
Christian ethic is, undoubtedly, a noble "good" in and of itself;
the reality remains, nevertheless, that it has been used in
various ways--throughout the whole of Western civilization,
especially in American society--to protect in large measure, the
power, wealth, and privilege of the ruling class, of white
Anglo-Saxon Protestants and their descendants. Indeed, the
specific historical and sociological conditioning of white
theology and ethics vis-a-vis the black religious experience
renders yet another interesting result: the perpetration of a
fierce ethic of monopolistic competition and bourgeois individualism
where the socio-economic domination and control of blacks by
the white power structure becomes virtually complete. Eldridge
Cleaver, in *Soul on Ice*, alluded to this moral dilemma inherent
in the socio-economic system of America, as he critically observed
how the ethic of bourgeois individualism functions in the exploitation of the poor and dispossessed. He describes the situation

this way:

> In a culture that secretly subscribes to the piratical
> ethic of "every man for himself"...in our dog-eat-dog
> economic system of profit and loss, and in our
> adversary system of justice wherein truth is secondary
> to the skill and connections of the advocate--the logical
> culmination of this ethic, on a person-to-person level,
> is that the weak are seen as the natural and just prey
> of the strong.[23]

Thirdly, we may observe that Christian ethics, in terms of
effective dialogue with corpus of Black Theology, is ambiguous
and problematic because of its failure to remain sensitive to
the redeeming and living faith of the Christian community. It
seems to me that far too many theologians and ethicists on the
contemporary American scene exhibit a tendency toward a purely
rationalistic understanding of ethical reality. The result of
this is a kind of ethico-theological exclusivism and theoretical
abscurantism; both elements, I might add, appear to alienate
the Christian believer from the heart and pulse of the living
faith. The ethical life of the Christian is a fruit of faith.[24]
Of course, the ethical sensitive person must also admit that the
"living faith" is not an easy phenomenon to discern in religio-
moral discourse. Indeed, the word "faith" itself is somewhat
ambiguous because it is used in so many different ways. For
example, the theologian or ethicist may speak of faith with
reference to the affirmation of certain fundamental religious
beliefs: "I believe in God, the Father Almighty, Maker of heaven
and earth, and in his Son Jesus Christ..." Or, in another context, faith may mean a sort of moral confidence in the basic
democratic principles and social creeds of America relative to
the aspirations and hopes of an oppressed minority. Martin Luther
King, Jr., for instance, expressed a mode of faith by emphatically
proclaiming: "I have a dream that one day this Nation will rise
up and live out the true meaning of its creed: we hold these
truths to be self-evident that all men are created equal..."

In still another way, the theologian or ethicist of the
black religious experience may interpret faith in terms of a sense
of radical dependence and reliance upon Jesus. The "Gospel-song
tradition" of the Black Church expresses this perspective on
faith in these words from a familiar song:

> I learned how to lean and depend on Jesus;
> He is my Friend and He is my Guide.
> I learned how to lean and depend on Jesus,
> For I found out, if I trust, He will provide!

The point I am trying to elucidate here is a simple one, that is to

say, the element of faith is a significant center of gravity for
Christian ethics and Black Theology. Furthermore, I think that
a viable Christian ethic must be, at every juncture, organically
related to the dynamics of faith and the radicalization of the
faith element in history, particularly as individuals and social
groups seek to achieve the "good" in light of their existential
situation.

Fourthly, it would seem that the authentic claims of Christian
ethics, from the perspective of Black Theology, tend to be tem-
porarily obscured by what may well be an *over-commitment* to the
principle of love as the paradigm of the moral life--especially
in light of the realities of oppression and suffering in modern
society. While the ethically sensitive person cannot deny the
importance of the love principle as a central feature of the ethics
of Jesus,[25] there is far too little attention given to the idea of
justice as a requirement of love, particularly in regard to the
black man's struggle for status, social respectability, equality,
and full personhood in the American cultural system. For example,
there are far too few writers in Christian ethics who emphasize,
in matters pertaining to race, ethnicity, and conscience, the
fact that justice is an integral part of love; that justice as a
social value is built into the very constitution of love. Radically
conceived, the Christian ethic affirms that love and justice are
the same: that in the struggle of the oppressed for authentic
freedom, justice is not only a requisite for human community, but
a fundamental ethical imperative of love. In short, there is a
failure of perspective in the thinking of the agent whenever he
defines Christian ethics narrowly to be only a love ethic (too often
misunderstood as sentimentality) separated from justice and
other moral principles crucial to the total life of the community.
In any event, the conceptual error, as I see it, is obvious in
our formal patterns of ethical and theological discourse: there
is an apparent overcommitment to the love principle without careful consideration of what it demands that we do in a society deeply
implicated in the guilt of social injustice and racial prejudice.

After having critically reflected upon some of the inherent
problematics in Christian ethics as it engages Black Theology,
I believe that further consideration must be given to the development of a constructive statement on Black Christian Social
Ethics of the community.

TOWARD A BLACK CHRISTIAN SOCIAL ETHIC

In our attempt to provide a constructive statement on the
relation of ethics and Black Theology, we recognize that the task

is not an easy one. There are certain critical ethical and
theological problems which each theologian and morally earnest
person of the black community must deal with. Theoretically
discerned, one of these problems, to be sure, is the issue of
methodology. In the first place, it would seem that the moral
agent has to decide on whether or not it is viable to begin self-
critical reflection from formal ethical systems, on the one hand;
or to begin with an ethical posture that symbolizes the essential
claims of the poor and the oppressed on the other. I would
venture to suggest that if hindsight is any indicator as to the
future direction of the black liberation struggle, then the
question of methodology will be a crucial consideration for all
oppressed peoples. Perhaps the hindsight of black ethical wisdom
would suggest that the agent must not necessarily begin with so-
called formal reationally tailored moral systems; rather, the
agent must begin, as it were, with the nitty-gritty sounds and
cries of the oppressed themselves and their attempt to make sense
out of life. Indeed, black folk themselves must decide the question
of methodology as well as the specific shape of the "engendering
ethical deed," if we are to seriously consider the development
of a Black Christian social ethic. Moreover, such an ethical
posture must be relevant enough to keep us on the pathway to
liberation or authentic freedom; and at the same time, it must be
true enough to the best of our African religio-cultural heritage
without losing sight, inadvertently, of the prophetic vision
implicit in biblical faith and its inherent possibilities for
the creation of a new social order in America. To be sure, this
is not an easy "ethico-theological act" to pull off. It requires
serious reflection on the part of the black theologian upon a
number of difficult questions, one of which can be simply put--
namely: "What is the actual meaning of Black Christian social
ethics in the context of a people acquainted with so much suffering
and oppression?"

In order to find an answer to the question, we may need to
distinguish, for a moment, between two modes of theoretical response.
Black Christian social ethics can mean, in the first place, the
search for a new beginning in the agent's reflection upon the black
religious experience in America. For the black theologian and
moral thinker, it can mean the development of a normative, systematic
framework in the quest for religio-cultural roots. Accordingly,
the idea of a Black Christian social ethic may refer therefore to
that matrix of social values and rules which determine the identity
of the oppressed, the pattern of mutual relationships with reference
to persons in community, whether or not particular values and
rules are given an exact formulation.

In contrast, the idea of a Black Christian social ethic, in
the second sense, may refer or encompass specific insight into the
ethical reality of oppressed blacks themselves, in light of their

professed goals and socio-religious value claims. In this case, the structure of ethical reflection upon the black religious experience can be viewed or defined in the following way: *that Black Christian social ethics is essentially an ethic of radical freedom for the moral life, initiated by the agapeistic love of God as disclosed in Jesus Christ, and in his concern for the poor and dispossessed in human community.* Thus we may say that Black Christian social ethics is aimed, deliberately and forthrightly, at the creation of community wherein persons have the moral freedom and obligation of caring, of sharing, and responding to the needs of others. Like any other discipline, Black Christian social ethics arises out of black people's own existential and social experience in their attempt to think through the meaning and value of human life, in light of the Christian faith. Perhaps in this seminal idea abides the foundation for a new beginning relative to the community of the oppressed. Of course, we are obligated naturally to recognize that ethics in any context is always concerned with man's basic freedom and dignity, and with the preservation of the ultimate values of the human spirit. And in this sense, ethics takes man as a center of value.[26]

If we are to seriously consider doing ethics from the perspective of the oppressed black community, there are, I believe, at least three vital dimensions which may claim our attention and normative reflection relative to the corpus of Black Theology. The three aspects in our conceptual framework on, and consideration of, a Black Christian social ethic include:

1. *foundational* sources;
2. *intentional* focus; and
3. *central-norm* or organizing principle.

Here it is important to point out from the beginning that the notion of a Black Christian social ethic is not an attempt essentially to "blackenize" Christian ethics based on the assumption that white folks in general, and the white moral philosopher in particular, have not dealt squarely with blacks in America. Although such a claim is not without ethic-theological legitimacy, a black Christian social ethic cannot be, and for that matter, must not be merely a nicely packaged, well-thought-out, and rationally construed corollary to counterbalance a "white Christian ethic." Neither can a Black Christian social ethic, in my own moral judgment, be merely a prescriptive-analytical tool to gauge accurately the pulse and tempo of Black Theology, to keep it within the temperance zone, to prescribe in a manner of speaking a proper value diet for right conduct, of proper behavior vis-a-vis the community of the oppressed in America. Nor can it be conceptualized fully as a sort of treaty principle or moral-theology dictionary where the individual can easily find the answers as to what he ought to do, or must do in every moral situation. Indeed, moral logic would suggest that a Black Christian social ethic cannot be a "super-watchdog" for Black Theology, to make sure that it stays on the right tract, on the straight and narrow way. Rather, the seminal idea of a Black Christian social ethic, in a descriptive and functional sense, must take a disciplined and serious look at the whole Gospel, the biblical faith, and at the implications of God's divine revelation in Jesus Christ, particularly with reference to the demoralization and exploitation experienced by blacks and other dispossessed minorities in American society. Professor Herbert O. Edwards puts the matter succinctly by contending:

> To do *Black Christian Social Ethics* is to analyze and
> actively respond to the black situation in the light
> of Biblical, theological and sociological inter-
> pretations of the liberating acts of God, taking into
> account previous assumptions and presuppositions of
> those who have sat and sit where the oppressors sit,
> and those who have sat and sit with the oppressed.[27]

Thus our theoretical orientation into the development of a Black Christian social ethic is in part an attempt to understand the moral principles of the Christian faith in light of their applicability to the need of the oppressed for liberation or authentic freedom. Therefore, we may cogently and relevantly speak of *Christian belief* as one of the foundational sources of a Black Christian social ethic. Here I feel that it is important to recognize--theologically and biblically considered--that the black Christians of the community do not, for the most part, debate about God's moral or existential presence in the world. Rather, they assume God's existence as a given, as an ever-present reality in history. From the posture of ethical belief in his Holy Word, they assume that God acts; that he lives. Though some-times strange and mysterious, they believe that God acts in history in a redemptive and reconciling way on the behalf of the poor and outcast, the despised and lowly. Ethically speaking, there is a sense in which blacks believe and affirm God by believing and affirming their own humanity and worth as persons. Accordingly, the oppressed can respond to God because God himself first responded to them through a profoundly revolutionary and redemptive act on the cross. It is this ethical spirit of the Black Christian community that affirms: because God lives, we live. Because God has acted and continues to act in history, we can live free and act responsibly in human community.

Furthermore, there is a sense in which the central authority of a Black Christian social ethic comes, ultimately, from God's humanizing and liberating activity in the world. To be sure, there is a manner in which Christian belief, as a foundational source for the development of a Black Christian social ethic, provides a fresh start for the understanding of real freedom and its radical

143

significance for the unfree. So then, the black Christian tends
to believe that God cares desperately about what happens to him
in this life, about the trials and tribulations blacks suffer in
history. Perhaps the real ethical significance of belief in God
is captured in this religious dictum of the Black Church: "God
may not come when you want Him, but He's always on time!" Professor J. Deotis Roberts speaks cogently about this God-consciousness
relative to ethics and Black Theology in an article entitled:
"Black Consciousness in Theological Perspective." Concerning the
importance of black belief in God as an ethical indicator for
right conduct, Professor Roberts hold that:

> the God of Jesus who identified himself with those of
> low estate, must be a God who cares for and loves all
> men....He casts his lot with the needy, the sinful,
> and the disinhereited.[28]

He further asserts that:

> A black theology must develop this theme of a God who
> is ever-present, a God who cares, who rules, who
> guides and gives us "strength for the day." But this
> God must no longer be understood as a means of escape
> from life, but as one who enables us to stand up to
> life....Black theology, in asserting the presence of
> God, must be positive and aggressive, rather than
> passive, quietistic, and escapist.[29]

A second foundational source for the development of a viable
Black Christian social ethic, in relation to Black Theology, is
the actual experiences of the oppressed black man in American
society. For the black Christian, I contend that it is the actual
socio-economic and historical and cultural conditions of the disinherited that require understanding and constructive ethical
analysis on the part of all morally sensitive persons. Through
the process of critical reflection, the black theologian and
Christian ethicist alike have the difficult task of trying to make
sense out of the social, religious and moral experiences of black
people as they struggle, day by day, to create a more palatable
future. Here part of the task, from an ethico-theological perspective, involves coming to grips with inherent thought forms,
cultural patterns as well as the matrix of social and moral values
of blacks vis-a-vis their existential predicament. Ralph Ellison
enables us to discern more clearly the complexity of the black man's
existential predicament in America when he once remarked:

> For even as his life toughens the Negro, even as it
> brutalizes him, sensitizes him, dulls him, goads him
> to anger, moves him to irony, sometimes fracturing
> and sometimes affirming his hopes...it conditions him

to deal with his life and with himself. Because it
is his life and not mere abstraction in someone's head.
He must live it and try consciously to grasp its
complexity until he can change it;...he is a product
of interaction between his racial predicament, his
individual will and the broader American cultural freedom in which he finds his ambiguous existence...[30]

The third major foundational source in our conception of a
Black Christian social ethic is the Holy Spirit. Ethics in the
New Testament is full of references to the Spirit (Gk. *pneuma*).
New Testament scholars have given undue attention to the contrast
between the abundance of references to the Spirit in connection
with the main events in the moral life of Jesus and the Spirit's
work in wider Christian community.[31] Here we are ethically concerned with the implications of the latter--the Spirit's redemptive work in the life of the community. The expressed purpose
of the Spirit, (i.e., the Spirit of God in Christ), is to equip
the believer with power to overcome his existential predicament.
We may say theologically that the Spirit sets the believer free
from the legalistic clinging to the letter of the law or to any
culturally oppressive norm; the Spirit is the Spirit of Christ
the Liberator.[32] In this context, therefore, the fact of social
and political heteronomy, guidance from an external source,
cannot be the only accepted norms if the oppressed black man is
to be morally free. While ethics in a black Christian context
places emphasis upon Christian belief and religious experience
as important sources, it is the Spirit of God--functioning in a
practical way as a guide in the presence--that inspires and
compels the oppressed and downtrodden to start afresh; to
literally keep on pushing on the long journey toward genuine
freedom and full human dignity.

Ethically, it is the work of the Spirit that brings us into
new relationships with each other as a community of faith.[33]
For the poor and oppressed, it is a force which gives the human
spirit courage to confront every moral situation by providing a
greater sense of unity and solidarity in the common quest for
liberation. So then, it is the Spirit's work that set into perspective, ultimately, the dialectical character of ethics and
Black Theology. "Now the Lord is that Spirit: and where the
Spirit of the Lord is, there is freedom." (II Cor. 3:17) It is
reasonable to assume that the crucial question here is not
whether Black Theology can adequately proceed without due consideration to the Spirit as a vital source for ethical insight,
but whether it can proceed at all without moral sensitivity to,
without being guided by, the sounds of the Spirit of God as disclosed in black religious experience. Thus it is conceivable
that the motivation undergirding the moral struggle for liberation
may find its source, ultimately, in the Spirit of God. In short,

those who do Black Theology and those who are concerned about the plight of dispossessed must never lose sight of the fact that God is Spirit; that God's divine word is an indispensable ethical source for liberation in earthen form.

Now the second consideration in our discussion of the development of a viable Black Christian social ethic, in relation to the structure of Black Theology, is the *intentional focus*. Here it is my fundamental contention that to do ethics in a black theological context means to be oriented toward the creation of the beloved community.[34] The ethical spirit of the black Christian rests on the hope implicitly and explicitly disclosed in the notion of the beloved community. Obviously, one of the implications of this ethical conception is the recognition of the poor and oppressed as moral agents of social change. Accordingly, the oppressed of the land are encouraged to believe that "what is" (i.e., their present state of alienation, victimization, and demoralization) need not be, necessarily, determinative in terms of future hope and ethical promise. Ethics in a black theological context must affirm the possibility of the "beloved community" because the future of America may depend on how well Christians, both black and white, can appropriate the biblical, moral, and socio-cultural implications of this pivotal concept with regard to the kinds of changes needed in our social system. Thus the *intentional focus*--a vital dimension in the development of a Black Christian social ethic--is the creation of community. I believe that it is only in community where the human values of trust, love, mutuality, self-respect and freedom can take shape and form. Neither theological exclusivism nor cultural exclusivism can be acceptable to the ethically sensitive person; for the "beloved community" is, in essence, the *inclusive* community. In short, the intentional focus of ethics in a black theological context must be upon the vision of the "beloved community": a vision of community wherein authentic freedom, love, justice, and the righteousness of God can be actualized in history.

We now come to the matter of the *central norm* as the distinctive element in our discussion of a Black Christian social ethic. Christian writers in Black Theology find it helpful, on occasions, to delineate between "source" and "norm." In the context of ethics and Black Theology, some writers have referred to "source"[35] to mean relevant data for the ethical task. However, the term "source" in theological discourse can also be used to refer to the broad character of black religious experience itself--and to its complex nucleus of value presuppositions and postulates. Accordingly, the source, in this sense, becomes not only relevant data for ethical and critical reflection, but the *grass roots* from which the black man as moral agent can begin to build a new ethic for a new social order. Theoretically, we may say that the *norm* differs from the source in that it becomes a sort of ethical

barometer or gauge as to how the agent will actually use the
source. In any event, the advantage of having a norm, seemingly,
is the fact that it provides concrete standards not only for particular types of situations, but for the moral life in general.

Thus the *norm* is a measuring rod or criterion of judgment to
which human moral action is subjected. For Christians of the
oppressed black community, I propose, therefore, that the *central
norm* of Black Christian social ethics is the norm of Jesus Christ
as the Liberator and Reconciler. Those serious about the business
of doing ethics and Black Theology affirm Jesus as the Christ.
In a black context, Jesus as the Christ means that he liberates
and reconciles whomsoever he pleases: for a redemptive and
humanizing purpose in history, so that former slaves and former
slave masters may come to the awareness that human oppression
anywhere is a perennial threat to human justice everywhere. As
for black-white relations, I think that one of the ethical implications here arises from the awareness that Christ liberates
blacks from the bondage of oppression and powerlessness, while at
the same time, he liberates whites--if they renounce the sin of
racism and turn to him in repentance and faith--from the burden of
guilt, fear, and shame. In essence, our understanding of Jesus
Christ as the central norm of Black Christian social ethics means
that he gives the community of oppressed blacks a new radical
imperative, viz., *become who you are*: a free and responsible
people. Further, we must recognize that while the black theologian's
interpretation of foundational sources may change--depending on
the cultural milieu in which they develop--the central norm of
Black Christian social ethics remains the key paradigm in the
ethical life of the black Christian in human community. This is
true, I believe, largely because the ethical life of the black
Christian, not unlike that of the Black Church community as a whole,
must continue to be a life of faith, of trust, of forgiveness,
of earnest struggle for the realization of authentic freedom and
mutual sharing of the burden of responsibility in the world.

An Unstructured Ethic of Responsibility

In our current discussion, the theme we are concerned with is
the meaning of responsibility in the context of ethics and Black
Theology. Here I wish to elaborate the view that there is a need
to distinguish between what may be called an "unstructured ethic" of
responsibility vis-a-vis a more conventional understanding of
responsibility in moral and theological discourse. In examining the
matter of an unstructured ethic of responsibility in a highly complex
and structured society would seem, at first glance, totally absurd.
Indeed, some Christian moralists argue that the word "ethic" itself

147

would presuppose a certain type of rational-normative structure peculiar to the human spirit; and the inclusion of the word "unstructured" borders on being tautology. However, my own experiences, as a black man in white America, force me to reflect upon not only the meaning of responsibility in ethical theory, but to put in proper perspective what being "black" in this society is all about: moral alienation, suffering, oppression, insensitivity to the cries and sounds of the poor; but it also means, at the deeper levels of the black man's soul, the proclamation of the liberation gospel of Jesus Christ through teaching, preaching, living, dying, and being born anew in order that God's kingdom of righteousness and love might be actualized in history.

In terms of the black religious experience, an unstructured ethic of responsibility calls for a major restructuring of the ethical problematic, i.e., the basic moral strategy for radical social change in our value system must begin with the oppressed themselves, with the so-called "misfits," "nobodies," of society, and begin to interpret God's divine love and righteousness in light of their concrete existential situation. In a black context, the restructuring of the ethical problematic, as a key expression of the idea of responsibility, means that black people themselves must reorder their blackness, their socio-religious value orientation.

Furthermore, the black theologian and Christian social ethicist alike must participate in the difficult task to restructure the "ethical problematic," to reorder the basic character of blackness in such a way that the oppressed no longer see themselves as mere "pawns" or "victims" in an alienative social system; but rather to discern the essence of their being as representative of a new moral consensus in America. However, it is precisely at this juncture that we can see the agonizing moral dilemma of responsibility for blacks in this country: paradoxically, we are at once asked by the larger normative culture to be responsible, when responsibility itself is based in part upon recognition and power,[36] upon the acknowledgment of the equal worth and common humanity of the black man in the community of humankind. Ralph Ellison, almost three decades ago, put his finger upon the moral dilemma in terms of the historical predicament of black people in this country. In *Invisible Man*, Allison argues that the black man is *invisible* in regard to equal participation in the social, economic, and political institutions of our corporate life. "Can we expect, in any reasonable manner, an 'invisible' man to be responsible?" In struggling with this question, it would seem that the ethically sensitive person may come to the painful awareness that it is the black man's own invisibility which illuminates his blackness, his essence as a human being. With ironic precision Allison makes a cogently relevant observation of what it means to be responsible by asserting: "...even the invisible victim is responsible for the fate of all."[37] I believe that Allison's ethical

148

disposition here would serve notice that each person of the black
community has a "measure" of moral responsibility relative to the
state of his own existential condition and the moral plight of the
other.

However, the Christian moralist and theologian are compelled
to recognize that so long as social and cultural *victimization*,[38]
to a greater or lesser degree, functions as a significant factor
in the historical existence of blacks, the society at large must
share in the burden of ameliorating the total socio-economic and
religio-cultural conditions of the poor and disadvantaged. Despite
this important fact of our collective existence, I believe that
a constructive Black Theology must begin to emphasize more forcibly
the idea of blacks taking moral responsibility for their own human
welfare and destiny. Analytically, it is my basic conviction that
a constructive Black Theology is essentially an *ethical* theology;
it is a theology of concern and moral action. A constructive Black
Theology, as I see it, must be a theology of ethical responsiveness
to the needs of the disinherited in their plight for true freedom
and for the right to lay hold and moral claim upon the abundant
life. Theologically considered, a constructive Black Theology is
one of loyalty to and faith in Jesus Christ; and the ethical
realization that loyalty to him does make, can make, and ought to
make a difference in the moral lives of the members of the black
Christian community. In a manner of speaking therefore, a constructive Black Theology in the future must not simply be "anti-
white" but "pro-black," not simply reactive in character, but
"pro-active"; not simply a theology arising from socio-cultural
victimization, but one which aims at a new kind of moral, social,
and spiritual revitalization of the wider society wherein the
oppressed can find real hope and eschatological promise as a people
of God. It seems to me, in the first place, that nothing can,
perhaps, be more revolutionary in our reflection upon an unstructured
ethic of responsibility than for the oppressed to recognize that
even a slave has moral choice. Radically discerned, the man at
the bottom, though the risks are higher, is never fully deprived
of moral choice. For example, we may say that man as moral agent
is the only being who deliberately chooses his end--i.e., those
values or things which serve as directives for his own finite
existence. Perhaps nothing is more potentially revolutionary in
building a constructive Black Theology than the ethics of moral
choice (viz., the stubborn capacity and courage to say "YES" or
"NO" even in the face of imminent death). This is not, I believe,
an impetuous ethical stance because many black slaves historically
knew very well the risks inherent in "moral choice." Thus an
unstructured ethic of responsibility must encompass the element of
moral choice. Without the presence of moral choice, the idea of
responsibility makes no sense at all, especially as a viable stance
of the oppressed black man in American society.

149

Secondly, an unstructured ethic of responsibility means that
the black community must develop, increasingly, moral sensitivity
to the fact that there are no ready-made or neatly packaged
solutions to the complex problems of survival and black progress
in the modern world. Besides the obvious need of caring, sharing,
and enabling, the black community at large--especially the Black
Church as a change agent--must begin to redirect the values,
rational energy, and physical resources of black people in such
a way that would enhance black survival. I am in basic agreement
with Sterling D. Plumpp's observation that

>Black survival demands that Black people take the fate
>of all Black people into Black hands; this means that
>Black churches must initiate and sustain actions needed
>to unify Black people and needed for Black people to
>survive.[39]

Plumpp goes on to articulate more precisely the meaning of "black
survival" in light of the moral responsibility of the Black Church.
He states:

>Black survival means educating Black people to see
>dangers to their existence when those dangers are not
>as obvious as pre-dawn raids...or preventive detentions.
>It means educating the people to their position in this
>country and to their position in the world. For Black
>people must understand that as long as somebody else
>decides for them...those people cannot be their friends.
>The black church has the capacity...to equip Black people
>with a worldview pragmatic enough to allow them means
>for survival yet spiritual enough from becoming
>technological monsters sacrificing their whole being
>for the gain of a few.[40]

Thirdly, an unstructured ethic of responsibility accents what
has been traditionally described in the Black Church as "keeping-
the-charge." I believe that it was no accident of history that
pioneers of the Black Church, in particular, tended to interpret
the idea of responsibility both theologically and sociologically.
Theologically considered, the black man--not unlike the rest of
humanity--is ultimately responsible to God for what happens, for
the totality of his experiences in history; he is also responsible
to community for what happens to his neighbor. More concretely,
the element of the "charge" as an expression of responsibility
is described in the words of an old Black Spiritual: "A Charge
to Keep, I Have, A God to Glorify." From an ethico-theological
perspective, I contend that this notion of the "charge" not only
refers to a binding moral claim of the black Christian believer with
the Divine, but it also indicates a sort of partnership with God
for the purpose of making human life more free and human on the

part of the dispossessed, particularly in light of the ethical
principles of the Christian faith. In this sense, the black
Christian community perceives the charge politically--that is to
say, to be oriented essentially around the goal of freedom.
(In the last section of this chapter, we will examine critically
the modern dilemmas of "freedom" in contemporary Black Theology
and ethical thought.)

In any event, the "charge" element implicit in the ethics of
responsibility urges the oppressed to hold fast to the faith,
to believe that God's liberating work in history will not die,
come what may! Because God is righteous and just, he abides with
the oppressed. Because God is loving and merciful, his redemptive
activity--in and through the oppressed--is open ethically to all.
From the perspective of the black religious experience therefore,
all morally sensitive persons are called to keep the "charge"--
i.e., to be loyal and faithful to almighty God.

Thus far we have examined at least descriptively some of the
salient aspects of the meaning of responsibility in a black
context. Comparatively speaking, we may now look at a few implications of what can be called a more "structured" or theoretical
understanding of the idea of responsibility in theological discourse vis-a-vis the black struggle. Accordingly, the reader may
find H. Richard Niebuhr's book, *The Responsible Self*, to be
instructive at this juncture in our discussion. Professor Niebuhr
delineates what it means to be responsible in both personal and
social relationships of the normative Christian community. From
an ethico-theological perspective, he speaks of what it means to
be responsible in terms of man's own radical freedom in the world.
Man being made in the image of God, (*Imago Dei*), may not only be
perceived as *Homo-religiosis*--i.e., having a religious impulse or
persuasion--but generic man is also *Homo-ethicus*.[41] The image of
man as *Homo-ethicus* is not simply one wherein he perceives the
"Good," the "Right," or the "Just" through the exercise of critical
moral judgment, but also one wherein he is compelled to act
responsibly in human community. Thus the image of man as *Homo-
ethicus* means that he is not only a moral thinker who contemplates
the necessary conditions for human freedom, but an "answerer" as
well; one who must give account for his historical deeds before
God. "What is implicit in the idea of responsibility," says
Niebuhr, "is the image of man-the-answerer, man engaged in dialogue,
man acting in response to action upon him....To be engaged in dialogue,
to answer questions addressed to us, to defend ourselves against
attacks, to reply to injunctions, to meet challenges--this is
common experience."[42]

If our current analysis bears any legitimate weight at all
relative to the black liberation struggle, it is that the use of
symbolism of responsibility in ethics and Black Theology must be

one of the ground rules for moral action on the part of the
oppressed. The symbol of responsibility means that the oppressed
themselves must begin to appropriate their struggle in a different light. What I am suggesting here is that the oppressed must
not think of themselves as "helpless victims" but as *aggressive-
responsive beings*, capable of responding in a creative way to the
multifaceted realities of the black condition in American society.
Ethically, I feel that Professor Niebuhr is essentially correct
in his view that man as agent must be concerned about the "fitting
response" relative to the social forces that bear upon his historical situation. He asserts that the "fitting action, the one
that fits into a total interaction as response and as anticipation
of further response, is alone conducive to the good and alone is
right."[43]

There is another relevant note, I believe, which the morally
sensitive person may observe in Niebuhr's typology on the meaning
of responsibility: namely, a viable ethic of responsibility must be
inclusive of--among other elemental considerations--the motifs of
accountability and social solidarity.[44] Certainly, many Christian
moralists and black theologians would agree that these motifs,
to be sure, are nothing new in the fields of ethics, philosophy,
and theology. What is of crucial importance, as I see it, is
the precise manner in which black theologians and ethicists
evaluate these motifs in their interpretation and clarification
of fundamental life-death issues of the black religious experience
in white America. For instance, H. Richard Niebuhr points out,
and I think rightly so, that the ethical burden of responsibility
rests not primarily with the individual person but the group. It
stands to reason, therefore, that the ethical burden of liberation
falls ultimately with the social group itself; it falls within
the boundary of the precise manner in which the oppressed use the
principle of "social solidarity" as a revolutionary expression of
moral responsibility and persistent struggle for authentic freedom.

In short, the idea of responsibility must begin not with the
objectification of social reality of the external world, but
rather with a critical understanding of the subjective feelings,
moods, trials and tribulations of black people themselves in light
of their own religious, spiritual, and cultural values in the
context of the black community in American society. Whatever else
we may say about the notion of responsibility and how it fits into
our scheme of reflection on ethics and Black Theology, we may conclude that the black man as moral agent is responsible, ultimately,
to Almighty God and to the community for his own ethical action,
as well as accountable for the kind of future he shapes for himself.
As Bonhoeffer indicated so well, in *Ethics,* that man's conduct
becomes responsible and takes on higher ethical meaning only in
relationship to Jesus Christ and the community of men.[45] Bonhoeffer
puts it succinctly: "I stand for Christ before men and for men

before Christ. The responsibility which I assume for Christ in speaking to men is also my responsibility for men in speaking to Christ."[46] He further states:

> The structure of the responsible life is conditioned by two factors; life is bound to man and to God and a man's own life is free. It is the fact that life is bound to man and to God which sets life in the freedom of a man's own life. Without this bond and without this freedom there is no responsibility.[47]

In essence, the structure of the responsible life is dynamically interwoven with the life of radical freedom in God and Jesus Christ. So then, the precise moment in history the oppressed black man decides to be ethically responsible, he has in the same breath made the choice to be ethically free under God.

SEARCH FOR A UNIFIED THEORY OF FREEDOM

Perhaps there is no singular ethical concept more crucial for the health and viability of the black community than the concept of freedom. Ethically, freedom is the essence of liberation; and liberation the essence of freedom. Since the appearance of Black Theology on the contemporary American scene, black writers in religion, Christian ethics, and social sciences have been struggling to understand and clarify the idea of freedom, both in terms of theory and practice. However, it seems that part of the current task of the black minister and the black community--particularly if we are to be sensitive theologically to the need for moral and social change in America--would be to provide guidance as to what freedom "is" and what it requires at this moment in history. Obviously, there is no consensus of opinion among the scholars on this vital question. Yet the survival of the black church and the progress of the wider society may well depend on how we come to grips theologically with a unified perspective of freedom.

In analyzing the task of the black minister and the black church as change agents, Dr. Shelby Rooks makes a cogently relevant comment on one of the dilemmas in our ethico-theological perception of freedom in a black context. He asserts:

> Black ministers will never be whatever expectations the black church and community hold about their activity as change agents, unless the goals of that activity are clearer than they are today. It is undoubtedly true

153

that the ultimate goal of the black community is
freedom. But neither the content of that freedom,
what it means, nor the methods of achieving it are
clear. At one point, freedom simply meant freedom
from the chains of slavery. At another it meant freedom
from legal segregation and discrimination. Today,
both slavery and legal segregation are gone. What
then is the present goal of the freedom and liberation
we talk so much about? And how shall blacks achieve
it?[48]

Critically discerned, one of the perennial problematics inherent in
the structure of black theological discourse is the tendency by
some black thinkers to define the essence of Black Theology in
terms of freedom *from*. Any cursory glance or informal survey of
black theological literature in recent years reveals the interesting
fact that the material itself tends to be marred by such phrases
or interfused slogans as: "We want freedom from white control,"
"freedom from oppression and exploitation," "freedom from white
racism and injustice," "freedom from dehumanization"--Freedom
from...! Freedom *from*...! Freedom *from*...! The list goes on and
on.

Paradoxically, it would seem that Black Theology has gotten
itself into the peculiar moral dilemma of almost exclusively
defining its existence or reason for being over against what some
call "white theology." If the agent perceives liberation to be
the primary center of gravity of Black Theology, does it logically
follow that the center itself must be critically interpreted in
order to move the discussion beyond the static paradigm of freedom
from? In light of the black Christian's struggle to achieve full
personhood in a community of equals, perhaps the crucial question
can be put quite simply, "Should we recognize only a freedom *from*?"
It is my basic contention and ethical conviction that freedom is
more than the absence of restraint. Indeed, the search for a
unified theory of freedom would suggest to all of us that while
freedom *from* is a necessary condition for human dignity and the
realization of human potentiality; it alone is not sufficient. It
is probable, therefore, that a greater theoretical clarification
of the concept of freedom in Black Theology is imperative in order
to extricate the negatory moral isolationism implicit in the terminology freedom *from*.

To this end, I wish to elaborate a perspective of freedom
which embraces at least three ethical considerations:

1. the need for the development of a religio-cultural
   framework which is supportive of a freedom *for*;

2. an idea or theory of freedom which encompasses a

154

freedom *to*; and

3. the demand for an organic mode of freedom that expresses itself as freedom *in community*.

Regardless of what one's methodological orientation may be in ethics and Black Theology, whether it be purely functional and sociological, deontological or teleological, the apparent desire, I believe, for a more unified perspective of freedom is a moral imperative of human existence. There is no desire more persistently peculiar to the human spirit than the craving for freedom. Freedom is not only a moral value,[49] as some theologians and philosophers would contend, it is a moral mandate of man's basic nature. The essence of man is freedom; but not a form of freedom which is purely mechanistic or negative. Thus the idea of freedom *for* in the structure of black ethical and theological thought points toward the need to provide concrete religio-moral directives for oppressed blacks in American society. To be quite candid about the matter, I think that freedom *for* means that the poor and socially outcast of every ethnic group in this society need not understand their condition--psychologically considered--totally from the posture of powerlessness and oppression; nor their particular modes of victimization as being sociologically determinative. In one sense, I am suggesting that the notion of freedom *for* implies a "change in attitude" and the parallelistic realization that the things that be need not be; that even the "feeble" action of the socially outcast can lead to a higher good.

In another respect, we may say that the idea of freedom *for* ans participation on the part of the agent through creative self-expression. It is precisely at this point, I believe, where freedom and responsibility converge in order to see more clearly the relationship of ethics and Black Theology, where the inner and outer boundaries of the human spirit come together so that the oppressed black man can discern more cogently what he is about in a white-dominated society; and perhaps more pertinently, what he is capable of becoming--a fully liberated human being. Thus the idea of freedom *for* transcends a mere freedom *from*, essentially because it offers the agent real hope, ethical promise, and to a greater extent indeterminate possibilities for achieving the good in history. Further, there is the recognition in our discussion that in some respect these "indeterminate possibilities" are undoubtedly bound up in our reflection upon the nature of man-- especially man as a moral creature. Reinhold Niebuhr has pointed out that "man requires freedom in his social organization because he is essentially free, which is to say, that he has the capacity for indeterminate transcendence over the processes and limitations of nature."[50]

Secondly, it is my contention that any ethico-theological

155

stance of the black community which fails to come to terms with
a *freedom to* is conceptually deficient and methodologically
inadequate. Ethically speaking, freedom *to* implies "I can."
Sometimes this view is expressed theologically and religiously in
the black community by the black Christian when he affirms: "I
can do all things through Christ who strengthens me." Sometimes
it is expressed socially when one "soul" brother says to another
in profound ethical seriousness: "Man, I gotta keep on *pushing*!"
For the oppressed black community, the notion of freedom *to* always
incites within us a certain definiteness, character of being
that mitigates against power inertia and enables us to become
what we ought to be.

Theoretically, it would seem that the idea of freedom *to* in
black ethical and theological thought tells the oppressed something
about the right to participate in the decision-making process.
Perhaps it is only by the agent's ability to act and respond in
the process of decision-making, that we can begin to critically
understand and discern what freedom *to* really means. To be free means
that the moral agent has the capacity for deliberate decision and
self-determined action. Now in terms of black-white relations in
America, I contend that this perspective of freedom *to* does not mean
the freedom to be *somebody else*, to somehow escape the social, religious, and cultural boundaries of one's own existential existence.
Rather, this level of freedom is the power of liberation, the power
to grow, to interact with the other, to participate and challenge.
In the book *The Black Community: Diversity and Unity*, James E.
Blackwell puts it this way:

> Liberation means the complete freedom of black American
> and entails "equal distribution of decision-making power,"
> the liberated black is more concerned about freedom as an
> individual and of blacks as a group of people than he
> is about physical proximity to white people. He is
> especially concerned about his capacity to obliterate
> white oppression as well as his ability to challenge
> cherished American values that are inconsistent with the
> black experience in white America.[51]

Than Blackwell goes on to argue concerning the black man as moral
agent:

> He is committed to the unity of blacks as a people living
> in a nation that is as much his as it is that of any
> other group of people inhabiting it.[52]

Thus the ethical conception of freedom *to* implies that black people
must have the power to participate fully and equally in the possibilities of this society.

Thirdly, I believe that the subject matter of freedom in the structure of ethics and Black Theology must be more clearly delineated in light of the community. Here the concept of the *ought*, as I see it, has always had an implicit reference to freedom *in community* in the whole structure of ethical inquiry. For instance, the idea of *ought* in ethical discourse implies *can*,[53] and the notion of *can* is not only consistent with the ethics of freedom but *is* freedom, to the extent that freedom is the power of self-determination, in and through community. Normatively, freedom really means belonging to the community (a point which we have stressed especially in the treatment of the ethics and theology of Martin Luther King, Jr.). The use of the terminology freedom *in community*, then, suggests to us that the worth and dignity of all people, all races and classes can only be authenticated in a relationship of trust, mutuality, justice, and love. Freedom *in community* means the affirmation of the posture of self-respect; it means that there is no place for an "I-IT" relationship. In black-white relations, it means that there is no room for the classical sociocultural syndrome of "superordination/subordination." Normatively, all are free and equal because each has the power of moral choice and the capacity to respond to the other's needs.

Perhaps what is uniquely characteristic of freedom *in* is its emphasis upon the "we relationship." For the structure of our analysis and reflection upon the black religious experience, there is no factor or component more important than the "we relationship." Indeed, I think that the ethical mandate for freedom can only be qualitatively appropriated when oppressed blacks themselves meet, struggle, and interact with each other and the oppressor in the context of community. Therefore, we may observe that freedom means not only the capacity to respond to the totality of human claims, but the power to respond creatively to the divine liberating presence of God in community. So then, the essence of freedom *in* relative to the humanity of the oppressed can be best expressed in terms of "we relationship" and our capacity to respond to the claims and counterclaims of God and man in love. Undoubtedly, it is in the "we relationship" where the essential core of the humanity of the oppressed black can best be sustained and reinforced in practical ways.

In the final analysis, it would appear that the ethical concept of freedom *in* points toward the interdependent character and mutuality of all human existence. In a word, neither the oppressed nor the oppressor can ultimately find full personhood, happiness, human wholeness or moral responsiveness apart from community. To be sure, the future of Black Theology in America may well depend on how it comes to terms with a unified perspective of freedom inclusive enough to respond to the organic pluralism of the wider cultural ethos, and at the same time, particularized enough to meet the needs of the poor and dispossessed who still cry daily in the marketplace of the world community for social justice and human liberation.

Questions for Additional Study

1. Does Black Theology really make sense to the typical lay-
   person who may be involved in the day-to-day life of the
   Christian community?

2. What can religious leaders and scholars do to relativize
   "theological language" and "ethical speech" with reference to
   the meaning of the Christian faith for the moral life?

3. Does the ethical spirit and moral spontaneity characteristic
   of black church workship emanate essentially from a biblical
   understanding of God's liberating Word?

4. In light of the critical social issues of perennial racism
   and sexism, can Black Theology be ethical? If so, how?

5. Can ethics make a positive difference in clarifying our understanding of what God is doing in the world? *Who* is he doing
   it with? And for what *purpose*?

6. List several ways by which an ethic of "responsible freedom"
   can speak to the current grassroot conditions of the poor
   and dispossessed in America and elsewhere in the world
   community.

7. Is the central ethical question confronting Black Theology today
   one of *how* we've "come thus far by faith?" or *where* do we go
   from here as the community of faith seeks to appropriate the
   biblical norms of liberation and redemptive love to the concrete
   social conditions of oppression in human society?

Related Readings

Alves, Rubem, A *Theology of Human Hope*. Washington, D. C.:
Corpus Books, 1969.

_____, *Tomorrow's Child*. New York: Harper and Row,
Publishers, 1972.

Blassingame, John, *The Slave Community*. New York: Oxford
University Press, 1972.

Bonhoeffer, Dietrich, *The Cost of Discipleship*. Trans, R. H.
Fuller, New York: Macmillan Co., 1959.

Brandon, S. G. F., *Jesus and the Zealots*. New York: Charles
Scribner's Sons, 1967.

Cone, James H., *God of the Oppressed*. New York: The Seabury
Press, 1975.

Gutierrez, Gustavo, A *Theology of Liberation*. Maryknoll, New York:
Orbis Books, 1973.

Kasemann, Ernst, *Jesus Means Freedom*. Philadelphia: Fortress
Press, 1972.

Lehmann, Paul, *Ethics in a Christian Context*. New York: Harper
and Row, Publishers, 1973.

_____, *The Transfiguration of Politics*. New York: Harper
and Row, Publishers, 1975.

Miguez, Bonino, Jose, *Doing Theology in a Revolutionary Situation*.
Philadelphia: Fortress Press, 1975.

Niebuhr, Reinhold, *The Nature and Destiny of Man*. Vol. II,
New York: Charles Scribner's Sons, 1943.

Roberts, J. Deotis, A *Black Political Theology*. Philadelphia:
The Westminster Press, 1974.

Yoder, John H., *The Politics of Jesus*. Grand Rapids: Wm. B.
Eerdmans, 1972.

NOTES

CHAPTER I. THE PROBLEM OF ETHICS AND THE BLACK RELIGIOUS EXPERIENCE

[1]Cf. After a careful assessment of the ethical alternatives of the American cultural system, Professor Williams
strongly suggests that oppressed blacks ought to be loyal to God;
and that one's primary motivation for engagement in the Black
Revolutionary Struggle should reflect inclusive norms and universal principles which take into account the human rights of
all men. Thus he perceives the principle of "promise-keeping"
to be the first essential for the liberation of the oppressed
black man; and subsequently, "a recognition by white Americans
that black Americans have a full claim upon American ideals and
resources and that this claim cannot be wholly determined by the
capricious white will." See Preston N. Williams, "The Problem
of a Black Ethic," *The Black Experience in Religion*, C. Eric
Lincoln, ed., (New York: Anchor Press/Doubleday, 1974), pp. 181-
183ff.

[2]Paul Deats, Jr., "The Quest for a Social Ethic," *Toward a
Discipline of Social Ethics*, Paul Deats, Jr., ed., (Boston:
Boston University Press, 1972), pp. 21-23ff.

[3]Cited in Ronald W. Walters, "Toward a Definition of Black
Social Science," *The Death of White Sociology*, Joyce A. Ladner,
ed., (New York: Vintage Books, 1973), p. 206.

[4]Here the notion of "digging" as a concept to depict the heart
of the ethical task was often used by F. D. Maurice and appreci-
ated by H. Richard Niebuhr. James Gustafson speaks of it as being
important in understanding the nature of ethical inquiry. In reflecting upon the black religious experience, however, the term
"digging" seems to be ethically relevant because it invites a
critical explication of the meaning of Black presence in the
larger context of American society. When one begins to "dig" into
the funky facts of black life, it is plain to see, then, that all
is not well for blacks and other exploited minorities in our so-
called land of "liberty, equality, and justice." H. Richard
Niebuhr, *The Responsible Self*, (New York: Harper and Row, Publishers, 1963), pp. 14-15ff.

[5]Lerone Bennett, *The Challenge of Blackness*, (Atlanta: Institute of the Black World, Black Paper No. 1, April, 1970), pp. 3-4. A note of caution is needed also. Perhaps some theoretical distinction should be made between what Lerone Bennett calls "false universality of white concepts" or those principles which masquerade under the guise of authenticity, on the one hand; and the apparent need to recognize certain universal principles common to all humanity, on the other. The need to work out a system of moral values, wherein the whole of humankind can participate, has already been alluded to in a commend made earlier by Professor Williams, of which I am in agreement. In any case, there is no theoretical inconsistency here in affirming "genuine universal principles," while at the same time rejecting a kind of "false universality" implicit in much of Euro-American intellectual and religious thought.

[6]See James M. Gustafson, "Moral Discernment in the Christian Life," *Norm and Context in Christian Ethics*, Gene H. Outka and Paul Ramsey, eds., (New York: Charles Scribner's Sons, 1968), esp. pp. 26-36.

[7]*Ibid.*, p. 24.

[8]Cf. Enoch H. Oglesby, "Ethical and Educational Implications of Black Theology in America," *Religious Education*, (Vol. LXIX July-August, 1974), p. 411.

[9]*Ibid.*, pp. 410-412.

[10]Paul Lawrence Dunbar, "We Wear the Mask," *On Being Black: Writings by Afro-American from Frederick Douglass to the Present*, Charles T. Davis and Daniel Walden, eds., (Greenwich, Conn.: Fawcett Publications, Inc., 1970), pp. 89-90.

[11]James H. Cone, *Black Theology and Black Power*, (New York: The Seabury Press, 1969), p. 149.

[12]*Ibid.*, pp. 150-151ff.

[13]Cf. Herbert O. Edwards, "Toward a Black Christian Social Ethic," *The Duke Divinity School Review*, (Spring, 1975), p. 106.

[14]Cf. Lerone Bennett, *Op. Cit.*, p. 4.

[15]Joseph A. Johnson, Jr., *The Soul of the Black Preacher*, (Philadelphia: A Pilgrim Press Book, United Church Press, 1971), p. 155.

[16]Cf. Howard Thurman, *Jesus and the Disinherited*, (New York: Abingdon Press, 1949), p. 29.

[17]See John C. Diamond, "David Walker's Appeal: A Theological Interpretation," *The Journal of the Interdenominational Theological Center*, (Vol. III, No. 1, Fall, 1975). After an astute ethico-theological assessment of the Walker's Appeal, Professor Diamond concludes that "...the central theological concern of Walker's Appeal is, in fact, the justice of God, or better, the problem of evil, and Walker has demonstrated his 'solution' to the problem. Fundamental to this solution is Walker's faith that God is the Stern, Powerful, Just, Sovereign Lord of the Universe, who punishes disobedience--sin--whether it arises from the hand of blacks or whites." (p. 39)

[18]David Walker, "Walker's Appeal, in Four Articles," *Black American Literature*, Ruth Miller, ed., (Beverly Hills, Calif.: Glenco Press, 1971), pp. 119-124ff.

[19]Cf. David Walker, *Ibid.*, p. 126.

[20]Walter G. Muelder, *Moral Law in Christian Social Ethics*, (Richmond, Va.: John Knox Press, 1966), p. 46.

[21]Andrew Billingsley, *Black Families in White America*, (Englewood Cliffs, New Jersey: Prentice-Hall, Inc., 1968), pp. 27-28.

[22]*Ibid.*, pp. 28ff.

[23]Alain Locke, "The Negro's Contribution," *On Being Black*, C. T. Davis and D. Walden, eds., pp. 106-107.

[24]*Ibid.*, pp. 109-110.

[25]Benjamin Brawley, A *Social History of the American Negro*, (New York: The Macmillan Co., 1921, also 1970), p. 384.

[26]*Ibid.*, pp. 384ff. In my opinion, it is, undoubtedly, morally relevant to note that a strong "ethic of achievement" accounts in part for the black man's psychobiological and spiritual survival in America. When you are "down and out" and literally suppressed by the white power structure, there is really no way to go but up. To do this, I think, requires strong internal moral strength and the expressed view that "I can achieve," "I can overcome." Seemingly, blacks have always possessed this kind of moral perspective; especially in their struggle to deal with the ironies of being "black" in white America. In recent years, for example, black leaders like Dr. Leon Sullivan, an outstanding community person who helped to organize the O.I.C., has stressed an "ethic of achievement" in his concept of "Build, Brother, Build" rather than "Burn, Baby, Burn!" See also, Benjamin Quarles, *The Negro in the Making of America*, (New York: Collier Books, 1964);

Edgar A. Toppin, *Blacks in America: Then and Now,* (Boston: The Christian Science Publishing Society, 1969); Agnes McCarthy and L. Reddick, *Worth Fighting For,* (New York: Zenith Books, 1965).

[27]Waldo Beach and H. Richard Niebuhr, *Christian Ethics,* 2nd ed. (New York: The Ronald Press Co., 1973), pp. 14-16ff.

CHAPTER II. THE BLACK CHURCH AND MORAL DISCOURSE

[1]Albert B. Cleage, Jr., *The Black Messiah,* (New York: Sheed and Ward, 1968), pp. 233ff. As a radical community leader, Albert Cleage is perhaps known nationwide in black theological and political circles; he is pastor of the Shrine of the Black Madonna in Detroit, Michigan. Theologically, he advocates the "Black Messiah" as an integrative religious symbol of the Black Revolutionary struggle. Cleage also is critical of the traditional Negro Church for its conservative theological posture.

[2]*Ibid.,* p. 233. Perhaps the traditionalist as a social type is symbolized best in this comment made by some black church folks: "We have always done it this way, the old way is the right way; we have always had Sunday school books depicting Jesus as 'white'--i.e., with straight blonde hair and blue eyes-- because after all, what difference does color make? We don't need no 'black' Jesus for purposes of social identity." "We don't need no tampering with Jesus' 'color' around here at this church!"

[3]C. Eric Lincoln, *The Black Church Since Frazier,* (New York: Schocken Books, Inc., 1974), p. 108.

[4]W. E. B. DuBois sets forth an intriguing thesis here, and I believe correctly so, that a careful reading of history would strongly suggest or validate the claim that the sources of ethical guidance of the Black Church are not necessarily or dis- tinctively "Christian" sources; but rather a complex pattern of interaction between a variety of religious beliefs and moral values--some of which are more uniquely African; others may well be essentially Biblical in character; and still others are colored by the peculiar manner or as a result of the way in which the black man was enslaved and brought to the New World. In any event, it would appear that the "distinctively ethical tone" of the Black Church--especially in terms of its historical and evo- lutionary growth and development--is not wholeheartedly "Christian." See *The Negro Church,* by W. E. B. DuBois, (Atlanta: The Atlanta University Press, 1903), p. iv.

[5]Benjamin E. Mays and Joseph W. Nicholson, *The Negro's Church,* (New York: Russell and Russell, 1933), p. 278. It may be helpful to note in our analysis that C. Eric Lincoln's work, *The Black Church Since Frazier,* makes a rather interesting distinction between the "Negro Church" and the "Black Church." He argues essentially that the "Black Church" is basically a by-product of the Black Revolution of the sixties--with its complex convergence of radical political, social, cultural, moral, and religious forces in America. "Ironically, the white Church in America is the principal *raison d'etre* for the Black Church," says Lincoln, "for just as the white Church permitted and tolerated the Negro Church, it made the Black Church necessary for a new generation of Black people who refuse to be 'Negroes' and who are not impressed by whatever it means to be white." (p. 110)

[6]*Ibid.,* p. 278.

[7]Cf. W. E. B. DuBois, *The Negro Church,* p. 5.

[8]Mays and Nicholson, *Op. Cit.,* p. 281.

[9]Mays and Nicholson, *Op. Cit.,* p. 281.

[10]In our ethical analysis of the term "up-tight," it is important to point out--which is perhaps less obvious to some social thinkers--that many American psychologists and counselors associate the term "up-tight" with certain types of mental depression, tension, emotional stress, and social pressure as a result of one's vocation or career. However, the present use of the popular slogan by many blacks is suggestive of "moral positiveness" rather than a kind of negative social syndrome in American culture.

[11]Carter G. Woodson, *The History of the Negro Church,* (Washington: Associated Publishers, 1921), pp. 280-284ff.

[12]*Ibid.,* p. 284.

[13]*Ibid.,* pp. 272-275ff.

[14]Mays and Nicholson, *Op. Cit.,* pp. 58-59ff.

[15]Mays and Nicholson, *Op. Cit.,* pp. 66-69.

[16]Joseph A. Johnson, Jr., *The Soul of the Black Preacher,* p. 151.

[17]*Ibid.,* p. 151.

[18]James W. Johnson and J. R. Johnson, *The Books of American Negro Spirituals*, (New York: The Viking Press, Inc., 1925), pp. 11-13ff.

[19]Cf. John W. Work, ed., *American Negro Songs and Spirituals*, (New York: Bonanza Books, 1940), p. 2.

[20]James W. Johnson and J. R. Johnson, *Op. Cit.*, p. 14.

[21]Cf. The ethical disposition, as we have seen, of many of the Spirituals is essentially biblical in character. Therefore, the slave's rendering of the song "We Are Walking in de Light," may very well be referring to, or evaluative reflection upon, the scripture that says: "Let us walk honestly, as in the day; not in rioting and drunkenness, not in chambering and wantonness, not in strife and envying." (Rom. 13:13). It is obvious that the influence of the Christian faith is stamped upon the Spirituals, given their peculiar historical development. "...The Negro seized Christianity....the result," writes J. W. Johnson, "was a body of songs voicing all the cardinal virtues of Christianity--patience, forbearance, love, faith and hope-- through a necessarily modified form of primitive African music. The Negro took complete refuge in Christianity, and the Spirituals were literally forged of sorrow in the heat of religious fervor." See J. W. Johnson and J. R. Johnson, *The Books of American Negro Spirituals*, p. 20.

[22]Cf. R. Nathaniel Dett, ed., *Religious Folk Songs of the Negro*, (Hampton, Va: Hampton Institute Press, 1927), p. 26.

[23]Cf. Here it is important to point out that Dr. Howard Thurman provides the reader with a brilliant theological moral, and existential interpretation of the Black Spirituals, with an unusually penetrating focus concerning the meaning of "life and death." "The clue to the meaning of the Spirituals," says Thurman, "is to be found in religious experience and spiritual discernment." He touches also a morally relevant note, with regard to the existence of freedom of choice on the part of the slave, by maintaining: "A man is not compelled to accept life without reference to the conditions upon which the offering is made." See H. Thurman, *The Negro Spiritual Speaks of Life and Death*, (New York: Harper and Brothers, 1947), pp. 12-15ff.

[24]James H. Cone, *The Spirituals and the Blues*, (New York: The Seabury Press, 1972), p. 96.

[25]LeRoi Jones, *Blues People*, (New York: William Morrow and Co., 1963), p. 80.

166

Chapter III. Can Black Religion Be Ethical?

[1]Robert McAffe Brown, *Religion and Violence.* (Philadelphia: The Westminster Press, 1973), p. 3.

[2]Robert C. Monk, et. al., *Exploring Religious Meaning.* (Englewood Cliffs, N. Y.: Prentice-Hall, 1973), p. 19.

[3]Richard L. Means, *The Ethical Imperative.* (New York: Doubleday and Company, Inc., 1970), p. 2.

[4]Richard L. Roe, *Society Today.* (Del Mar, Ca.: CRM Books, 1971), p. 17.

[5]James Cone, *Black Theology and Power.* (New York: The Seabury Press, 1969), p. 6.

[6]*Rogets International Thesaurus.* (New York: Thomas Y. Crowell Co., 1962), pp. 542-544.

[7]Joseph R. Washington, Sr., "How Black is Black Religion?" in *Quest for a Black Theology*, J. J. Gardiner and J. D. Roberts, eds. Philadelphia: Pilgrim Press, 1971), p. 31.

[8]Gayraud Wilmore, *Black Religion and Black Radicalism,* (New York: Anchor Books, 1973), p. 4.

[9]*Ibid.*, pp. 4-6.

[10]W. E. B. DuBois, *The Gift of Black Folk.* (Boston: The Stratford Company, Publishers, 1924), pp. 238-239.

[11]G. S. Wilmore, *Black Religion and Black Radicalism.* (New York: Anchor Books, 1973), p. 302.

[12]*Op. Cit.*, pp. 325-326.

[13]*Op. Cit.*, p. 321.

[14]Will Herberg, *Protestant-Catholic-Jew: An Essay in American Religious Sociology.* (New York: Doubleday and Co., 1955), pp. 92-102.

[15]*Op. Cit.*, p. 310.

[16]*Op. Cit.*, p. 327.

[17]James M. Gustafson, *Christian Ethics and the Community.* (Philadelphia: United Church Press, 1971), pp. 94ff.

[18]Joseph Washington, *Black Religion: The Negro and Christianity in the United States*. (Boston: Beacon Press, 1964), p. 33.

[19]C. Eric Linclon, *The Black Experience in Religion*. (New York: Anchor Books, 1974), p. 68.

[20]Cecil W. Cone, *The Identity Crisis in Black Religion*. (Nashville: AMEC, 1975), pp. 143-144.

CHAPTER IV. NEW NOTES ON BLACK POWER: HISTORICAL ROOTS

[1]Nathan Wrights, Jr., *Black Power and Urban Unrest*. (New York: Hawthorn Books, Inc., 1967), pp. 12-14.

[2]Carleton Mabee, *Black Freedom*. (London: The Macmillan Company, 1970), pp. 6-8.

[3]Harold Cruse, *The Crisis of the Negro Intellectual*. (New York: William Morrow and Co., Inc., 1967), p. 5.

[4]*Ibid.*, p. 5.

[5]Dorothy Sterling, *The Making of an Afro-American*. (New York: Doubleday and Co., Inc., 19710, p. 98.

[6]Martin R. Delany, *The Condition, Elevation, Emigration and Destiny of the Colored People of the United States*. (Philadelphia: 1852; (reprinted: New York: Arno Press, 1968), p. 183.

[7]Quoted in Edwin S. Redkey, *Black Exodus*, (New Haven: Yale University Press, 1969), p. 27.

[8]Barbara Ritchie, *The Mind and Heart of Frederick Douglass*. (New York: Thomas Y. Crowell, Co., 1968), pp. 83-84.

[9]Benjamin Quarles, *Frederick Douglass*. (Washington: The Associated Publishers, Inc., 1948), p. 124.

[10]*Ibid.*, p. 124.

[11]Frederick Douglass, "No Progress Without Struggle!" 1849 in Floyd Barbour, ed., *The Black Power Revolt*. (Boston: Porter Sargent Publisher, 1968), p. 42.

[12]Barbara Ritchie, *Op. Cit.*, pp. 89-90.

[13]Carleton Mabee, *Black Freedom*. (London: The Macmillan Company, 1970, pp. 4-5.

[14]Quoted in Carleton Mabee, *Ibid.*, p. 65.

[15]Quoted in Dorothy Sterling, *The Making of an Afro-American: Martin R. Delany, 1812-1885*, p. 156.

[16]Quoted in Carter G. Woodson, *The Mind of the Negro as Reflected in Letters Written During the Crisis: 1800-1860*. (Washington: The Assoc. for the Study of Negro Life and History, Inc., 1929), p. 293.

[17]Claude McKay, "If We Must Die," in Ruth Miller, ed., *Black American Literature*. (Beverly Hills, California: Glenco Press, 1971), p. 334.

[18]Harold Cruse, *The Crisis of the Negro Intellectual*, p. 283.

[19]DuBois, *Dusk of Dawn*. (New York: Harcourt, Brace, 1940), p. 96.

[20]Harold Cruse, *Op. Cit.*, p. 283.

[21]Edmund D. Cronon, *Black Moses: The Story of Marcus Garvey and the Universal Negro Improvement Association*. (Madison: The University of Wisconsin Press, 1966), p. 171.

[22]Amy Jacques-Garvey, ed., *Philosophy and Opinions of Marcus Garvey*. (New York: The Universal Publishing House, 1923), p. 7.

[23]*Ibid.*, p. 52.

[24]Quoted in Edmund D. Cronon, *Black Moses*, p. 172.

[25]W. E. B. DuBois, *The Souls of Black Folk*. (Greenwick: Fawcett Publications, Inc., 1961), pp. 16-17.

[26]W. E. B. DuBois, *Ibid.*, p. 17.

[27]W. E. B. DuBois, *Ibid.*, p. 17.

[28]Phillip S. Foner, ed., *W. E. B. DuBois Speaks*. (New York: Pathfinder Press, 1970), pp. 275-276.

[29]W. E. B. DuBois, *The Souls of Black Folk*, p. 17.

[30]John H. Clarke, et. al., *Black Titan: W. E. B. DuBois.* (Boston: Beacon Press, 1970), p. 145.

[31]John H. Franklin, *From Slavery to Freedom.* (New York: Alfred A. Knoph, Inc., 1967), p. 215.

[32]*Ibid.*, p. 214.

[33]Benjamin Quarles, *Frederick Douglass.* (Washington: Associated Publishers, Inc., 1948), p. 90.

[34]Harold Cruse, *The Crisis of the Negro Intellectual.* (New York: William Morrow & Co., Inc., 1967), p. 238.

[35]*Ibid.*, p. 238.

[36]Harold Cruse, *Ibid.*, pp. 238-239.

[37]E. D. Cronon, *Op. Cit.*, pp. 220-221.

[38]E. D. Cronon, *Op. Cit.*, p. 186.

CHAPTER V. CURRENT SECULAR AND THEOLOGICAL DEVELOPMENTS OF BLACK POWER

[11]Melvin Drimmer, Ed., *Black History Reappraisal.* (New York: Doubleday & Co., Inc., 1968), p. 440.

[2]John H. Franklin, *From Slavery to Freedom.* (New York: Alfred A. Knopf, Inc., 1969), 3rd ed., p. 576.

[3]*Ibid.*, p. 576.

[4]*Ibid.*, p. 579. Lerone Bennett notes that another important action initiated by the federal government in matters relating to majority-minority relations was President Truman's Executive Order 9981, in July 1948. This Executive Order advocated that "equality of treatment and opportunity: be given to blacks in the armed forces, (L. Bennett, Jr., *Before the Mayflower*, Chicago: Johnson Publishing Co., Inc., 1962), p. 367.

[5]Gunnar Myrdal, et al., *An American Dilemma.* (New York: Harper and Row, Publishers, 1944), p. lxxi.

[6]*Ibid.*, p. lxxvii.

[7]Benjamin Quarles, *The Negro in the Making of America.* (New York: The Macmillan Co., 1969), 3rd ed., p. 265.

170

[8]J. R. Washington, Jr., *Black and White Power Subreption*. (Boston: Beacon Press, 1969), p. 66.

[9]Nathan Wright, Jr., *Black Power and Urban Unrest*. (New York: Hawthorn Books, Inc., 1967), p. 13.

[10]J. R. Washington, Jr., *Black and White Power Subreption*, p. 66. NAACP (National Association for the Advancement of Colored People); CORE (Congress of Racial Equality); and SNCC (Student Nonviolent Co-ordinating Committee).

[11]Bryan Fulks, *Black Struggle*. (New York: Dell Publishing Co., 1969), p. 313.

[12]S. Carmichael, "Black Power," in J. Grant, ed., *Black Protest*. (New York: St. Martin's Press, 1970), p. 460.

[13]Martin L. King. Jr., *Where Do We Go From Here: Chaos or Community?* (Boston: Beacon Press, 1968), p. 48.

[14]Bayard Rustin, "Black Power and Coalition Politics," in *Black Protest*, J. Grant, ed., p. 466.

[15]S. Carmichael and C. Hamilton, *Black Power*. (New York: (Alfred A. Knopf, Inc., 1967), p. 60.

[16]*Ibid.*, p. 60.

[17]S. Carmichael, *Stokely Speaks*. (New York: Vantage Books, Random House, 1971), p. 36.

[18]*Ibid.*, p. 78.

[19]S. Carmichael and C. Hamilton, *Black Power: The Politics of Liberation in America*. (New York: Vintage Books, Random House, 1967), pp. 79-80.

[20]*Ibid.*, p. 78.

[21]S. Carmichael, *Stokely Speaks*, pp. 36-37.

[22]James H. Cone, *Black Theology and Black Power*. (New York: The Seabury Press, 1969), p. 17.

[23]S. Carmichael, *Stokely Speaks*, p. 37.

[24]*Ibid.*, p. 39.

[25]Alvin F. Poussaint, "The Negro American: His Self-Image and Integration," in Floyd B. Barbour, ed., *The Black Power Revolt*, p. 94.

[26]Nathan Wright, "The Crisis Which Bred Black Power," in Floyd B. Barbour, ed., *The Black Power Revolt*, p. 114.

[27]Quoted in L. M. Killian, *The Impossible Revolution?* (New York: Random House, 1968), pp. 132-133.

[28]*Ibid.*, p. 133.

[29]*Ibid.*, p. 112.

[30]Carmichael, "What We Want," *The New York Review of Books*, September 22, 1966, p. 5.

[31]Washington, *Black and White Power Subreption.* (Boston: Beacon Press, 1969), p. 82.

[32]*Ibid.*, p. 85.

[33]R. L. Scott and W. Brockriede, *The Rhetoric of Black Power*, (New York: Harper & Row, Publishers, 1969), p. 195.

[34]S. Carmichael and C. Hamilton, *Black Power*, p. 50.

[35]Quoted in Chuck Stone, *Black Political Power in America.* (New York: Dell Publishing Co., 1968), p. 17.

[36]*Ibid.*, p. 17

[37]*Ibid.*, p. 16.

[38]*Ibid.*, p. 16.

[39]Harold Cruse, *The Crisis of the Negro Intellectual.* (New York: William Morrow & Co., 1967), p. 545.

[40]The term "provisional disengagement" derived from an interview which the writer had with Professor Gayraud Wilmore concerning the "black power" philosophy of Stokely Carmichael in terms of strategy and methodology for black liberation.

[41]Chuck Stone, *Op. Cit.*, p. 18.

[42]*Ibid.*

[43]*Ibid.*

[44]*Ibid.*, pp. 18-19.

[45]Charles E. Silberman, *Crisis in Black and White*. (New York: Vintage Books, Random House, 1965), p. 165.

[46]Chuck Stone, *Op. Cit.*, p. 20.

[47]Joseph Washington, *Black and White Power Subreption*. (Boston: Beacon Press, 1969), p. 171.

[48]R. L. Scott and W. Brockriede, *The Rhetoric of Black Power*, (New York: Harper and Row, Publishers, 1969), p. 130.

[49]*Ibid.*, p. 130.

[50]*Ibid.*, p. 130.

[51]*Ibid.*, pp. 130-131.

[52]David Danzig, "Black Power and 'the movement': Two Views in Defense of Black Power" in Endo and Strawbridge, ed., *Perspectives on Black America*. (New York: Prentice-Hall, Inc., 1970), p. 191.

[53]*Ibid.*, p. 191.

[54]V. Harding, "The Religion of Black Power" in Donald Cutler, ed., *The Religious Situation: 1968*. (Boston: Beacon Press, 1968), p. 4.

[55]G. S. Wilmore, *Black Religion and Black Radicalism*. (New York: Doubleday and Company, Inc., 1972), p. 289.

[56]J. O. Killens, "Symposium on Black Power," *Negro Digest*, November, 1966.

[57]M. J. Jones, "Black Awareness: Theological Implications of the Concept," in *Religion in Life*, Autumn, 1969, p. 393.

[58]Major J. Jones, "Black Awareness: Theological Implications of the Concept," *Religion in Life*, Autumn, 1969, (Nashville: Abingdon Press), p. 393.

[59]*Ibid.*, p. 394....

[60]Major J. Jones, *Black Awareness: A Theology of Hope*. (Nashville: Abingdon Press, 1971), p. 132.

[61]S. Carmichael, "Power and Racism," in Floyd B. Barbour, *The Black Power Revolt*. (Boston: Porter Sargent Publisher, 1968), p. 68.

[62]*Ibid.*, p. 70.

[63]N. Wright, *Black Power and Urban Unrest.* (New York: Hawthorn Books, Inc., 1967), p. 136.

[64]*Ibid.*, p. 136. Here the term "authentic black existence" as used by the writer refers to a quality of experience in community which supports the black man's integrity and self-esteem by providing the necessary freedom for the realization of his God-given potentiality.

[65]A Statement by the National Committee of Black Churchmen on "Black Power," quoted in *The Black Power Revolt*, F. B. Barbour, ed., p. 264.

[66]Gayraud S. Wilmore, *Black Religion and Black Radicalism*, (New York: Doubleday & Co., Inc., 1972).

[67]Bradford Chambers, ed., *Chronicles of Black Protest.* (New York: The New American Library, Inc., 1968), p. 33.

[68]James H. Cone, *Black Theology and Black Power.* (New York: The Seabury Press, 1969), p. 94.

[69]James H. Cone, *A Black Theology of Liberation.* (New York: J. B. Lippincott, Co., 1970), p. 23.

[70]*Ibid.*, pp. 23-24.

[71]Joseph A. Johnson, Jr., "Jesus, the Liberator," in *Quest for a Black Theology*, Roberts and Gardiner, eds. (Philadelphia: United Church Press, 1971), pp. 98-99.

[72]*Ibid.*, p. 71.

[73]*Ibid.*, p. 62.

[74]James H. Cone, *Black Theology and Black Power*, p. 117.

[75]Roberts and Gardiner, *Op. Cit.*, p. 69.

[76]*Ibid.*, p. 65.

[77]Henry P. Fairchild, ed., *Dictionary of Sociology.* (Totowa, New Jersey: Littlefield, Adams and Co., 1968), p. 259.

[78]*Ibid.*, p. 259.

[79]Joseph Washington, *Black and White Power Subreption*, p. 122.

[80]*Ibid.*, pp. 120-121.

Chapter VI. Martin Luther King., Jr.: Liberation Ethics in a Christian Context

[1]Martin Luther King, Jr., *The Trumpet of Conscience.* (New York: Harper and Row, Publishers, 1967), pp. 4ff.

[2]Cf. E. U. Essien-Udom, *Black Nationalism.* (New York: Dell Publishing Co., Inc., 1962), pp. 23ff.

[3]Charles F. Sleeper, *Black Power and Christian Responsibility.* (Nashville: Abingdon Press, 1969), pp. 26-27.

[4]David L. Lewis, *King: A Critical Biography.* (New York: Praeger Publishers, 1970), p. 315.

[5]Martin Luther King, Jr., *Op. Cit.*, pp. 5-6.

[6]H. E. Stotts and P. Deats, *Methodism and Society: Guidelines for Strategy.* (New York: Abingdon Press, 1962), pp. 28ff.

[7]See Talcott Parsons and Kenneth B. Clark, eds., *The Negro American.* (Boston: Houghton Mifflin Co., 1965), p. xi.

[8]Martin Luther King, Jr., *Where Do We Go From Here: Chaos or Community?* (Boston: Beacon Press, 1968), pp. 37ff.

[9]Cf. J. Deotis Roberts, "Black Theological Ethics: A Bibliographical Essay," in *The Journal of Religious Ethics,* (Spring, 1975), p. 86.

[10]Cf. Martin Luther King, Jr., *Strength to Love.* (New York: Harper and Row, Publishers, 1963), pp. 44ff.

[11]Martin Luther King., Jr., *The Rumpet of Conscience,* p. 73.

[12]Vincent Harding, "The Religion of Black Power," in Donald Cutler, ed., *The Religious Situation: 1968.* (Boston: Beacon Press, 1968), pp. 4ff.

[13]J. Deotis Roberts, *Op. Cit.*, p. 86.

[14]Martin Luther King, Jr., *The Trumpet of Conscience,* p. 78.

[15]*Ibid.*, p. 64.

¹⁶Martin Luther King, Jr., *Why We Can't Wait*. (New York: Harper and Row, Publishers, 1963), pp. 76-80.

¹⁷*Ibid.*, pp. 81ff.

¹⁸Reinhold Niebuhr, *An Interpretation of Christian Ethics*. (New York: Meridian Books, 1960), pp. 37ff.

¹⁹Reinhold Niebuhr, *The Children of Light and the Children of Darkness*. (New York: Charles Scribner's Sons, 1944), p. xiii.

²⁰Cf. R. Niebuhr, *The Nature and Destiny of Man*, Vol. 2. (New York: Charles Scribner's Sons, 1943), pp. 254ff.

²¹M. L. King, *Strength to Love*, p. 81.

²²*Ibid.*, p. 78.

²³*Ibid.*, p. 111.

²⁴Cf. Kenneth L. Smith and Ira G. Zepp, Jr., *Search for the Beloved Community: The Thinking of Martin Luther King, Jr.*, (Valley Forge, Pa.: Judson Press, 1975), pp. 119-130.

²⁵Cited in K. L. Smith and I. G. Zepp, *Search for the Beloved Community*, p. 131.

²⁶Martin Luther King, Jr., *Strength to Love*, pp. 49ff.

²⁷Cited in William R. Miller, *Martin Luther King, Jr.: His Life, Martyrdom and Meaning for the World*. (New York: Avon Books, 1968), p. 66.

²⁸Martin Luther King, Jr., *Stride Toward Freedom*. (New York: Harper and Row, Publishers, 1958), p. 87.

²⁹Martin Luther King, Jr., *The Trumpet of Conscience*, p. 68.

³⁰*Ibid.*, p. 68.

Chapter VII. Sounds of Ethics and Black Theology

¹Quoted in Lerone Bennett, Jr., *The Challenge of Blackness*, (Chicago: Johnson Publishing Co., 1972), p. 192.

²Readers will observe that the term "soul" is a black value concept which means different things to different people,

depending on the concrete factors of the black man's social situation. While this notion requires greater theoretical clarity for the oppressed, Leonard E. Barrett provides the agent with insight as to its ethical importance. He writes: "...'Soul' signifies the moral and emotional fiber of the Black man that enables him to see his dilemmas clearly and at the same time encourages and sustains him in struggle." (p. 1). See, L. E. Barrett, *Soul-Force: African Heritage in Afro-American Religion.* (New York: Anchor Press/Doubleday, 1974).

[3]Cf. William K. Frankena, *Ethics.* (Englewood Cliffs, N. J.: Prentice-Hall, Inc., 1963), esp. Chap. I, "Morality and Moral Philosophy," pp. 3-5.

[4]Cf. Eliseo Vivas, *The Moral Life and the Ethical Life.* (Chicago: The University of Chicago Press, 1950), p. 265.

[5]C. H. Whiteley, "On Defining 'Moral,'" in *The Definition of Morality,* G. Wallace and A. D. M. Walker, Eds. (London: Methuen and Co., Ltd. 1970), p. 22.

[6]Cf. Elliot Liebow, *Talley's Corner: A Study of Negro Street-corner Men.* (Boston: Little, Brown and Co., 1967), p. 214.

[7]Larry L. King, *Confessions of a White Racist.* (New York: The Viking Press, 1969), pp. 5-8ff.

[8]*Ibid.*, p. 19.

[9]In my opinion, the "moral way" in our conceptual framework must be equated with the reality of "blackness" because blackness itself in the view of the oppressed represents a key form of moral strength and cultural identity. We have already suggested that the terminology "moral way" refers largely to the actual socio-historical experience of blacks in America, and how they relate to, and interact with themselves and others; and how they cope with the many frustrations, social and normative conflicts, hopes and dreams in their day-to-day existence. The internal and external forces of the "moral way" betray a terrifying pain in the soul of black folks because we have never fully understood, at least by any rational criterion, exactly *why* we have been and still are the victims of so much oppression in the modern world. Cf. C. T. Davis and Daniel Walden, eds., *On Being Black.* (Greenwich, Conn.: Fawcett Publications, Inc., 1970). See also *White Racism: A Psychohistory,* by Joel Kovel. (New York: Vintage Books, 1971), esp. chapter 8.

[10]R. S. Browne, "A Negro is Still a Nigger," in *Is Anybody Listening to Black America?* by C. Eric Lincoln, ed. (New York: The Seabury Press, 1968), p. 131.

[11]Cf. We may point out that Kierkegaard himself distinguished between three interrelated levels of life: the
"aesthetic" stage, the "ethical" stage, and the "religious"
stage. To a degree, I think that his typology or theoretical
construct is relevant to our analysis of the black religious
experience. At the "aesthetic" stage, the individual person
lives essentially for happiness, pleasure, and fun. The agent's
existence and activity, so to speak, are set into motion by
hedonistic desires--with not much concern for social responsibility. At the "ethical" stage, however, the individual person
is called to responsibility and maturity; according to Kierkegaard,
the principles of duty and maturity reflect, in part, the
ethical. He asserts: "When with all his energy a person has
felt the intensity of duty he is then ethically mature, and in
him duty will emerge of itself." See Soren Kierkegaard,
Either/Or, Vol. 2, trans. by Walter Lowrie, (New York: Doubleday
and Co., Inc., 1959), p. 269.

[12]Ibid., pp. 274ff.

[13]For further discussion and analysis of the ethical significance of what God is doing on behalf of the oppressed in the
world, see J. Deotis Roberts' A Black Political Theology.
Professor Roberts, one of the leading exponents of Black Theology,
argues that the experiences of oppressed blacks have great ethical and theological import in terms of God's activity in
history. Indeed, he believes that what God is doing in the
world for man must be ethically interpreted in a political context. The force of the ethical points always, in varying
degrees, to liberation and humanization of broken relations between persons; it points toward building a new human order. Thus
there is, in Roberts' view, a political context of the Christian
faith. J. D. Roberts, A Black Political Theology. (Philadelphia:
The Westminster Press, 1974), pp. 24-36ff.

[14]Cf. Roger L. Shinn, "Some Ethical Foundations of Christian
Theology," Union Seminary Quarterly Review, (Jan. 1960, p. 101).

[15]N. H. G. Robinson, The Groundwork of Christian Ethics.
(Grand Rapids: William B. Eerdmans Publishing Co., 1971).

[16]For a further discussion of Christian ethics and theology
in light of the New Testament teachings about the life of Jesus,
see W. D. Davies, "Ethics in the New Testament," in Interpreter's Dictionary of the Bible, Vol. 2, (New York and Nashville).
In a discussion on the importance of Jesus' life as a central
paradigm, Davies observes: "the ethics of Jesus is best thought
of as the demands which are placed upon those who have accepted
God's rule, as Jesus proclaimed and lived it." (p. 172). See

also Jack T. Sanders, *Ethics in the New Testament: Change and Development*. (Philadelphia: Fortress Press, 1975).

[17]Cf. Robinson, *Op. Cit.*, p. 14.

[18]Cf. Robinson, *Op. Cit.*, p. 15

[19]Cf. Robinson, *Op. Cit.*, p. 15.

[20]Cf. James M. Gustafson, *Christian Ethics and the Community*. (Philadelphia: A Pilgrim Press Book, 1971), esp. Chapter I: "Christian Ethics in America," pp. 23-33ff.

[21]James H. Cone, *God of the Oppressed*. (New York: The Seabury Press, Inc., 1975), pp. 199-200.

[22]James H. Cone, *Ibid.*, p. 200.

[23]Cf. Eldridge Cleaver, *Soul on Ice*. (New York: Dell Publishing Co., Inc., 1968), pp. 84ff.

[24]Cf. Roger Mehl, *Catholic Ethics and Protestant Ethics*. (Philadelphia: The Westminster Press, 1971), p. 119.

[25]Cf. T. W. Manson, *Ethics and the Gospel*. (New York: Charles Scribner's Sons, 1960), esp. Chapter 4, "The Foundation of Christian Ethics: Following Christ." When the question is raised, "What is the differentia of Christian ethics?" the answer most frequently expressed on the part of many theologians is the "love-principle" or the promulgation of the dual ethical commandment: the love of God and neighbor. Yet I think that the problems of social morality in modern society--largely aggravated by the ideology of race--make the love ethic of Jesus almost an impossible ethical idea; despite the fact that it is, for the Christian believer, the epitome of the moral life. In a cogent way, Reinhold Niebuhr spoke of this same ethical problematic in candor: "The absolutism and perfectionism of Jesus' love ethic sets itself uncompromisingly not only against the natural self-regarding impulses, but against the necessary prudent defenses of the self, required because of the egoism of others." Reinhold Niebuhr, *An Interpretation of Christian Ethics*. (New York: Meridian Books, 1958), pp. 45ff.

[26]Cf. James R. Simmons, *The Quest for Ethics*. (New York: Philosophical Library, Inc., 1962), p. 3.

[27]Cf. Herbert O. Edwards, "Toward a Black Christian Social Ethic," *The Duke Divinity School Review*. (Spring, 1975), pp. 107ff.

[28]J. J. Gardiner, S. A. and J. D. Roberts, Jr., eds. *Quest for a Black Theology.* (Philadelphia: A Pilgrim Press Book, 1971), p. 69.

[29]*Ibid.,* p. 69.

[30]Cf. Quoted in T. Parsons and K. B. Clark, eds., *The Negro American.* (Boston: Houghton Mifflin Co., 1965), p. 160.

[31]J. D. Douglas, ed., *The New Bible Dictionary.* (Grand Rapids, Michigan: Wm. B. Eerdmans Publishing Co., 1973), pp. 532ff.

[32]*Ibid.,* p. 534.

[33]Cf. Ellis H. Richards, "The Source of Christian Ethics," in *The Center,* Vol. 5, No. 2., (Spring, 1964), pp. 26ff.

[34]One of the fundamental themes in the ethics and theology of Dr. Martin Luther King, Jr. was the conception of the "beloved community." Although we have referred to this ethical-theological-eschatological paradigm in our text earlier, we feel that the notion is also crucial in the development of a viable Black Christian Social Ethic with regard to the community of the oppressed. In Dr. King's prophetic vision of the "beloved community," we have a blueprint of a new ethic for a new social order where all races, classes, and ethnic groups can have their full measure of freedom and human dignity. See *Strength to Love,* by M. L. King, Jr., (New York: Harper & Row Publishers, 1963).

[35]Cf. Herbert O. Edwards, *Op. Cit.,* p. 107.

[36]Cf. Ralph Ellison, *Invisible Man.* (New York: New American Library, Inc., 1947), p. 16.

[37]*Ibid.,* p. 17.

[38]Cf. Readers will note that a more elaborate discussion of the concept of "victimization" can be found in St. Clair Drake's essay, "The Social and Economic Status of the Negro in the United States," in Parsons and Clark, eds., *The Negro American.* Drake argues that blacks are *victims* in the American socio-cultural system not only because of class considerations-- i.e., having or not having money, education, power, technical skills, etc.,--but also because of caste-color considerations, which drastically affect the "life chances" of the poor for real success. Drake enables us to understand subtle aspects of the moral dilemma in black-white relations by distinguishing between *direct victimization* and *indirect victimization.* The former is defined as "the operation of sanctions which deny access to power...sustain job discrimination, permit unequal pay for

similar work, or provide inferior training or no training at all." The latter is "revealed in the consequences which flow from a social structure which decreases 'life chances,' such as high morbidity and mortality rates, low longevity rates...or the persistence of personality traits...which impose disadvantages in competition or excite derogatory and invidious comparisons with other groups." (pp. 5ff)

[39]Cf. Sterling D. Plumpp, *Black Rituals*. (Chicago: Third World Press, 1972), p. 78.

[40]*Ibid.*, pp. 79ff.

[41]Cf. Calvin E. Bruce, "Refocusing Black Religious Education: Three Imperatives," in *Religious Education*, (July-August, 1974), pp. 427-429.

[42]See H. R. Niebuhr, *The Responsible Self*. (New York: Harper and Row Publishers, 1963), p. 57.

[43]*Ibid.*, p. 61.

[44]*Ibid.*, p. 65.

[45]Cf. Dietrich Bonhoeffer, *Ethics*, (New York: The Macmillan Co., 1955), p. 222. For a comparative and socio-ethical analysis of the idea of responsibility--especially in the light of social science--see, Gibson Winter's *Elements for a Social Ethic*, (New York: The Macmillan Co., 1966), Chapter 7, "An Ethic of the Social World."

[46]*Ibid.*, p. 223.

[47]*Ibid.*, p. 224.

[48]An address by Dr. C. Shelby Rooks on the theme: "The Minister as a Change Agent," The Pre-Inaugural Conference, the Interdenominational Theological Center, Atlanta, Ga. (October 5, 1976).

[49]Cf. Vernon J. Bourke, *Ethics in Crisis*. (Milwaukee: The Bruce Publishing Co., 1966), pp. 45-48ff.

[50]Cf. Quoted in Tryon Edwards, et al., *The New Dictionary of Thought*. (New York: Standard Book Co., 1960), p. 221.

[51]Cf. James E. Blackwell, *The Black Community: Diversity and Unity*. (New York: Dodd, Mead, and Co., 1975), p. 285.

[52]*Ibid.*, p. 285.

[53]Melvin Rader, *Ethics and the Human Community*. (New York: Holt, Rinehart and Winston, 1964), pp. 4ff.

SELECTED BIBLIOGRAPHY

Ahmann, Mathew, ed. *Race: Challenge to Religion.* Chicago: Henry Regnery Co., 1963.

Arendt, Hannah. *On Violence.* New York: Harcourt, Brace and World, Inc., 1969.

Barbour, Floyd B., ed., *The Black Power Revolt.* Boston: Porter Sargent Publisher, 1968.

_____. *The Black Seventies.* Boston: Porter Sargent Publishers, 1970.

Barker, Ernest. *The Political Thought of Plato and Aristotle.* New York: G. P. Putnam's Sons, 1906.

Benedict, Stewart H., ed. *Blacklash: Black Protest in Our Time.* New York: Popular Library, 1970.

Bennett, Lerone, Jr. *Black Power U.S.A.* Chicago: Johnson Publishing Co., Inc., 1967.

_____. *Confrontation: Black and White.* Baltimore: Penguin Books, 1965.

_____. *Before the Mayflower.* Chicago: Johnson Publishing Co., Inc., 1962.

_____. *The Negro Mood.* Chicago: Johnson Publishing Co., Inc., 1964.

Bingham, June R. *Courage to Change.* New York: Charles Scribner's Sons, 1961.

Brockerick, Francis L. *W. E. B. DuBois: Negro Leader in a Time of Crisis.* Stanford, Calif.: Stanford University Press, 1959.

Brockriede, Wayne and Scott, Robert L. *The Rhetoric of Black Power.* New York: Harper and Row, Publishers, 1969.

Carmichael, Stokely. *Stokely Speaks Black Power: Back to Pan-Africanism.* New York: Random House, 1965.

Carmichael, Stokely and Hamilton, Charles V. *Black Power: The Politics of Liberation in America*. New York: Random House, 1967.

Chambers, Bradford, ed. *Chronicles of Black Protest*. New York: The New American Library, Inc., 1968.

Clark, Kenneth B. *Dark Ghetto*. New York: Harper and Row, Publishers, 1965.

Clarke, John H. et al., eds. *Black Titan: W. E. B. DuBois*. Boston: Beacon Press, 1970.

Cleage, Albert B., Jr. *The Black Messiah*. New York: Sheed and Ward, 1968.

_____. *Black Christian Nationalism*. New York: William Morrow and Co., Inc., 1972.

Cone, James H. *Black Theology and Black Power*. New York: The Seabury Press, 1969.

_____. *A Black Theology of Liberation*. New York: J. B. Lippincott Co., 1970.

_____. *The Spirituals and the Blues*. New York: The Seabury Press, 1972.

Cronon, Edmund David. *Black Moses*. Madison, Wisconsin: The University of Wisconsin Press, 1955.

Cruse, Harold. *Crisis of the Negro Intellectual*. New York: William Morrow and Co., Inc., 1967.

Cullen, Countee. *The Black Christ*. New York: Harpers, 1929.

Cutler, Donald R., ed. *The Religious Situation: 1968*. Boston: Beacon Press, 1968.

Deats, Paul K. Jr., ed. *Toward a Discipline of Social Ethics: Essays in Honor of Walter George Muelder*. Boston: Boston University Press, 1972.

Delany, Martin R. *The Condition, Elevation, and Destiny of the Colored People of the United States*. New York: Arno Press, Inc., 1968.

Delany, Martin R. and Campbell, Robert. *Search for a Place: Separatism and Africa 1860*. Ann Arbor: The University of Michigan Press, 1969.

184

Drimmer, Melvin, ed. *Black History Reappraisal*. New York: Doubleday and Co., Inc., 1968.

DuBois, W. E. B. *Dusk of Dawn*. New York: Harcourt, Brace and World, Inc., 1940.

_____. *The Souls of Black Folk*. Greenwich: Fawcett Publications, Inc., 1961.

Ebersole, Mark C. *Christian Faith and Man's Religion*. New York: Thomas Y. Crowell Co., 1961.

Endo, Russell and Strawbridge, William, eds. *Perspectives on Black America*. Englewood Cliffs: Prentice-Hall, Inc., 1970.

Essien-Udom, E. U. *Black Nationalism*. New York: Dell Publishing Co., Inc., 1962.

Fackre, Gabriel. *The Promise of Reinhold Niebuhr*. New York: J. B. Lippincott Co., 1970.

Fager, Charles E. *White Reflections on Black Power*. Grand Rapids: William B. Eerdman's Publishing Co., 1967.

Fairchild, Henry Pratt, ed. *Dictionary of Sociology*. Totowa, New Jersey: Littlefield, Adams and Co., 1968.

Flynn, James J. *Negroes of Achievement in Modern America*. New York: Dodd, Mead and Co., 1970.

Foner, Philip S., ed. *W. E. B. DuBois Speaks*. New York: Pathfinder Press, 1970.

Franklin, John Hope. *From Slavery to Freedom*. 3rd ed., New York: Vintage Books, Random House, Inc., 1969.

Frazier, E. Franklin. *The Negro Church in America*. New York: Schocken Books, Inc., 1963.

Freire, Paulo. *Pedagogy of the Oppressed*. New York: Herder and Herder, 1970.

Fulks, Bryan. *Black Struggle*. New York: Dell Publishing Co., Inc., 1969.

Gardiner, James J, SA, and Roberts, J. Deotis, eds. *Quest for a Black Theology*. Philadelphia: United Church Press, 1971.

185

Garvey, Marcus. *Philosophy and Opinions of Marcus Garvey*. Vol. I, New York: Arno Press, Inc., 1968.

_____. *Philosophy and Opinions of Marcus Garvey*. Vol. II, New York: Arno Press, Inc., 1968.

Grant, Joanne, ed. *Black Protest History, Documents and Analysis*. New York: St. Martin's Press, 1970.

Grimes, Alan P. *Equality in America*. New York: Oxford University Press, 1964.

Harland, Gordon. *The Thought of Reinhold Niebuhr*. New York: Oxford University Press, 1960.

Harvey, Van A. *A Handbook of Theological Terms*. New York: The MacMillan Co., 1964.

Hessel, Dieter T. *Reconciliation and Conflict*. Philadelphia: The Westminster Press, 1969.

Hough, Joseph C. Jr. *Black Power and White Protestants*. New York: Oxford University Press, 1968.

Jones Major J. *Black Awareness: A Theology of Hope*. New York: Abingdon Press, 1971.

Kegley, Charles W. and Bretall, Robert W., eds. *Reinhold Niebuhr: His Religious, Social and Political Thought*. New York: The Macmillan Co., 1956.

Kelsey, George D. *Racism and the Christian Understanding of Man*. New York: Charles Scribner's Sons, 1965.

Killian, Lewis M. *The Impossible Revolution?* New York: Random House, 1968.

King, Coretta Scott. *My Life with Martin Luther King, Jr.* New York: Avon Books, 1969.

King, Martin Luther, Jr. *The Measure of a Man*. Philadelphia: United Church Press, 1958.

_____. *Strength to Love*. New York: Harper and Row, 1963.

_____. *Stride Toward Freedom*. New York: Harper and Row, 1958.

_____. *Where Do We Go From Here: Chaos or Community?*
New York: Harper and Row, 1967.

_____. *Why We Can't Wait.* New York: Harper and Row, 1964.

Lafarge, Rene. *Jean-Paul Sartre: His Philosophy.* Notre Dame:
University of Notre Dame Press, 1970.

Lewis, David L. *King: A Critical Biography.* New York: Praeger
Publishers, 1970.

Lincoln, C. Eric. *The Black Muslims in America.* Boston: Beacon
Press, 1961.

Lincoln, C. Eric, ed. *Martin Luther King, Jr.: A Profile.*
New York: Hill and Wang, 1970.

Lomax, Louis E. *The Negro Revolt.* New York: Harper and Row,
1962.

Mabee, Carleton. *Black Freedom: The Nonviolent Abolitionists
from 1830 Through the Civil War.* London: The Macmillan
Co., 1970.

Merton, Robert K. *Social Theory and Social Structure.* Rev. ed.,
New York: The Free Press, 1968.

Miller, Ruth, ed. *Black American Literature.* Beverly Hills:
Glencoe Press, 1971.

Miller, William Robert. *Martin Luther King, Jr.: His Life,
Martyrdom and Meaning for the World.* New York: J. H. Kok
N. V. Kampen, 1958.

Myrdal, Gunnar. *An American Dilemma.* New York: Harper and
Row, 1944.

Niebuhr, Reinhold. *The Children of Light and the Children of
Darkness.* New York: Charles Scribner's Sons, 1944.

_____. *Christianity and Power Politics.* New York: Charles
Scribner's Sons, 1940.

_____. *Christian Realism and Political Problems.* New York:
Charles Scribner's Sons, 1954.

_____. *Faith and History.* New York: Charles Scribner's
Sons, 1949.

_____. *Faith and Politics* by Ronald H. Stone, ed. New York:
George Braziller, Inc., 1968.

_____. *An Interpretation of Christian Ethics*. New York:
Harper and Brothers, Publishers, 1935.

_____. *The Irony of American History*. New York: Charles
Scribner's Sons, 1952.

_____. *Love and Justice*. by D. B. Robertson, ed., New York:
The World Publishing Co., 1957.

_____. *Man's Nature and His Communities*. New York: Charles
Scribner's Sons, 1965.

_____. *Moral Man and Immoral Society*. New York: Charles
Scribner's Sons, 1932.

_____. *The Nature and Destiny of Man*. Vol. I, New York:
Charles Scribner's Sons, 1941.

_____. *The Nature and Destiny of Man*. Vol. II, New York:
Charles Scribner's Sons, 1943.

_____. *The Structure of Nations and Empires*. New York:
Charles Scribner's Sons, 1959.

Oden, Thomas C. *The Promise of Barth*. New York: J. B.
Lippincott Co., 1969.

Osborn, Robert T. *Freedom in Modern Theology*. Philadelphia:
The Westminster Press, 1967.

Parsons, Talcott and Clark, Kenneth B., eds. *The Negro
American*. Boston: Houghton Mifflin Co., 1965.

Peeks, Edward. *The Long Struggle for Black Power*. New York:
Charles Scribner's Sons, 1971.

Pettigrew, Thomas F. *Racially Separate or Together?* New York:
McGraw-Hill Book Co., 1971.

Powledge, Fred. *Black Power: White Resistance*. Cleveland:
The New World Publishing Co., 1967.

Proctor, Samuel D. *The Young Negro in America, 1960-1980*.
New York: Association Press, 1966.

Quarles, Benjamin. *The Negro in the Making of America*. Rev.
ed., New York: The Macmillan Co., 1969.

_____. *Frederick Douglass*. Washington: The Associated
Publishers, Inc., 1948.

Ramsey, Ian T., ed. *Christian Ethics and Contemporary Philosophy.*
London: SCM Press, 1966.

Ramsey, Paul, ed. *Faith and Ethics.* New York: Harper and
Brothers, 1957.

Redkey, Edwin S. *Black Exodus.* New Haven: Yale University
Press, 1969.

Reimers, David. *White Protestantism and the Negro.* New York:
Oxford University Press, 1965.

Richards, Henry J., ed. *Topics in Afro-American Studies.*
Buffalo, N.Y.: Black Academy Press, 1971.

Ritchie, Barbara. *The Mind and Heart of Frederick Douglass.*
New York: Thomas Y. Crowell, Co., 1968.

Roberts, J. Deotis. *Liberation and Reconciliation: A Black
Theology.* Philadelphia: The Westminster Press, 1971.

Ruether, Rosemary. *Liberation Theology.* New York: Paulist
Press, 1972.

Sharp, Gene. *Exploring Nonviolent Alternatives.* Boston: Porter
Sargent Publisher, 1970.

Silberman, Charles E. *Crisis in Black and White.* New York:
Random House, Inc., 1965.

Simpson, George E. and Yinger, J. Milton. *Racial and Cultural
Minorities.* 3rd ed. New York: Harper and Row, 1965.

Sleeper, Charles F. *Black Power and Christian Responsibility.*
Nashville: Abingdon Press, 1969.

Spike, Robert. *The Freedom Revolution and the Churches.*
New York: Association Press, 1965.

Sterling, Dorothy. *The Making of an Afro-American: Martin
R. Delany: 1812-1885.* New York: Doubleday and Co.,
Inc., 1971.

Stone, Chuck, ed. *Black Political Power in America.* New York:
Dell Publishing Co., Inc., 1968.

Stone, Ronald H. *Reinhold Niebuhr.* Nashville: Abingdon
Press, 1972.

Stotts, Herbert E. and Deats, Paul K., Jr. *Methodism and Society: Guidelines for Strategy.* New York: Abingdon Press, 1962.

Tillich, Paul. *Love, Power, and Justice.* London: Oxford University Press, 1954.

Washington, Joseph, Jr. *Black and White Power Subreption.* Boston: Beacon Press, 1969.

_____. *Black Religion.* Boston: Beacon Press, 1964.

_____. *The Politics of God.* Boston: Beacon Press, 1967.

Williams, Daniel Day. *God's Grace and Man's Hope.* New York: Harper and Row, 1949.

Wilmore, Gayraud S. *Black Religion and Black Radicalism.* New York: Doubleday and Co., Inc., 1972.

Woodson, Carter G. *The Mind of the Negro as Reflected in Letters Written During the Crisis: 1800-1860.* Washington: The Association for the Study of Negro Life and History, Inc., 1929.

Wright, Nathan, Jr. *Black Power and Urban Unrest.* New York: Hawthorn Books, Inc., 1967.

Wright, Richard. *Black Power.* New York: Harper and Brothers, 1954.

ABOUT THE AUTHOR

ENOCH H. OGLESBY is Associate Professor of Theology
and Ethics at Eden Theological Seminary in St. Louis, Missouri.
Dr. Oglesby came to Eden from a teaching position at the Inter-
denominational Theological Center in Atlanta, Georgia, where he
served as the Andrew W. Mellon Assistant Professor of Christian
Social Ethics, and Chairman of the Department of Church and
Society. Prior to his appointment to the faculty of the Interdenominational Theological Center, he was Assistant Professor of
Religion at Wittenberg University in Springfield, Ohio;
Instructor at North Shore Community College in Beverly, Massachusetts; Program Coordinator and Instructor of Afro-American
Studies at the Margaret Fuller House in Cambridge, Massachusetts;
and has served as Pastor of the Zion Baptist Church in Lynn,
Massachusetts. In terms of professional experience, he has pub-
lished in a number of theological and educational journals on
such topics as "Religion and Racism in America," and "Christian
Ethics and Black Theology."

Dr. Oglesby earned the Doctor of Philosophy Degree from
Boston University Graduate School, a Master of Theology Degree
from Boston University School of Theology, and a Bachelor of
Arts Degree from Lane College. He is the recipient of numerous
honors and awards, including the Rockefeller Doctoral Fellowship
in Religion. Dr. Oglesby is also active in community social
change in the greater St. Louis area. He resides in Webster Groves,
Missouri, with his wife and their two young sons, Josten and
Derek.

Dr. Enoch H. Oglesby

DATE DUE

JAN 2 8 1983		
FEB 1 5 1983		
MAR 1 6 1983		
JUL 1 3 1983		
FEB 1 1 1988		
OCT 1 8 1988		
FEB 2 9 2000		
DEC 0 7 2000		
GAYLORD		PRINTED IN U.S.A.